TEXT — CASES — PROBLEMS

ON

THE ADJUDICATION OF SOCIAL ISSUES

By

EDWIN WALLACE TUCKER

Professor of Business Law, University of Connecticut

ST. PAUL, MINN.

WEST PUBLISHING CO.

1971

Tucker, Adjudication Social Issues Pamph. MCB

PREFACE

Extensive changes in the American social, economic, and political structure have been brought about within the framework of the judicial process. Proponents of reform, as well as militant advocates of revolution, have called upon the nation's courts to act as their protectors and champions. At times, it has been government, and at other times individual proponents or opponents of change, who have instituted proceedings which have led to judicial adjudication of social issues.

As the selected arbiter in social, economic, and political confrontations courts have spoken out on such issues as the rights of the poor, the shelter deprived, the young, the student, the activist, the debtor, the consumer, the conscientious objector, and discrimination against non-whites. Simultaneously called upon to respond favorably to the supporters and opponents of a new ordering of rights and duties judges have been obliged to probe questions dealing with abortion, family planning, sexual morality, forms of sexual behavior, privacy, welfare rights, women's rights, pollution, obscenity, drug addiction, alcoholism, political representation, and the right to criticize public officials. Judicial response has been marked by abandonment of long established legal principles and espousal of new legal doctrines. Courts have proceeded to fashion freshly designed procedures to facilitate enforcement of their newly announced substantive rules.

As judges go about their job of adjudicating social issues it is essential that they keep their own house in order. The ultimate measure of judicial achievement in the adjudication of social issues is inescapably intertwined with the overall state of health of the judicial process. Defects in judicial administration such as lengthy delays and blatant incompetency of lawyers or judges must detract from the contribution courts can make to resolving social problems. Such defects also impair the value of our courts as a significant force in bringing about orderly change and protecting valued features of our society.

Courts must be free to judiciously proceed with the work at hand. Judges must not be stymied by schemes concocted by litigants, counsel, or others which are intended to thwart their efforts. If not properly contained chicanery and shrewd ploys can undermine the effectiveness of the judicial system. In the course of litigation which touches upon, or has at its very heart the disposition of delicate social issues in an age of social turmoil, the very existence of the tribunal in which the case is being tried may come under attack. In such cases a judge may find that he must resort to special procedures to insure the orderly administration of justice and the court's continued existence. But courts must take great care, in spite of the tumultuous setting in which they must go about their affairs, that the litigant's rights are protected. The task of keeping a proper balance between society's best interests and individual rights is extremely difficult. Should our courts fail to successfully meet the challenges made to their properly performing the functions assigned to them in time they will be replaced by a new forum and a new arbiter who will then pass judgment on the kinds of social issues our courts presently decide.

This volume has been prepared with four purposes in mind: (1) to call attention to the kinds of social issues presently being adjudicated in the nation's courts; (2) to focus attention on the manner in which courts have dealt with some of today's most pressing social issues; (3) to give the reader an opportunity to examine the procedures and remedies our courts have formulated and follow so that they can fairly arrive at their decisions and enforce their judgments; and (4) to assist the reader to evaluate the role of our courts as arbiters in resolving today's social issues.

I express my thanks to the many persons whose questions, answers, and ideas have guided me in the preparation of this book. Special thanks are extended to my parents whose insights into the American way of life and their endless queries and recommendations instilled, and continue to instill in their children, a desire to dig beneath the surface of contemporary relationships and structures within our society and to explore the probabilities and possibilities of fomenting change. My wife Gladys, whose awareness of social problems and understanding of human behavior, whose positive and perceptive attitudes toward all human beings, but especially young people, whose incisive analysis of the past, present, and future, whose cogency in presentation is seldom equalled, has helped me to carefully draw the line between the sorts of issues which do and do not warrant inclusion in a law text. My teenage son Sherwin, whose incessant insistence that his parents and teachers seek out answers to old and new problems, has motivated me to search for those types of materials which shed light on questions of vital concern to today's young people. He has been a most demanding taskmaster. My almost teenage daughter Pamela is not as yet able to succinctly verbalize all of her views about contemporary society. But her basic humanistic intuitive sense of ethical behavior and fairness has convinced her parents that she, like millions of other pre-teenagers across the land, will as a young woman, and then as an adult, work to promote and nurture the best in mankind and strive to eliminate that which is the least desirable. Materials which will be of concern to her as a young woman and an adult are included in this volume. For more than fifteen years I have had the cherished privilege to teach college students. Their probing of the society in which they live, the challenges they have made and continue

PREFACE

to make to the institutions and standards which proclaim what they may and may not do, and the carefully thought out queries and solutions so many of them have communicated to me in the classroom, in the hallways, on the steps, on the walkways of our sprawling campus whatever the weather may be, in my office, and in my home, and their insistence that I respond, have inestimably contributed to my writing of this volume and to making college teaching a sheer delight.

EDWIN WALLACE TUCKER

Storrs, Connecticut
June, 1971

•

TABLE OF CONTENTS

TABLE OF CASES

The principal cases are in italic type. Cases cited or discussed are in roman. References are to Pages.

TEXT—CASES—PROBLEMS

ON

THE ADJUDICATION OF SOCIAL ISSUES

Part One

JUDICIAL ADMINISTRATION

Chapter 1

ADMINISTRATION OF JUSTICE

The nature of the issues placed before a court for adjudication influence the procedures the court must use in order to fulfill its function. To properly administer the law a court at times must invoke procedures which call for the stringent control or punishment of certain types of behavior engaged in during the proceedings by a party, counsel, witnesses, spectators, or other persons. Such special procedures have to be employed to promote or protect selected societal objectives. These procedures are independent of usually followed court procedures and the substantive rules of law which the tribunal will ultimately rely upon to adjudge the rights and duties of the litigants.

Lawsuits in which courts are called upon to decide such questions as a party's contractual rights, ownership of property, the correct amount or validity of a tax assessment, or who is entitled to the proceeds of a trust fund are generally bland affairs. In such cases each litigant cherishes a victory, counsel ardently go about their tasks, there are some heated moments, some torment, some elation and some dismay, the court expends great and careful effort to arrive at a correct result, but invariably reason reigns. For the most part the participants hold their emotions at bay. Few, if any persons, not directly connected with the lawsuit, have more than a passing interest in the outcome.

1

Contrast such suits and their attendant behavior with the setting in which the adjudication of controversial social rights and responsibilities frequently takes place. Perhaps the court has been asked to decide if a black man or woman has a right to be buried in an all white cemetery, or if a woman has a right to have an abortion, or if the defendant is guilty of murder because he performed a "mercy" killing, or if the possession of marijuana should be treated as a criminal act. In such cases emotional outbursts may abound. Litigants, lawyers, spectators, and even judges occasionally appear to be bereft of reason. Interest in the proceedings is widespread. Comment, criticism, and deep diverse feelings are not confined to the courtroom. Press, radio, and television extensively report on the progress of the suit. Persons who usually remain silent feel compelled to speak out. Yet in such cases, as in all other cases, the court is obliged to dispassionately and correctly administer the law. Judges are required to see that reason and fairness determine the outcome of litigation.

To insure that justice is done, a court may have to invoke procedures specially designed to bar emotional outbursts and ranting which if left uncontrolled may precipitate a capricious or irrational result. Shouts of "political trial," or "fascist pig," or "repression" may invite rejection of rational behavior by counsel, jury, judge, witnesses, and the parties. In a tense, heated, turbulent atmosphere rampant with outrage the very procedures designed to insure reasonable action may be perverted. A result which is the product of emotion, arbitrary action, or whim may not stand. The Constitution requires that it be set aside.

Judges and jurors must be free to properly perform the tasks society has assigned to them. Courts must be allowed to properly administer the law and to enforce their mandates. For these reasons courts are empowered and obliged to formulate and enforce rules and take such steps as may be reasonably necessary to protect the integrity of the judicial process. They may punish persons who interfere with or obstruct or subvert the work of the court, or disobey a lawful order of the court, or demean the manner in which a judge goes about his official duties. A person who commits any one of the aforementioned acts is known as a contemner and is said to be guilty of contempt of court.

A contempt of court may be civil or criminal. Civil contempt occurs when the contemner violates an order of the court and the court imposes a penalty to (1) coerce him to comply with the order, (2) remedy the situation, or (3) compensate a party. For instance, a witness may refuse to obey a lawful order that he testify before a grand jury. If the judge wishes to coerce the witness he may order he be imprisoned for a period of time or until he testifies. Imprisonment is not intended to punish but to obtain sought after testimony. The contemner can gain his freedom at any time by simply obeying the court's order that he testify. Once the contemner can no longer offer testimony, such as when the grand jury has been discharged, he must be released. His imprisonment can no longer be productive. The imposition of a fine on a contemner who fails to obey an order intended to benefit another party is another example of the kind of punishment which may be meted out to one guilty of civil contempt. The fine is payable to the other party to the suit to compensate him for the damage caused him by the contemner's disobedience of the court's order.

In the case of a criminal contempt the court uses its power to punish the contemner for his behavior rather than to coerce him, remedy a wrong, or to compensate a party. One may be charged with criminal contempt if he attempts, or in fact does, obstruct or impair the administration of justice. Assume that a judge directs that a witness only answer the questions put to him and not to go into long proclamations unrelated to a question posed to him by counsel. If the witness disobeys the order the judge may charge him with criminal contempt and fine or imprison him. Here the purpose is to punish rather than to coerce the witness. The witness's later willingness to comply with the court's order will not entitle him to a refund of the fine or a release from prison.

One charged with civil or criminal contempt must be afforded due process of law. Unless required by statute or court rule one charged with civil contempt is not entitled to a trial by jury. In cases of criminal contempt if a sentence of more than six months can be imposed upon the alleged contemner he has a constitutional right to a jury trial.

There is a category of criminal contempt which may be punished summarily. This means that the accused can be punished without enjoying the usual requisites of due process such as the opportunity to cross-examine in the course of the hearing. In this category falls behavior which occurs within the sight or hearing of the judge and which disrupts the decorum of the court or prevents the orderly, dispassionate, speedy administration of justice. Examples of such behavior are verbal attacks on the integrity of the court or the judge, attacks on the judge's competency, and disorderly or violent behavior. In these cases the judge is personally aware of all of the facts. He is empowered to protect the orderly administration of justice. But even in such cases the accused is entitled to an unbiased judge. If it appears that the judge who convicted the contemner acted out of passion, animosity, or emotional reflex rather than with the dispassionate cool one might properly expect of a jurist, or if the judge who convicted the alleged contemner had been the object of such a cruel personal attack carried on against him by the accused that it does not appear likely that he was capable of impassionately considering the guilt or innocence of the accused, the conviction cannot stand. Due process requires that another judge, in a public trial, rule on the propriety of the accused's behavior.

The circumstances determine whether one charged with criminal contempt for his conduct during a trial should be dealt with the instant he supposedly misbehaves or only after the end of the trial. Instant punishment of an attorney might greatly prejudice his client's case and may therefore be properly delayed. On the other hand, when other persons are involved, the Supreme Court has stated that instant punishment might be the "only wise course" to follow. But whenever the trial, and whether the charge be civil or criminal contempt, if it appears that the defendant was dealt with in an arbitrary or oppressive fashion, his conviction cannot stand.

A number of legal doctrines, intended to permit governmental officials to effectively perform their assigned duties, shield government and governmental officials from suit. One such doctrine is sovereign immunity. When strictly followed it bars lawsuits against any branch of the federal or state government or any governmental official. Viewing the doctrine as archaic and unrealistic, and alert to the hardship it can work on one injured by official action or inaction, courts and legislatures have, within the last several decades, significantly narrowed its applicability.

The conditions under which one injured by the federal government may sue the government for relief is found in Congressional legislation and federal court decisions. Since states have adopted various approaches to limiting the use of the doctrine state court decisions and statutes must be scrutinized to determine when, in a particular state, one can obtain relief for a wrong committed by state or local officials. Even when allowed to sue the government a plaintiff is usually subject to restraints not placed on other litigants, such as (1) the need to promptly file a notice of claim, (2) suit must be commenced within a relatively short period of time after the occurrence of the wrong, and (3) a prescribed maximum sets a limit on the amount of money one can recover regardless of the extent of his injuries.

Generally, sovereign immunity is no longer a defense to suits based on breach of contract or tortious behavior. Injunctions may be granted to prohibit unconstitutional or unlawful conduct by governmental officials. Sovereign immunity commonly remains a defense to suits against officials who unwisely use their discretionary powers. In some jurisdictions this doctrine is invoked to protect judges, legislators, and administrative officers from suit who are charged with having improperly performed their duties.

Executive immunity is akin to sovereign immunity. Like sovereign immunity it shields governmental officials from suit. The federal courts invoke this doctrine in place of sovereign immunity in suits against federal officials. Like sovereign immunity, it is a court created doctrine and can be altered or done away with by court or legislative action. Under it an official is immune from suit for injuries he has caused to another as a result of his poor judgment, negligence, or malicious conduct if the complained of conduct occurred while the official was acting within the outer perimeter of his official duties. Courts have expressed the opinion that officials who need have no fear of being sued are encouraged to vigorously and diligently go about their tasks. The advantages of the immunity to the public are seen as outweighing the denial of relief to one who has suffered injury at the hands of a malicious or negligent federal officer.

It has been held that when a private business enterprise is entrusted with the same kind of task as a governmental official in a sensitive area such as safeguarding the secrecy of information vital to the nation's defense, that enterprise is imbued with executive immunity. It, like a federal official, is immune from suit for even malicious misbehavior which takes place while it goes about the business of preventing unauthorized disclosure of classified information.

Closely related to the executive immunity doctrine is the state secret privilege. This privilege is much narrower than sovereign or executive imunity. It is a rule of evidence. When recognized, it denies a litigant access to information which is in the possession of the government. To make use of the privilege the government must make a formal demand on the court that disclosure be barred. The demand must be made by the head of the department which has control of the sought after material. To decide whether or not the privilege may be used the court must, without forcing a disclosure, determine if disclosure would be dangerous to the national interest. If the court reasonably concludes that it would be, the information need not be disclosed, regardless of the adverse impact non-disclosure may have on the party requesting disclosure. Military secrets and espionage data are examples of materials which fall under the protection of the state secret privilege.

Contempt, sovereign and executive immunity, and the state secret privilege are illustrative of principles which may be invoked by or on behalf of government. The defense of entrapment and the liberal treatment of the standing to sue doctrine are examples of concepts which may be used to promote societal interests by allowing individuals to challenge particular kinds of governmental action. The first four principles limit individual freedom, the latter two concepts promote individual rights.

Federal and most state courts recognize entrapment as a defense to a criminal charge. Entrapment is the manufacture of a crime by the government. But for the action of the government the defendant would not have carried out the criminal act with which he is charged. Entrapment takes place when a governmental officer originates the idea, implants it in the accused's mind, and arranges for the performance by the accused of the unlawful act. It is not entrapment to merely present one who independently planned to commit a crime with the opportunity to carry it out. It is entrapment to "trap the unwary innocent" but it is not entrapment to "trap the unwary criminal." Contrary to the generally held view, some courts allow a defendant to use entrapment as a defense when the entrapment scheme was concocted and carried out by a private citizen.

One cannot challenge governmental action in a lawsuit unless he has standing to sue. In federal courts this means that the contesting party must have a personal stake in the outcome of the suit. Limiting the right to challenge the action taken by government to persons who would be injured if such action is not halted insures adversity. Courts see adversity as serving the purpose of sharpening and illuminating the issues they are being asked to adjudicate.

The required personal stake is present if there is a "logical nexus" between the contesting party's status and the alleged governmental wrongdoing. A logical nexus is not present if the plaintiff, on the ground that he is a taxpayer, objects to a statute he claims is unconstitutional because it wrongfully regulates another person's business, or if he objects to a federal statute on the ground that it violates the power of states over intrastate commerce, or if he objects to a taxing statute because it violates another person's right to practice medicine. In each of these instances there is said to be no logical connection between the plaintiff's status as a taxpayer and the basis for his objecting to what the government has done.

A taxpayer has standing to challenge an act of Congress which makes funds available for religious purposes on the ground that the use of the government's power to tax or to spend may not be used to favor one religion over another or to support religion in general. In such a case there is a logical connection between the plaintiff's status as a taxpayer and the governmental behavior to which he objects. Similarly, a voter may challenge an election procedure which he claims gives less weight to his vote than to the vote of other persons casting a ballot in the same election.

Statutes commonly provide that an "aggrieved" party may ask a court to rule on the propriety of agency action. One is ordinarily said to be an "aggrieved" party if the action he wishes the court to review affects one of his "legal interests." One's legal interest is affected if agency action has an economic, aesthetic, conservational, or recreational impact upon him or interferes with some other legally protected value. When a statute reveals that Congress intended to confer a benefit upon, or to protect a particular interest of a class of persons, any member of that class who claims that he may be or has been injured by agency action qualifies as an "aggrieved" party.

States differ as to the degree of personal interest one must have in the outcome of litigation to satisfy the state's standing to sue requirement or to qualify as an aggrieved person under state law. Recently state lawmakers and judges, like their federal counterparts, have chosen to take a more flexible approach to each of these criteria. This has been done with full recognition of the fact that the broader the interpretation of the "standing to sue" requisite and the more loosely "aggrieved" is construed, the greater the opportunity for individuals to make use of the courts to challenge unpopular federal and state policies.

Growing concern with the manner in which governmental officials go about their tasks and increased insistence that greater care be taken to protect individual liberties have brought forth vocal and forceful demands that new procedures and means be introduced to curb the abuse of official power and to effectively vindicate individual rights. In response, some jurisdictions have provided for the use of ombudsmen. These officials are charged with the task of seeing to it that government and governmental officers properly go about their duties. To accomplish their task ombudsmen are empowered to make inquiries, conduct investigations, and invoke prescribed procedures at the behest of private citizens. They may or may not resort to the courts to assist them in their work.

ILLINOIS v. ALLEN

Supreme Court of the United States, 1970.
90 S.Ct. 1057, 397 U.S. 337, 25 L.Ed.2d 353.

Allen, during the course of his trial in an Illinois court on a charge of armed robbery, was removed from the courtroom after he repeatedly argued with the judge, told him that "when I go out for lunchtime, you're [the judge] going to be a corpse here," threw the file papers of his court assigned lawyer on the floor, and when warned by the judge that if there was "one more outbreak of that sort" he would be removed from the courtroom told the judge "there's not going to be no trial." After lunch he was brought back into the courtroom. He asserted "there is going to be no proceeding," and said "I'm going to start talking and I'm going to keep on talking all through the trial." He was again removed from the courtroom and was kept out while the prosecution presented its case. He was then allowed to return and remained in the courtroom after promising he would behave. The jury returned a verdict of guilty. He was sentenced to 10 to 30 years. He petitioned the Federal District Court for a writ of habeas corpus, claiming he had been denied his constitutional right to confront witnesses. His petition was dismissed. The Court of Appeals reversed. The Supreme Court granted certiorari.

MR. JUSTICE BLACK delivered the opinion of the Court.

The Confrontation Clause of the Sixth Amendment to the United States Constitution provides that "In all criminal prosecutions, the accused shall enjoy the right * * * to be confronted with the witnesses against him * * *." We have held that the Fourteenth Amendment makes the guarantees of this clause obligatory upon the States. * * * One of the most basic of the rights guaranteed by the Confrontation Clause is the accused's right to be present in the courtroom at every stage of his trial. * * *

The Court of Appeals felt that the defendant's Sixth Amendment right to be present at his own trial was so "absolute" that, no matter how unruly or disruptive the defendant's conduct might be, he could never be held to have lost that right so long as he continued to insist upon it, as Allen clearly did. Therefore the Court of Appeals concluded that a trial judge could never expel a defendant from his own trial and that the judge's ultimate remedy when faced with an obstreperous defendant like Allen who determines to make his trial impossible is to bind and gag him. We cannot agree that the Sixth Amendment, the cases upon which the Court of Appeals relied, or any other cases of this Court so handicap a trial judge in conducting a criminal trial. The broad dicta in Hopt v. Utah and Lewis v. United States, * * * that a trial can never continue in the defendant's absence has been expressly rejected. * * * We accept instead the statement of Mr. Justice Cardozo who, speaking for the Court in Snyder v. Massachusetts, 291 U.S. 97, 106, 54 S.Ct. 330, 332, 78 L.Ed. 674 (1938), said: "No doubt the privilege [of personally confronting witnesses] may be lost by consent or at times even by misconduct." Although mindful that courts must indulge every reasonable presumption against the loss of constitutional rights, * * * we explicitly hold today that a defendant can lose his right to be present at trial if, after he has been warned by the judge that he will be removed if he continues his disruptive behavior, he nevertheless insists on conducting himself in a manner so disorderly, disruptive, and disrespectful of the court that his trial cannot be carried on with him in the courtroom. Once lost, the right to be present can, of course, be reclaimed as soon as the defendant is willing to conduct himself consistently with the decorum and respect inherent in the concept of courts and judicial proceedings.

It is essential to the proper administration of criminal justice that dignity, order, and decorum be the hallmarks of all court proceedings in our country. The flagrant disregard in the courtroom of elementary standards of proper conduct should not and cannot be tolerated. We believe trial judges confronted with disruptive, contumacious, stubbornly defiant defendants must be given sufficient discretion to meet the circumstances of each case. No one formula for maintaining the appropriate courtroom atmosphere will be best in all situations. We think there are at least three constitutionally permissible ways for a trial judge to handle an obstreperous defendant like Allen: (1) bind and gag him, thereby keeping him present; (2) cite him for contempt; (3) take him out of the courtroom until he promises to conduct himself properly.

* * *

* * * Allen's behavior was clearly of such an extreme and aggravated nature as to justify either his removal from the courtroom or his total physical restraint. Prior to his removal he was repeatedly warned by the trial judge that he would be removed from the courtroom if he persisted in his unruly conduct, * * * the record demonstrates that Allen would not have been at all dissuaded by the trial judge's use of his criminal contempt powers. Allen was constantly informed that he could return to the trial when he would agree to conduct himself in an orderly manner. Under these circumstances we

hold that Allen lost his right guaranteed by the Sixth and Fourteenth Amendments to be present throughout his trial.

It is not pleasant to hold that the respondent Allen was properly banished from the court for a part of his own trial. But our courts, palladiums of liberty as they are, cannot be treated disrespectfully with impunity. Nor can the accused be permitted by his disruptive conduct indefinitely to avoid being tried on the charges brought against him. It would degrade our country and our judicial system to permit our courts to be bullied, insulted, and humiliated and their orderly progress thwarted and obstructed by defendants brought before them charged with crimes. As guardians of the public welfare, our state and federal judicial systems strive to administer equal justice to the rich and the poor, the good and the bad, the native and foreign born of every race, nationality and religion. Being manned by humans, the courts are not perfect and are bound to make some errors. But, if our courts are to remain what the Founders intended, the citadels of justice, their proceedings cannot and must not be infected with the sort of scurrilous, abusive language and conduct paraded before the Illinois trial judge in this case. The record shows that the Illinois judge at all times conducted himself with that dignity, decorum, and patience that befits a judge. Even in holding that the trial judge had erred, the Court of Appeals praised his "commendable patience under severe provocation."

* * *

Reversed.

BLOOM v. ILLINOIS

Supreme Court of the United States, 1968.
88 S.Ct. 1477, 391 U.S. 194, 20 L.Ed.2d 522.

In a non-jury trial Bloom was found guilty of having filed a petition requesting that a will he knew to be forged be admitted to probate. Under state law this act was classified as a criminal contempt. Bloom was sentenced to 24 months in prison. He claimed that he had been denied his constitutional right to a trial by jury. The state supreme court affirmed his conviction. The Supreme Court granted certiorari.

MR. JUSTICE WHITE delivered the opinion of the Court.

* * *

* * * Our deliberations have convinced us, * * * that serious contempts are so nearly like other serious crimes that they are subject to the jury trial provisions of the Constitution, now binding on the States, * * *. We accept the judgment of *Barnett* and *Cheff* that criminal contempt is a petty offense unless the punishment makes it a serious one; but, in our view, dispensing with the jury in the trial of contempts subjected to severe punishment represents an unacceptable construction of the Constitution, "an unconstitutional assumption of powers by the [courts] which no lapse of time or respectable array of opinion should make us hesitate to correct." * * * The Constitution guarantees the right to jury trial in state court prosecutions for contempt just as it does for other crimes.

Criminal contempt is a crime in the ordinary sense; it is a violation of the law, a public wrong which is punishable by fine or imprisonment or both. In the words of Mr. Justice Holmes:

> "These contempts are infractions of the law, visited with punishment as such. If such acts are not criminal, we are in error as to the most fundamental characteristic of crimes as that word has been understood in English speech." * * *

Criminally contemptuous conduct may violate other provisions of the criminal law; but even when this is not the case convictions for criminal contempt are indistinguishable from ordinary criminal convictions, for their impact on the individual defendant is the same. Indeed, the role of criminal contempt and that of many ordinary criminal laws seem identical—protection of the institutions of our government and enforcement of their mandates.

Given that criminal contempt is a crime in every fundamental respect, the question is whether it is a crime to which the jury trial provisions of the Constitution apply. We hold that it is, primarily because in terms of those considerations which make the right to jury trial fundamental in criminal cases, there is no substantial difference between serious contempts and other serious crimes. Indeed, in contempt cases an even more compelling argument can be made for providing a right to jury trial as a protection against the arbitrary exercise of official power. Contemptuous conduct, though a public wrong, often strikes at the most vulnerable and human qualities of a judge's temperament. Even when the contempt is not a direct insult to the court or the judge, it frequently represents a rejection of judicial authority, or an interference with the judicial process or with the duties of officers of the court.
            * * *

* * * Prosecutions for contempt play a significant role in the proper functioning of our judicial system; but despite the important values which the contempt power protects, courts and legislatures have gradually eroded the power of judges to try contempts of their own authority. In modern times, procedures in criminal contempt cases have come to mirror those used in ordinary criminal cases. Our experience teaches that convictions for criminal contempt, not infrequently resulting in extremely serious penalties, * * * are indistinguishable from those obtained under ordinary criminal laws. If the right to jury trial is a fundamental matter in other criminal cases, which we think it is, it must also be extended to criminal contempt cases.

* * * We do not deny that serious punishment must sometimes be imposed for contempt, but we reject the contention that such punishment must be imposed without the right to jury trial. The goals of dispatch, economy, and efficiency are important, but they are amply

served by preserving the power to commit for civil contempt and by recognizing that many contempts are not serious crimes but petty offenses not within the jury trial provisions of the Constitution. When a serious contempt is at issue, considerations of efficiency must give way to the more fundamental interest of ensuring the even-handed exercise of judicial power. In isolated instances recalcitrant or irrational juries may acquit rather than apply the law to the case before them. Our system has wrestled with this problem for hundreds of years, however, and important safeguards have been devised to minimize miscarriages of justice through the malfunctioning of the jury system. Perhaps to some extent we sacrifice efficiency, expedition, and economy, but the choice in favor of jury trial has been made, and retained, in the Constitution. We see no sound reason in logic or policy not to apply it in the area of criminal contempt.
     *   *   *

     *   *   *   Under Illinois law no maximum punishment is provided for convictions for criminal contempt. *   *   *   In *Duncan* we have said that we need not settle "the exact location of the line between petty offenses and serious crimes" but that "a crime punishable by two years in prison is *   *   *   a serious crime and not a petty offense." *   *   *   Bloom was sentenced to imprisonment for two years. Our analysis of *Barnett* *   *   *   and Cheff v. Schnackenberg, *   *   * makes it clear that criminal contempt is not a crime of the sort that requires the right to jury trial regardless of the penalty involved. Under the rule in *Cheff*, when the legislature has not expressed a judgment as to the seriousness of an offense by fixing a maximum penalty which may be imposed, we are to look to the penalty actually imposed as the best evidence of the seriousness of the offense. *   *   *   Under this rule it is clear that Bloom was entitled to the right to trial by jury, and it was constitutional error to deny him that right. Accordingly, we reverse and remand for proceedings not inconsistent with this opinion.

     *   *   *

PROBLEMS

1.   Does a black defendant waive his constitutional right to challenge a state procedure which bars blacks from jury service, if his lawyer, fearful of arousing prejudice against his client intentionally fails to challenge this practice at the beginning of a state criminal proceeding?

2.   May a Congressman, who enjoys a constitutionally granted immunity from arrest while attending Congress or while going to or returning from a session of Congress in all cases except treason, felony, and breach of the peace, be served with a subpoena while traveling to Congress if his failure to obey the subpoena could render him liable to arrest?

3.   May an attorney be punished for contempt because of his failure to obey a judge's unlawful order that he sign a court document?

4.   May a judge cite a courtroom spectator for contempt if the spectator refuses to rise at the convening of the court, the spectator contending that his refusal was his way of expressing his protest against the injustices of the American legal system?

5.   Does a private citizen have standing to maintain an action to enjoin the Secretary of Defense and the Atomic Energy Commission from setting off nuclear weapons which produce radio active material?

6.   A witness in a criminal proceeding refused to obey the judge's directive that he respond to a question posed by the prosecutor. The witness told the judge he was "being 'badgered' and 'coerced' and that the court was 'suppressing evidence.' " The judge had previously warned the witness " 'to confine his answers to the questions' " and "he warned the witness that he would hold him to the natural consequences of his acts." After the trial, the judge charged the witness, because of the way he had conducted himself during the trial, with "willful and disruptive contempt of court." The judge tried the witness and "sentenced him to 10 days imprisonment and imposed a fine." The witness claimed that this procedure denied him due process of law since he was tried by the same judge he had "personally attacked" by his statement quoted above. Was the witness's contention correct?

7.   The defendant, having refused to answer questions before a grand jury, was found guilty of contempt and sentenced to a prison term of two years with the proviso that if he answered the questions before the expiration of his sentence he would be released. The grand jury was disbanded several months after he was sentenced. Insisting that his imprisonment was primarily intended to coerce him to testify before the grand jury he demanded he be released without having to complete his sentence. What judgment?

8.   At the request of the state prosecutor the trial judge discharged the plaintiff from jury service on the ground that his answers showed that he was "biased" and could not act fairly and impartially. The plaintiff sued the judge for money damages on the ground that he had been denied his constitutional right to serve as a juror. What judgment?

Chapter 2

COURT DELAY

Chapter 40 of the Magna Carta provides "we will not deny or defer to any man either justice or right." Lord Coke, the renowned seventeenth century English jurist condemned "prolonged detention without trial" of one charged with a crime. He saw delay in bringing an accused to trial as "contrary to the law and custom of England." Coke was of the opinion that "the delay in trial by itself, would be an improper denial of justice."

The Sixth Amendment to the Constitution guarantees individuals charged with a crime a speedy trial. The Fourteenth Amendment grants the same right to defendants in state criminal proceedings. Apart from the Fourteenth Amendment, state constitutions or statutes require that once formal charges are filed against an accused he be granted a speedy trial. But in spite of directives and universal agreement that the right to a speedy trial is a fundamental right under our legal system, extensive backlogs continue to plague the nation's criminal courts. For many defendants a speedy trial is nothing more than a bald ideal, often voiced but seldom realized.

At what point in time does the government's failure to bring an accused to trial violate his right to a speedy trial? With some exceptions courts have avoided a technical absolute yardstick which would "calendarize" this right. They have refused to prescribe the outermost limit of time beyond which a trial may not be delayed after the filing of an information or an indictment. To decide whether or not one has been denied a speedy trial courts employ a rule of reason. This is a factual test. It treats speed as a relative concept. Speed is regarded as consistent with some delay. When a defendant claims he has been denied a speedy trial the court closely scrutinizes the facts. If it appears that there has been an unreasonable delay in bringing the accused to trial he may not be prosecuted. To do otherwise would deny him his right to a speedy trial.

Under the rule of reason delay is condemned because it is oppressive, causes the accused unnecessary anxiety and concern, holds him suspect of wrongdoing for longer than necessary, and may make it more difficult for him to defend himself due to the dulling of memories, the loss of evidence, or the disappearance or death of witnesses. To determine whether or not a delay is lawful the court considers its length, the reasons for it, the blameworthiness of the government, the accused's reactions, and the prejudice, actual or supposed, it has caused the accused. A delay of five or more years *per se* should bar further prosecution. A delay of a year or less, if not specifically prohibited by statute or court rule, without any showing of actual prejudice caused by the delay, will not bar a trial. A delay deliberately caused by the government in order to work a hardship on the accused, even if of brief duration, would call for a dismissal of the charges. A delay consented to or not objected to by the accused does not deprive him of his right to a speedy trial.

The right to a speedy trial does not mean that a defendant can be forced to proceed to trial with such great haste that he will be denied an opportunity to conduct a meaningful defense. Speed alone does not insure fair treatment. Think of a lynching. Concern with speed cannot be allowed to overshadow other legitimate interests of the accused such as allowing him to discuss his case with his attorney and to do whatever else may be reasonably necessary for his defense. The defendant's right to a speedy trial may not deny society, acting through its officials, the opportunity to prepare for trial. The government, like the accused, must be given a reasonable opportunity to ready itself for trial, even if this necessitates some delay.

Individuals involved in civil litigation, like the government and the accused in a criminal proceeding, may rightfully insist that justice delayed is justice denied. While life and personal liberty are not at stake in civil suits in many cases the stakes for one or both of the parties may still be high. Basic civil rights, for example, may be denied or substantially altered simply because of delay. Grievously injured persons may ultimately go uncompensated should there be a long time lapse between injury and trial. When courts find that they are especially bogged down in handling criminal cases they may divert all of their available resources to the trial of criminal cases. While such action helps to expedite the disposition of criminal cases it serves to even further delay the trial of civil suits.

Many steps have been taken, some only within the last decade, to reduce court delay. A Federal Judicial Center has been created to probe problems involved in the administration of justice. An administrative office has been established within the federal court system and in a large number of state court systems. Such an office is charged with examining and reporting on the flow of cases through the courts and with making suggestions as to how the courts may more efficiently go about their work. Judicial councils, composed of judges, study the reports and proposals submitted by the administrative office and undertake to bring about improvements in court management. Administrative judges have the task of seeing to it that trial judges conscientiously and diligently perform their duties. To expedite the processing of cases the length of the judge's working day has been extended and judges' vacations have been shortened. Judges periodically gather together to consider new procedures intended to promote speed and efficiency. Newly appointed or elected judges may be obliged to attend classes carried on under the direction of experienced judges to quickly familiarize themselves with court procedures. Computers have found their place in the quest for speed. Not only do they help those who are involved in seeking out the causes of delay but they are also being used as a management tool to accelerate the flow of cases through the courts.

Various procedures are being used to promote the settlement of litigation under court auspices. Steps have been taken to facilitate the trial of cases which cannot be settled. In some jurisdictions the same judge now handles a case from its inception to its completion. Counsel are forcefully urged to agree upon as many facts as possible prior to trial. The fewer the facts to be proved during trial, the faster the trial can come to an end.

Those who have studied the causes of delay in dispensing justice have concluded that more and better qualified judges are needed to staff our courts. More courtrooms are required. Court staffs have to be enlarged. Mechanical routine chores now entrusted to judges should be done by other court officers. Some subject areas, such as traffic violations, housing code violations, and pollution law violations should be placed in the hands of administrative bodies. Care must be taken not to add to the current workload of the courts without making adequate provision for an increase in the number of judges, court officers, and courtrooms. Steps must be taken to refine court procedures so that attorneys seeking to delay the trial of a case are prevented from doing so.

Chief Justice Warren Burger has suggested that in criminal cases a period of sixty days between indictment and trial should become the order of the day. A somewhat longer period might be acceptable for civil suits. When a time lag of two or three months becomes commonplace only then can it be said that court delay is no longer a national problem.

KLOPFER v. NORTH CAROLINA

Supreme Court of the United States, 1967.
87 S.Ct. 988, 386 U.S. 213, 18 L.Ed.2d 1.

The petitioner was indicted in February, 1964. He was charged with having committed criminal trespass, a misdemeanor, in January, 1964. He was brought to trial in March, 1964. When the jury failed to agree on a verdict the court declared a mistrial and the case was continued. In April, 1965 the prosecutor's request that the case again be continued was granted. In August, 1965 the petitioner asked the trial court to permanently conclude the case as soon as possible, noting that 18 months had passed since he had been indicted. The prosecutor objected. He asked permission to take a *nolle prosequi*, with leave. Under state law this meant that the petitioner would be free to go wherever he wished, but that the state could later move the case for trial. No reason was given for the state's request. It was granted over the petitioner's objection. The petitioner appealed to the state supreme court on the ground that the trial court's decision deprived him of his right to a speedy trial under the Fourteenth Amendment. The appellate court affirmed.   Certiorari was granted.

*   *   *

Mr. Chief Justice Warren delivered the opinion of the Court.

*   *   *

The North Carolina Supreme Court's conclusion—that the right to a speedy trial does not afford affirmative protection against an unjustified postponement of trial for an accused discharged from custody—has been explicitly rejected by every other state court which has considered the question.   That conclusion has also been implicitly rejected by the numerous courts which have held that a *nolle prossed* indictment may not be reinstated at a subsequent term.

We, too, believe that the position taken by the court below was erroneous.   The petitioner is not relieved of the limitations placed upon his liberty by this prosecution merely because its suspension permits him to go "withersoever he will."   The pendency of the indictment may subject him to public scorn and deprive him of employment, and almost certainly will force curtailment of his speech, associations and participation in unpopular causes.   By indefinitely prolonging this oppression, as well as the "anxiety and concern accompanying public accusation," the criminal procedure condoned in this case by the Supreme Court of North Carolina clearly denies the petitioner the right to a speedy trial which we hold is guaranteed to him by the Sixth Amendment of the Constitution of the United States.

*   *   *

We hold here that the right to a speedy trial is as fundamental as any of the rights secured by the Sixth Amendment.   *   *   *

The history of the right to a speedy trial and its reception in this country clearly establish that it is one of the most basic rights preserved by our Constitution.

For the reasons stated above, the judgment must be reversed and remanded for proceedings not inconsistent with the opinion of the Court.   It is so ordered.

DICKEY v. FLORIDA

Supreme Court of the United States, 1970.
90 S.Ct. 1564, 398 U.S. 30, 26 L.Ed.2d 26.

On June 28, 1960, a motel in Gadsden County, Florida was robbed. Shortly thereafter Dickey was taken into custody in Jackson County, Florida on a federal robbery charge.   On the basis of the motel owner's description Gadsden authorities issued an arrest warrant for Dickey on July 1, 1960.   Although the Gadsden police knew that Dickey was in jail in Jackson County they did not request he be delivered into their custody for trial on the robbery charge.   On September 2, 1960, found guilty of the federal charge, Dickey was transferred to Leavenworth.   On the day of his transfer Gadsden authorities filed a detainer warrant with the Chief U. S. Marshal for the area, asking that Dickey be held for state prosecution after he served his federal sentence.

In 1962, while still in federal prison, Dickey petitioned the Gadsden County Court to order his presence before that Court and to try him on the motel robbery charge. His request was denied, in part on the ground that he was then in a federal prison because he had voluntarily committed a federal crime. Similar requests, made in 1963 and 1966, were also denied. On September 1, 1967, Dickey petitioned the Florida Court to dismiss the detainer warrant against him because he had been denied a speedy trial. His request was denied. Over his objection he was brought to trial in February, 1968, convicted, and sentenced to 10 years in prison, the sentence to run consecutively with his federal term. He appealed. The state appellate court affirmed. Certiorari was granted.

MR. CHIEF JUSTICE BURGER delivered the opinion of the Court.
   * * *

The record in this case shows that petitioner was available to the State at all times during the seven-year period before his trial. The State suggests no tenable reason for deferring the trial in the face of petitioner's diligent and repeated efforts by motions in the State court in 1962, 1963, and 1966 to secure a prompt trial. In the interval two witnesses died and other potential defense witnesses are alleged to have become unavailable. Police records of possible relevance have been lost or destroyed.

Florida argues that the right of the petitioner under the Federal Constitution did not arise until this Court's decision in Klopfer v. North Carolina, * * * and that not until Smith v. Hooey, 393 U.S. 374, 89 S.Ct. 575, 21 L.Ed.2d 607 (1969), was there a constitutional requirement that the State press for trial of a defendant in custody in another jurisdiction.

As noted by the Court in Smith v. Hooey, the holding of the *Klop-fer* case was that

"the Fourteenth Amendment, [applying] the Sixth Amendment right to a speedy trial is enforceable against the States as 'one of the most basic rights preserved by our Constitution.'" 393 U.S., at 374–375, 89 S.Ct. at 575.

From this the Court went on to hold that on demand a State had a duty to make a diligent and good-faith effort to secure the presence of the accused from the custodial jurisdiction and afford him a trial. In *Smith* we remanded the case to the State court without deciding whether the defendant, when available for trial in the State court, would be required to show prejudice arising from the delay.

Here the State of Florida brought the petitioner back to Florida, tried, and convicted him. Petitioner's challenge is directly to the power of the State to try him after the lapse of eight years during which he repeatedly demanded and was denied a trial.

The right to a speedy trial is not a theoretical or abstract right but one rooted in hard reality on the need to have charges promptly exposed. If the case for the prosecution calls on the accused to meet charges rather than rest on the infirmities of the prosecution's case, as is the defendant's right, the time to meet them is when the case is fresh. Stale claims have never been favored by the law, and far less so in criminal cases. Although a great many accused persons seek to put off the confrontation as long as possible, the right to a prompt inquiry into criminal charges is fundamental and the duty of the charging authority is to provide a prompt trial. This is brought sharply into focus when, as here, the accused presses for an early confrontation with his accusers and with the state. Crowded dockets, the lack of judges or lawyers, and other factors no doubt make some delays inevitable. Here, however, no valid reason for the delay existed; it was exclusively for the convenience of the state. On this record the delay with its consequent prejudice is intolerable as a matter of fact and impermissible as a matter of law.

In addition to exerting every effort to require the State to try him, there is present in this record abundant evidence of actual prejudice to petitioner in the death of two potential witnesses, unavailability of another, and the loss of police records. This is sufficient to make a remand on that issue unnecessary. We therefore reverse and remand to the District Court of Appeal of Florida, First District, with directions to vacate the judgment appealed from and discharge the petitioner from custody and from any further proceedings arising out of the charges on which that judgment was based.

Reversed and remanded with directions.

PROBLEMS

1. A Federal Court of Appeals entered an order directing that after a designated date all persons indicted by a federal grand jury sitting within the Circuit be tried within six months after an indictment was returned unless the defendant by his behavior had waived his right to a speedy trial. Any person not brought to trial within the six month period would be entitled to have the indictment against him dismissed. The United States Attorney in one of the Districts over which the Court of Appeals had jurisdiction challenged the constitutionality of the order on the ground that it denied the United States Government, and in turn the people of the United States, reasonable use of the police power since it required the release of persons even in those cases in which, because of shortage of staff or other resources, the United States could not proceed to trial within the prescribed six month period. What judgment?

2. The defendant, indicted on January 4, 1964, was arraigned shortly thereafter and released on a $50 cash bond. Five years later the state moved the case for trial. The defendant asked the court to dismiss the indictment because of the state's failure to move the case

within a reasonable period of time after the indictment had been returned. What judgment?

3. Seven months after the government completed its investigation of the defendant it presented its evidence to a grand jury. Shortly thereafter he was indicted. The defendant moved to dismiss the indictment on the ground that the government's delay denied him his constitutional right to a speedy trial. Is he correct?

4. A murder was committed in 1937. In 1939 the defendant was convicted of rape. Shortly thereafter, in a written confession, he admitted that he committed the 1937 murder. In 1953 a court ordered a new trial on the rape conviction. The following day the defendant was indicted for the 1937 murder. His first trial on the murder charge ended in a hung jury. He was retried in 1955 and sentenced to 199 years. On appeal, his only argument was that he had been denied a speedy trial and therefore his conviction should be set aside. What judgment?

5. The defendant, indicted in Massachusetts, was already serving a prison sentence in Georgia. He petitioned the Massachusetts court to bring him to trial within a reasonable period of time or to dismiss the indictment against him. The state opposed an immediate trial, arguing that if the request was granted it would be costly for the state to transport the prisoner to and from Massachusetts and it was only the defendant's misconduct which made his request necessary. The trial court denied the request. The defendant appealed. What judgment?

*

Part Two

LIFE AND THE QUALITY OF LIFE

Chapter 3

ABORTION AND EUTHANASIA

Abortion may be defined as "the expulsion of the fetus at a period of uterogestation so early that it has not acquired the power of sustaining independent life." Ordinarily a fetus can survive outside of the uterus once it has attained the age of twenty-eight weeks. At common law it was a crime to procure or to take part in the performance of an abortion if the fetus had already quickened. A fetus is said to be quickened once the mother feels its movement. Quickening normally occurs between the sixteenth and twentieth week after pregnancy. By statute a state may make it a crime to abort a fetus even prior to quickening. This approach prohibits abortion from the moment of conception.

A planned, deliberate, unjustified killing of a human being at any time after birth is treated as a wrong to society. One who commits such an act may be imprisoned or perhaps be put to death. Should one who destroys a fetus be treated as a murderer? Some persons say yes. They would outlaw all abortions. Others are of the opinion that at times an abortion is justifiable, as when it is necessary for the mother's well-being. An abortion performed under such circumstances is classified as therapeutic. Many states allow therapeutic abortions as well as abortions carried out when conception followed a rape or resulted from an incestuous relationship. A eugenic abortion is one performed to prevent the birth of a potentially defective child. A number of states permit such abortions.

A change in attitude toward the tenets of organized religion, unprecedented regard for the wishes of the pregnant woman, growing concern with overpopulation, and an awareness of the many and varied social, economic, and political problems which accompany a large population have contributed to present day widespread reconsideration of the extent to which society has an interest in protecting a fetus from destruction. A nineteenth century Pennsylvania court found that survival of a fetus was a matter of state concern. The court condemned abortion as a wrongful interference with, and a violation of, "the mysteries of nature in the process by which the human race is propagated and continued." Abortion, the court declared, is "a crime against nature which obstructs the fountains of life, and therefore, it is punished." This thinking is in sharp contrast to recent innovations in abortion law. For example, today, in New York, a fe-

when it couches its enactment in common law language, that its intent was to continue those rules in statutory form. * * * Perhaps the most influential statement of the "born alive" rule is that of Coke, in mid-17th century: "If a woman be quick with childe, and by a potion or otherwise killeth it in her wombe, or if a man beat her, whereby the childe dyeth in her body, and she is delivered of a dead childe, this is a great misprision [i. e., misdemeanor], and no murder; but if the childe be born alive and dyeth of the potion, battery, or other cause, this is murder; for in law it is accounted a reasonable creature, *in rerum natura*, when it is born alive." * * * In short, "By Coke's time, the common law regarded abortion as murder only if the foetus is (1) quickened, (2) born alive, (3) lives for a brief interval, and (4) then dies." * * *

By the year 1850 this rule of the common law had long been accepted in the United States. As early as 1797 it was held that proof the child was born alive is necessary to support an indictment for murder * * *, and the same rule was reiterated on the eve of the first session of our Legislature * * *.

We conclude that in declaring murder to be the unlawful and malicious killing of a "human being" the Legislature of 1850 intended that term to have the settled common law meaning of a person who had been born alive, and did not intend the act of feticide—as distinguished from abortion—to be an offense under the laws of California.

    * * *

It is the policy of this state to construe a penal statute as favorably to the defendant as its language and the circumstances of its application may reasonably permit; just as in the case of a question of fact, the defendant is entitled to the benefit of every reasonable doubt as to the true interpretation of words or the construction of language used in a statute. * * * We hold that in adopting the definition of murder in Penal Code section 187 the Legislature intended to exclude from its reach the act of killing an unborn fetus.

The People urge, however, that the sciences of obstetrics and pediatrics have greatly progressed * * * to the point where with proper medical care a normally developed fetus prematurely born at 28 weeks or more has an excellent chance of survival, i. e., is "viable"; that the common law requirement of live birth to prove the fetus had become a "human being" who may be the victim of murder is no longer in accord with scientific fact, since an unborn but viable fetus is now fully capable of independent life; and that one who unlawfully and maliciously terminates such a life should therefore be liable to prosecution for murder under section 187. * * *

    * * *

Whether to thus extend liability for murder in California is a determination solely within the province of the Legislature. For a court to simply declare, by judicial fiat, that the time has now come to prosecute under section 187 one who kills an unborn but viable fetus would indeed be to rewrite the statute under the guise of construing it.

The second obstacle to the proposed judicial enlargement of section 187 is the guarantee of due process of law. Assuming *arguendo* that we have the power to adopt the new construction of this statute as the law of California, such a ruling, by constitutional command, could operate only prospectively, and thus could not in any event reach the conduct of petitioner on February 23, 1969.

The first essential of due process is fair warning of the act which is made punishable as a crime. "That the terms of a penal statute creating a new offense must be sufficiently explicit to inform those who are subject to it what conduct on their part will render them liable to its penalties, is a well-recognized requirement, consonant alike with ordinary notions of fair play and the settled rules of law." * * * "No one may be required at peril of life, liberty or property to speculate as to the meaning of penal statutes. All are entitled to be informed as to what the State commands or forbids." * * *

Turning to the case law, we find no reported decision of the California courts which should have given petitioner notice that the killing of an unborn but viable fetus was prohibited by section 187. Indeed, the contrary clearly appears. * * *

We conclude that the judicial enlargement of section 187 now urged upon us by the People would not have been foreseeable to this petitioner, and hence that its adoption at this time would deny him due process of law.

Let a peremptory writ of prohibition issue restraining respondent court from taking any further proceedings on Count I of the information, charging petitioner with the crime of murder.

BABBITZ v. McCANN

United States District Court, E.D. Wisconsin, 1970.
310 F.Supp. 293.

In a state criminal proceeding the plaintiff, a physician, was charged with aborting, with the consent of the mother, an unquickened child in violation of a state abortion law. He brought this action to have the law adjudged unconstitutional and its enforcement enjoined. In part, the Wisconsin statute provided that any person, other than the mother, who destroyed the life of an unborn child might be punished by a fine of up to $5,000 or three years imprisonment, or both [§ 940.04(1)]. If the unborn child was quickened, imprisonment could be for a period of up to fifteen years. A physician might lawfully perform a therapeutic abortion when necessary to save the life of the mother [§ 940.04(5)]. The statute defined an unborn child as a human being from the time of conception.

PER CURIAM.

* * *

We hold that portions of the statute are constitutionally invalid, but we decline to enjoin the pending state prosecution of the plaintiff.

* * *

We believe we must apply the standard established in Douglas v. City of Jeanette, * * * there the Supreme Court observed that it was Congressional policy to leave to the state courts the trial of state criminal cases, and that such proceedings should be enjoined only in exceptional circumstances. We do not regard this as an exceptional case, and Dr. Babbitz is not entitled to injunctive relief. In the event that the state persists in the prosecution of Dr. Babbitz, we have no reason to doubt that the state courts of Wisconsin will fully vindicate his federal constitutional rights. * * *

Notwithstanding our denial of injunctive relief, a federal court is obliged to weigh separately the issue of declaratory relief. * * *

The ninth amendment to the United States Constitution provides:

"The enumeration in the Constitution, of certain rights, shall not be construed to deny or disparage others retained by the people."

In terms of the Wisconsin statute, we do not purport to decide the question of a woman's aborting a fetus which has already quickened. * * *

While problems of over-population, ecology and pollution have been brought to our attention, we deem them secondary as decisional factors in a judicial resolution of the issues at hand. So, too, we find it necessary to set aside arguments involving theological and ecclesiastical considerations.

Obviously, there is no topic more closely interwoven with the intimacy of the home and marriage than that which relates to the conception and bearing of progeny. Recent court cases have considered the sanctity of the right to privacy in home, sex and marriage; however, the concept of private rights, with which the state may not interfere in the absence of a compelling state interest, is one of long standing.

* * *

Recent decisions have asserted a judicial application of the ninth amendment to the matter of privacy in marital relations and contraception. In Griswold v. Connecticut, * * * the court struck down the Connecticut statute which forbade the use of contraceptives. * * * In the words of the Court, * * * many decisions by the Supreme Court "bear witness that the right of privacy which presses for recognition here is a legitimate one." * * *

In People v. Belous, * * * the California supreme court invalidated a state statute which made it illegal to perform an abortion on a woman unless it was necessary to preserve her life. The court said, * * *:

"The fundamental right of the woman to choose whether to bear children follows from the Supreme Court's and this court's repeated acknowledgment of a 'right of privacy' or 'liberty' in matters related to marriage, family, and sex."

* * *

It is clear that in order to justify the regulation of such fundamental private rights, the state must show a compelling need. * * *

The defendants urge that the state's interest in protecting the embryo is a sufficient basis to sustain the statute. Upon a balancing of the relevant interests, we hold that a woman's right to refuse to carry an embryo during the early months of pregnancy may not be invaded by the state without a more compelling public necessity than is reflected in the statute in question. When measured against the claimed "rights" of an embryo of four months or less, we hold that the mother's right transcends that of such an embryo.

We also find no compelling state interest in a need to protect the mother's life. At common law, abortion was not a crime unless the mother was quick with child. * * * This position was reflected in the original Wisconsin abortion statute, * * *

We are persuaded that a medical abortion during early pregnancy is not inherently dangerous to the mother. Nor do we find a compelling state interest in connection with the discouragement of non-marital sexual intercourse. The statute involved does not purport to distinguish between married and unmarried women.

We are invited to resolve the philosophical question, raised in some of the amicus curiae briefs, as to when an embryo becomes a child. For the purposes of this decision, we think it is sufficient to conclude that the mother's interests are superior to that of an unquickened embryo, whether the embryo is mere protoplasm, as the plaintiff contends, or a human being, as the Wisconsin statute declares.

There are a number of situations in which there are especially forceful reasons to support a woman's desire to reject an embryo. These include a rubella or thalidomide pregnancy and one stemming from either rape or incest. The instant statute does not distinguish these special cases, but in our opinion, the state does not have a compelling interest even in the normal situation to require a woman to remain pregnant during the early months following her conception.

Under its police power, the state can regulate certain aspects of abortion. Thus, it is permissible for the state to require that abortions be conducted by qualified physicians. The police power of the state does not, however, entitle it to deny to a woman the basic right reserved to her under the ninth amendment to decide whether she should carry or reject an embryo which has not yet quickened. The challenged sections of the present Wisconsin statute suffer from an infirmity of fatal overbreath.

The plaintiff is entitled to a declaratory judgment declaring § 940.04(1) and (5) violative of the United States Constitution. The plaintiff is not entitled to an injunction enjoining the defendants or their successors in office from prosecuting the plaintiff under § 940.04 (1) and (5).

It is so ordered.

PROBLEMS

1. May a mother recover damages for the destruction of an unquickened fetus resulting from an accident caused by the defendant's negligent operation of an automobile? Would your answer be the same if the fetus had quickened prior to its destruction? Would your answer be different if the fetus, quickened at the time of the accident, was born and later died because of the injuries which resulted from the accident?

2. Is a quickened fetus a "person" for the purposes of a statute which provides that the next of kin of deceased "persons" could recover damages from the one whose negligent behavior caused the deceased's death?

3. Is it constitutional for a state law to provide that if three licensed physicians certify that a person is suffering from a terminal disease and can live no longer than six months at the most should that person consent he or she can be put to death three days after the physicians' certificates are signed, or can be put to death with the consent of his or her next of kin if he or she is unable to communicate either consent or disagreement? Would your answer be the same if after the certificates were signed, but before the patient could be put to death, a court would have to hold an evidentiary hearing to determine if the prognosis is correct?

4. May a state compel pregnant women to undergo tests to determine if the fetus they are carrying will develop into a healthy infant and in those cases in which it is discovered that the fetus will probably not so develop, require the fetus to be destroyed at state expense?

5. Is a physician, who is convinced, for good and proper medical reasons, that his patient is to die within a short period of time, guilty of murder if he hastens, at the patient's request, his death by administering an overdose of pain relieving drugs? Would your answer be the same if the physician proceeded to cause the patient's death but only after the patient had repeatedly begged him to do so? Would your answer be the same if although the patient was unable to communicate with the physician it was clear to the physician that the patient was in great pain and would remain so for the rest of his life, which he believed could not exceed six months?

6. Is a physician guilty of malpractice if he fails to take every medical step possible under the circumstances to prolong the life of a patient who has been unconscious for six months and, who, by all standards of contemporary medical knowledge could at the outside remain alive no longer than a month? Six months? A year? Two years?

7. A statute which permitted a physician to abort a child when "necessary for preservation of the mother's life or health" was challenged as too vague and too broad to be constitutional? Is it?

8. The appellant was refused citizenship on the ground that he lacked "good moral character." The basis of the refusal was that he had intentionally administered a lethal dose of chloroform to his thirteen year old son who, because of brain damage, was destined to be an idiot and a physical monstrosity. He was malformed in all four limbs, blind, mute, and could not care for himself. When tried for manslaughter the jury found the appellant guilty of second degree manslaughter and recommended "utmost clemency." He was placed on probation. Except for this act, it was conceded that he was a good father to his four other children, a good husband, and of good moral character. Before the appellate court the appellant argued that the killing of his son was not immoral and that he did have "good moral character." What judgment?

Chapter 4

FAMILY PLANNING

A plethora of long established legal principles dealing with procreation, contraception, birth, annulment, marriage, and divorce are predicated on approval of the proposition that sexual intercourse and the birth and raising of children should all take place within the framework of a single unit, the family. For ages the concept of family served to satisfy a number of crucial individual and societal demands including religious dogma, economics, community established tests of right and wrong, and human physical, physiological, psychological, and philosophical needs and desires. But significant changes in thought, technology, the environment, values, and the social fabric, especially since the beginning of the twentieth century, have brought into question the validity, and even the desirability, of having marriage the nucleus around which sexual intercourse and parenthood should take place. As expected, the content of the law has been influenced by the appearance of new desiderata and the putting aside of ancient shibboleths in regard to the role of the family in contemporary civilized society. Within the next two decades further modifications will undoubtedly be made in the law's present constraints on extra-marital sexual intercourse and the begetting and rearing of children.

The term bastard is associated with grave wrongdoing. Birth of a child without the marriage of the child's parents conflicts with the idea of family. Traditionally bastards and their parents have been subjected to social disgrace and legal recriminations. Grave penalties have been imposed on the parents and serious legal disabilities have been placed on the illegitimate child. Today, in some quarters, the stigma once attached to illegitimacy is less intense. Many legal consequences which used to plague one who was born out of wedlock have also been abated.

The liberation of the illegitimate child has been greatly aided by a number of recent Supreme Court decisions. The Court has stated that illegitimate persons are not " 'nonpersons.' They are human, live, and have their being. They are clearly 'persons' within the meaning of the Equal Protection Clause of the Fourteenth Amendment." [1] On this basis the Court has struck down a state statute which allowed all persons but an illegitimate child to sue and recover money damages from the person who wrongfully caused the death of his or her mother. The Court has likewise ruled unconstitutional a state statute which denied the mother of an illegitimate child the right to sue and recover money damages against one whose negligence caused the child's death. The Court found no causal connection between the child's death and

1. Levy v. Louisiana, 88 S.Ct. 1509, 391
U.S. 68, 20 L.Ed.2d 436 (1968).

the " 'sin' " committed by the mother.[2] The Court has held that when a state takes part in a federally sponsored program to aid needy children the state may not, to discourage extra-marital sexual relations and illegitimacy, deny financial assistance to children otherwise qualified to receive assistance on the ground that the mother engaged in sexual intercourse with a man other than her husband. While a state may take reasonable steps to discourage immorality and illegitimacy and institute rehabilitation programs, it may not impose a penalty on a child on the basis of the nature of the sexual behavior engaged in by his or her mother.[3]

Does an individual possess a constitutional right to be free from governmental action designed to deprive him or her of the physical capacity to procreate? The response of the Supreme Court more than four decades ago was a qualified yes. Under certain circumstances the police power of government may be employed to compel sterilization. In the case in question state law called for forced sterilization in such cases as medical evidence established that the individual against whom state action was to be taken would, if a partner in an act of sexual intercourse which resulted in conception and birth, probably become the parent of an imbecile or a feeble-minded person. The medical evidence offered in the case was found to satisfy the statutory test. The surgical process prescribed to effect sterilization was assumed to be otherwise harmless. The Court ruled that so long as (1) the procedures used by the state to decide if the statutory test had been met satisfied the demands of due process and (2) the equal protection of the laws clause had not been violated, the state could resort to involuntary sterilization to prevent the birth of "degenerate offspring." [4]

In a subsequent challenge to a state sterilization law the Court found that the statute violated the equal protection of the laws clause. Under the statute one found guilty of repeatedly committing larceny could be sterilized but one repeatedly guilty of embezzlement could not be. The state's drawing of a distinction between larceny and embezzlement was condemned as "conspicuously artificial" and "invidious." The Court took the occasion to point out that the right to procreate was "one of the basic civil rights of man" and that procreation was a "basic liberty." [5]

If the right to procreate is a fundamental right, do individuals have a right to employ means to prevent conception while they engage in sexual intercourse? Religious doctrine may bar such behavior. Until very recently many states prohibited the sale of mechanical means designed to prevent conception. The Supreme Court has found that the decision of married persons to have or not to have children is a matter of personal decision-making. On this basis the Justices

2. Glona v. American Guarantee & Liability Co., 88 S.Ct. 1515, 391 U.S. 73, 20 L.Ed.2d 441 (1968).

3. King v. Smith, 88 S.Ct. 2128, 392 U.S. 309, 20 L.Ed.2d 1118 (1968).

4. Buck v. Bell, 47 S.Ct. 584, 274 U.S. 200, 71 L.Ed. 1000 (1927).

5. Skinner v. Oklahoma, 62 S.Ct. 1110, 316 U.S. 535, 86 L.Ed. 1655 (1942).

ruled that a state had no interest in, and therefore, might not bar, the distribution of contraceptive devices to a husband or a wife who wished to practice birth control.   This principle has now been applied to unmarried persons.   Presumably a state may not constitutionally prohibit a surgeon from performing an operation to sterilize either a man or a woman who wishes to put an end to his or her capacity to procreate.

When conception follows the artificial insemination of a husband's semen into his wife the child is treated as legitimate.   If a husband consents to the use of another man's semen to artificially inseminate his wife is the child born as a result of this procedure to be treated as the husband's child?   It has been held that (1) the child is illegitimate but (2) the husband is entitled to visit the child and (3) since the husband agreed to the artificial insemination he is obliged to support the child.

Persons lacking capacity to procreate may wish to adopt one or more children.   State statutes set forth the circumstances under which a court may approve an adoption.   Care must be taken not to deprive the natural father or mother of their parental rights.   Failure to accord either parent due process or equal protection of the laws would vitiate an adoption proceeding.

When deciding whether or not to allow an adoption the court must pay prime attention to the best interests of the child.   At one time state laws prohibited the adoption of a black child by white persons and the adoption of a white child by black persons.   Today this type of statute is unconstitutional.   A statutory test tied to racial considerations constitutes an invidious discrimination and violates the equal protection of the laws clause.   State statutes generally provide that the court charged with carrying out adoption proceedings should look with favor on the fact that the child and the persons wishing to adopt the child are of the same religious faith.   Courts have rejected the proposition that under no circumstances might an adoption be granted when the child's faith differs from the faith of the persons who have petitioned the court for permission to adopt the child.

Some legal principles governing the marital relationship, in use but three or four decades ago, are now no longer followed.   States which have effected the greatest change in their divorce laws have espoused a philosophy that a state should not deny either spouse a divorce when the marriage is in fact no longer a marriage in the true sense of the word.   Such states have rejected the view that divorce is based on guilt and that to obtain a divorce a spouse must prove that the other spouse has been guilty of the kind of wrongdoing which the legislature believes gives the innocent party a right to demand the termination of the marriage.   The de facto demise of the marital relationship, rather than guilt or innocence, is the standard used by these states to decide if a spouse should or should not be granted a divorce. In states in which an extreme departure from past practices has occurred, a divorce can be obtained by either spouse doing little more than following prescribed court procedures and waiting for the specified period of time to pass before requesting that the court enter a judgment formally declaring an end to the marriage.

A doctrine which is steadily disappearing from our law is that of intrafamily immunity. When broadly applied it bans one member of a family from suing any other family member. Today one spouse can sue the other spouse. The law has long recognized the right of a child to ask a court to adjudge his rights and the rights of his parents under a contract, a will, to property, or to an inheritance. More recently the right of a child to sue his parents for intentionally inflicting injury upon him has been recognized. The newest addition in this area has been acknowledgment of a right of a child to sue his parents for negligently causing him injury. In many such cases an insurance company rather than the parent will ultimately pay the amount of the judgment. Courts which have refused to completely put to rest the intrafamily immunity doctrine have allowed a child to sue his negligent parent under special circumstances, such as when (1) an insurance company will definitely pay the judgment, or (2) the injury caused to the child by the parent took place while the parent was engaged in a business activity, or (3) the injury did not take place while the parent was exercising parental authority over the child, or (4) the injury did not happen at a time when the parent was exercising his or her discretion in caring for the child, such as providing the child with food, clothing, shelter, medical or dental care.

GRISWOLD v. CONNECTICUT

Supreme Court of the United States, 1965.
85 S.Ct. 1678, 381 U.S. 479, 14 L.Ed.2d 510.

Each appellant was associated with a group known as the Planned Parenthood League of Connecticut. One was the group's director and the other its physician. In violation of state law they provided married persons with "information, instruction and medical advice * * * as to * * * means of preventing conception." They were fined $100. From a state supreme court decision affirming their conviction they appealed.

MR. JUSTICE DOUGLAS delivered the opinion of the Court.

* * *

We do not sit as a super-legislature to determine the wisdom, need, and propriety of laws that touch economic problems, business affairs, or social conditions. This law, however, operates directly on an intimate relation of husband and wife and their physician's role in one aspect of that relation.

The association of people is not mentioned in the Constitution nor in the Bill of Rights. The right to educate a child in a school of the parents' choice—whether public or private or parochial—is also not mentioned. Nor is the right to study any particular subject or any foreign language. Yet the First Amendment has been construed to include certain of those rights.

By Pierce v. Society of Sisters, * * * the right to educate one's children as one chooses is made applicable to the States by the force of the First and Fourteenth Amendments. By Meyer v. State of Nebraska, * * * the same dignity is given the right to study the German language in a private school. In other words, the State may not, consistently with the spirit of the First Amendment, contract the spectrum of available knowledge. The right of freedom of speech and press includes not only the right to utter or to print, but the right to distribute, the right to receive, the right to read * * * and freedom of inquiry, freedom of thought, and freedom to teach * * *— indeed the freedom of the entire university community. * * * Without those peripheral rights the specific rights would be less secure. And so we reaffirm the principle of the Pierce and the Meyer cases.

In NAACP v. State of Alabama, * * * we protected the "freedom to associate and privacy in one's associations," noting that freedom of association was a peripheral First Amendment right. Disclosure of membership lists of a constitutionally valid association, we held, was invalid "as entailing the likelihood of a substantial restraint upon the exercise by petitioner's members of their right to freedom of association." Ibid. In other words, the First Amendment has a penumbra where privacy is protected from governmental intrusion. In like context, we have protected forms of "association" that are not political in the customary sense but pertain to the social, legal, and economic benefit of the members. * * *

Those cases involved more than the "right of assembly"—a right that extends to all irrespective of their race or idealogy. * * *

The foregoing cases suggest that specific guarantees in the Bill of Rights have penumbras, formed by emanations from those guarantees that help give them life and substance. * * * Various guarantees create zones of privacy. The right of association contained in the penumbra of the First Amendment is one, as we have seen. * * *

The Fourth and Fifth Amendments were described in Boyd v. United States, * * * as protection against all governmental invasions "of the sanctity of a man's home and the privacies of life."

We have had many controversies over these penumbral rights of "privacy and repose." * * * These cases bear witness that the right of privacy which presses for recognition here is a legitimate one.

The present case, then, concerns a relationship lying within the zone of privacy created by several fundamental constitutional guarantees. And it concerns a law which, in forbidding the use of contraceptives rather than regulating their manufacture or sale, seeks to achieve its goals by means having a maximum destructive impact upon that relationship. Such a law cannot stand in light of the familiar principle, so often applied by this Court, that a "governmental purpose to control or prevent activities constitutionally subject to state regulation may not be achieved by means which sweep unnecessarily broadly and thereby invade the area of protected freedoms." * * * Would we allow the police to search the sacred precincts of marital bedrooms for telltale signs of the use of contraceptives? The very idea is repulsive to the notions of privacy surrounding the marriage relationship.

We deal with a right of privacy older than the Bill of Rights—older than our political parties, older than our school system. Marriage is a coming together for better or for worse, hopefully enduring, and intimate to the degree of being sacred. It is an association that promotes a way of life, not causes; a harmony in living, not political faith; a bilateral loyalty, not commercial or social projects. Yet it is an association for as noble a purpose as any involved in our prior decisions.

Reversed.

ARMSTRONG v. MANZO

Supreme Court of the United States, 1965.
87 S.Ct. 1187, 380 U.S. 545, 14 L.Ed.2d 62.

The petitioner and his wife were divorced. She was awarded custody of Molly, their only child, and he was granted visitation rights. The petitioner was ordered to pay $50 a month for Molly's support. One year after the divorce the petitioner's former wife married the respondent. Two years later the respondent started an adoption proceeding asking the court to make him Molly's legal father. State law provided that Molly could be adopted by the respondent without the petitioner's consent if the petitioner had not, commensurate with his financial ability, contributed substantially to her support for at least two years. The petitioner's ex-wife filed an affidavit with the court stating that the petitioner had failed to contribute to Molly's support for more than two years. On the basis of the affidavit, without a hearing of any kind, and without any notice to the petitioner, the court approved the adoption. The petitioner, after learning what the court had done, moved that the adoption decree be annulled. A hearing was held. The petitioner offered evidence to show that he had not failed to contribute to Molly's support commensurate with his financial ability. At the end of the hearing the court denied the petitioner's request. The state appellate court affirmed. Certiorari was granted.

Mr. JUSTICE STEWART delivered the opinion of the Court.

* * * It is clear that failure to give the petitioner notice of the pending adoption proceedings violated the most rudimentary demands of due process of law. "Many controversies have raged about the cryptic and abstract words of the Due Process Clause but there can be no doubt that at a minimum they require that deprivation of life, liberty or property by adjudication be preceded by notice and opportunity for hearing appropriate to the nature of the case." * * * "An elementary and fundamental requirement of due process in any proceeding which is to be accorded finality is notice reasonably calculated, under all the circumstances, to apprise interested parties of the

pendency of the action and afford them an oportunity to present their objections. * * * Questions frequently arise as to the adequacy of a particular form of notice in a particular case. * * * But as to the basic requirement of notice itself there can be no doubt, where, as here, the result of the judicial proceeding was permanently to deprive a legitimate parent of all that parenthood implies. * * *

The Texas Court of Civil Appeals implicitly recognized this constitutional rule, but held, in accord with its understanding of the Texas precedents, that whatever constitutional infirmity resulted from the failure to give the petitioner notice had been cured by the hearing subsequently afforded to him upon his motion to set aside the decree. * * * We cannot agree.

Had the petitioner been given the timely notice which the Constitution requires, the Manzos, as the moving parties, would have had the burden of proving their case as against whatever defenses the petitioner might have interposed. * * * It would have been incumbent upon them to show not only that Salvatore Manzo met all the requisites of an adoptive parent under Texas law, but also to prove why the petitioner's consent to the adoption was not required. Had neither side offered any evidence, those who initiated the adoption proceedings could not have prevailed.

Instead, the petitioner was faced on his first appearance in the courtroom with the task of overcoming an adverse decree entered by one judge, based upon a finding of nonsupport made by another judge. As the record shows, there was placed upon the petitioner the burden of affirmatively showing that he had contributed to the support of his daughter to the limit of his financial ability over the period involved. The burdens thus placed upon the petitioner were real, not purely theoretical. For "it is plain that where the burden of proof lies may be decisive of the outcome." * * * Yet these burdens would not have been imposed upon him had he been given timely notice in accord with the Constitution.

A fundamental requirement of due process is "the opportunity to be heard." * * * It is an opportunity which must be granted at a meaningful time and in a meaningful manner. The trial court could have fully accorded this right to the petitioner only by granting his motion to set aside the decree and consider the case anew. Only that would have wiped the slate clean. Only that would have restored the petitioner to the position he would have occupied had due process of law been accorded to him in the first place. His motion should have been granted. * * *

Reversed and remanded.

PROBLEMS

1. Does a child have a constitutional right to be classified legitimate when the child's mother, with her husband's consent, was impregnated by use of another man's semen?

2. May a high school bar sixteen year old married students from extracurricular activities?

3. The plaintiff's husband used a drug which was manufactured by the defendant. The drug rendered him impotent although he had not used the drug in order to become impotent. The plaintiff sues the manufacturer for money damages. What judgment?

4. A mother gave birth control instructions to her 16 year old unwed daughter after the daughter's third pregnancy. Because she gave such instructions she was charged with the crime of contributing to the delinquency of a minor. The mother defended her conduct on the ground that it was beyond the control of the state because of the constitutional guarantee of freedom of speech. Is she correct?

5. The infant plaintiff brought an action against the defendant asking for money damages on the ground that the defendant had induced one of his parents to leave the family. State law prohibited suits based on alienation of affections of any person, animal, or thing capable of feeling affection. Is the infant entitled to a judgment?

6. If Congress, wishing to control the size of the nation's population, enacted a law prohibiting a husband and wife from having more than two children, would the law be constitutional?

7. The defendant was found guilty of violating a state statute which prohibited the sale of contraceptive devices to unmarried persons. The defendant claimed that what the state was seeking to do was to regulate morality and to treat contraceptives as immoral *per se*. Such state action, he argued, conflicted with a fundamental human right and was therefore unconstitutional. Is he correct?

8. Husband and wife were Caucasians. After their divorce the wife was granted custody of their two children. She later married a black man and moved, with the children and her new husband, into a neighborhood inhabited predominantly by blacks. The children's father demanded that the court deny her future custody of the children. He asked the court to take into account the fact that if the children remained with their mother rather than with him they would be living in an area predominantly occupied by blacks. Should the court pay any attention to this fact?

9. Are children whose father was injured due to the defendant's negligence entitled to a judgment for money damages against the defendant for the loss of familial relationship they suffered while he was bedridden as a result of the accident?

Chapter 5

ENVIRONMENT

As late as the mid-1960's there was little general interest in conservation, preservation, aesthetics, demography, and ecology. Concern with the quality of man's habitat was overshadowed, almost to oblivion, by the overwhelming attention society, its leaders, and its institutions paid to individualism, property rights, economic growth, means of cheaply marshaling and utilizing natural resources, and the securing and enjoying of commercially tauted, personally sought after, or truly needed goods and facilities that could be made available only in a science oriented milieu in which extensive use is made of a highly developed and refined technology. Decision-makers, when called upon to choose between taking action to protect man's environment and taking action to protect individualism, property rights, business enterprise, or the wishes of consumers, in most instances decided to follow a course of action which paid little if any heed to what was best or essential to preserve or protect man's environment. The shielding of mankind's home from destruction ranked low on the nation's list of matters of vital importance.

By the latter part of the 1960's an increasing number of persons were displaying an awareness of the fact that if man continued to make short shrift of his environment the consequences of such misbehavior could be catastrophic. As the ranks of the environmentalists swelled the nation's legal institutions started to respond. Federal, state, and local law-making bodies, courts, governmental executive officers, and administrative agencies, in varying degrees, answered the call for change. The first Earth Day was celebrated in the Spring of 1970. Poignantly, Earth Day invited society, its institutions, and its leaders to proceed to take such steps as were necessary to satisfy mankind's critical need for a suitable and acceptable environment.

In the National Environmental Policy Act of 1969 Congress expressly called attention to "the profound impact * * * of population growth, high-density urbanization, industrial expansion, resource exploitation, and new and expanding technological advances" on the environment. It recognized the urgent need to restore and maintain "environmental quality." It declared that it "is the continuing policy of the Federal Government, in cooperation with State and local governments, and other concerned public and private organizations, to use all practicable means and measures, including financial and technical assistance, in a manner calculated to foster and promote the general welfare, to create and maintain conditions under which man and nature can exist in productive harmony, and fulfill the social, economic, and other requirements of present and future generations of Americans."

38

In the text of the Act Congress speaks of assuring "for all Americans safe, healthful, productive, and esthetically and culturally pleasing surroundings;" the desirability of preserving "important historic, cultural, and national aspects of our national heritage;" achieving "a balance between population and resource use which will permit high standards of living and a wide sharing of life's amenities;" and enhancing "the quality of renewable resources and [to] approach the maximum attainable recycling of depletable resources."

The Act requires the President to submit annually to Congress an "Environment Quality Report." A Council on Environmental Quality is established by the Act. The Council's duties include assisting and advising the President in the preparation of his annual report, to gather information concerning the condition of the environment, to evaluate existing programs, and to recommend to the President what action should be taken "to foster and promote the improvement of environmental quality to meet the conservation, social, economic, health, and other requirements and goals of the Nation."

Congress has enacted legislation dealing with such problems as air and water pollution, refuse disposal, and radiation. It has placed in the hands of governmental departments, such as the Department of Interior, and in administrative agencies, such as the Environmental Protection Agency, authority to deal with various sorts of injuries and potential dangers to the environment.

Many state and local legislative bodies, ever more sensitive to environmental problems, have passed laws dealing with air and water pollution, the protection of various kinds of animal life, the preservation of historical sites and landmarks, and the conservation of natural resources. Legislation having to do with thermal and noise pollution promises to become commonplace. Examples of recent innovations in environmental law are legislative prohibition of the sale of such items as detergents and non-returnable glass containers. The outlawing of throw away metal containers may be in the offing.

The power of government to enforce environmental legislation is predicated on its police power. This power authorizes government to take such action as is reasonably necessary for the protection of the health, safety, morals, or well-being of society and its members. Reasonable use of its police power permits government to restrict what one may do with his property. When properly exercising this power government is not obliged to compensate those persons who suffer a loss as a result of the demands government has imposed upon them.

When called upon to apply a principle of environmental law a court will generally probe the effect prompt and rigid enforcement will have on the challenged business activity. A judgment which directs an immediate closing of an enterprise can cause the loss of hundreds, if not thousands, of jobs. It may even decimate a significant factor in a community's economic life. To accommodate both environmental and economic considerations courts invoke a rule of reason. If convinced that the enterprise has acted reasonably and in good faith to comply with the law's demands, but has as yet failed to meet them, the court may grant the enterprise additional time to take those steps the law requires. Should it appear, however, that either the enterprise has not acted reasonably and in good faith, or that in spite of the laudable nature of the enterprise's response extensive damage will be done by permitting the enterprise to continue its operations, the court will order immediate compliance or the closing down of the unlawful operation.

It has been suggested that the Ninth Amendment grants every person a constitutional right to an environment free from pollution or risk to human life or individual well-being. Proponents of this position urge that this right, like the right to privacy, is a right enforceable by individuals against government and other persons. While the Supreme Court has recognized a right to privacy, to date it has not ruled that every person has a constitutional right to be free from other persons or government despoiling the environment. Several states, however, have passed laws which permit any individual to bring a lawsuit against it or private persons on the ground that the state or such private persons are guilty of violating some directive of environmental law.

The common law concept of nuisance may be invoked by one who has been, or is being injured, or unduly annoyed, because of what a property owner has done, or is doing, on or with his property. When a plaintiff objects to the use the defendant is making of his property the court weighs the rights of each of the parties. Should it appear that the defendant's behavior is reprehensible and society has an interest in shielding persons from such conduct, the injured party is entitled to money damages and, when suitable, an injunction directing the property owner to cease and desist from thereafter making such use of his property. For example, if one installs an exceptionally large air conditioner on his premises, one which emits such an unusually raucous noise that an adjoining home owner is caused great discomfort, a court will award that home owner a judgment for money damages to compensate him for his discomfort and enjoin future use of the air conditioner. Similarly, if a factory operated by a business enterprise discharges substances into the air which damage another's property, the injured party may be awarded money damages and an injunction. In each case the pollution caused by the land owner is recognized as a form of nuisance and may be banned.

UNITED STATES v. BISHOP PROCESSING CO.

United States Court of Appeals, Fourth Circuit, 1970.
423 F.2d 469, certiorari denied 70 S.Ct. 1695, 398 U.S. 904, 26 L.Ed.2d 63.

Between 1959 and 1965 the States of Delaware and Maryland unsuccessfully sought to bring an end to the malodorous air pollution caused by emissions coming from the defendant's animal reduction plant. In 1965 the United States Secretary of Health, Education and

Welfare, acting in accordance with the Clean Air Act, after holding a hearing, ordered that the defendant abate the pollution by a given date. When the defendant failed to do so the Secretary filed a complaint in March 1968 in a Federal District Court asking for a judgment enjoining the defendant from further discharging malodorous air pollutants. In November 1968 the case was settled. The defendant agreed to the entry of a decree it had suggested. The decree provided that the defendant would be required to "cease all manufacturing and processing" if the Director of Delaware's Air Pollution Control Division filed with the District Court an affidavit stating that the defendant's plant was discharging malodorous air pollution. Several months later the Director filed such an affidavit. He asked the Court for an order directing the defendant to cease all of its operations. The District Court, after holding an evidentiary hearing, found that there was substantial evidence that the defendant's plant was emitting malodorous air pollutants. It granted the Director's request. The defendant appealed.

SOBELOFF, CIRCUIT JUDGE:

* * *

The appellant presses the contention that the District Court erred in ruling that the Director performed his duties in accordance with the consent decree. Bishop argues that the decree was entered into with various "understandings" which contemplated certain procedures to be followed by the Director in his investigation. Specifically, Bishop asserts its "understandings" that (1) the Director was not to rely on citizen complaints or on testimony of representatives of the federal government in determining whether it committed air pollution and, (2) that the Director's finding was to be based upon "generally accepted sampling techniques."

Whatever merit this argument might have in other circumstances, it must fail here. The consent decree is plain in its terms. Nowhere and at no time was it intimated that any finding of air pollution was to be based upon unexpressed "understandings" with respect to the investigative procedures. Neither before the entry of the consent decree, nor when the judge held a hearing and announced his interpretation of the decree for the guidance of the parties did Bishop disclose the existence of any "understandings" or reservations on its part.

Bishop had ample opportunity to propose incorporation in the decree of any protection it may have felt necessary, and to object to procedures it deemed contrary to its understanding of the decree's terms. It cannot now ask the court to revise the decree by inserting language or to interpret it to embrace matters which, if present at all, were lurking in the recesses of Bishop's corporate mind.

* * *

Pollution is a severe and increasing problem of which the courts and other branches of government have become acutely conscious. The residents of the area in the neighborhood of Bishop's plant have the right to demand that the air they breathe shall not be defiled by what witnesses described as a "horrible" and "nauseating" stench.

The afflicted neighbors have striven long and in vain to vindicate that right. Relief is due them now.

The appellant cannot complain that the decree came suddenly, unexpectedly, or without awareness of the complaints, nor that it was denied full opportunity to meet them. In light of the entire history we perceive no inequity.

This court is not unmindful of the serious consequences to appellant's business from the District Court's order. It is, however, precisely the remedy which Bishop suggested and agreed to in order to avoid a trial, and seems inescapable since it has over a long period failed to take effective measures to solve the problem.

The order of the District Court is affirmed.

It is further ordered that if appellant applies to the Supreme Court for certiorari within 15 days from the filing of this opinion, the injunctive order of the District Court will be further stayed until final disposition of the case in the Supreme Court; otherwise the District Court's injunction shall become operative.

Affirmed.

[Certiorari denied.   90 S.Ct. 1695, 398 U.S. 904 (1970)]

———

GOLDBLATT v. TOWN OF HEMPSTEAD

Supreme Court of the United States, 1962.
82 S.Ct. 987, 369 U.S. 590, 8 L.Ed.2d 130.

Goldblatt owned a 38 acre tract of land. Since 1927 it was the site of a sand and gravel mine. By 1928 the excavation caused by the mining reached the water level. Over the course of decades the water-filled crater on the tract expanded, reaching 20 acres in size with an average depth of 25 feet. The town's population around the excavation increased. At the time of the trial there were more than 2200 homes and four public schools with an enrollment of 4500 pupils within a radius of 3500 feet of the water-filled crater. In 1958 the town enacted an ordinance which prohibited excavation below the water level and imposed a duty on landowners to refill any excavation then below that level. In 1959 the town brought an action to enjoin Goldblatt and his lessee from engaging in further mining. The defendants attacked the ordinance as unconstitutional. The trial court ruled that it was a valid exercise of the town's police power. The state appellate court affirmed. The defendants appealed.

MR. JUSTICE CLARK delivered the opinion of the Court.
* * *

Concededly the ordinance completely prohibits a beneficial use to which the property has previously been devoted. However, such a characterization does not tell us whether or not the ordinance is unconstitutional. It is an oft-repeated truism that every regulation necessarily speaks as a prohibition. If this ordinance is otherwise a valid exercise of the town's police powers, the fact that it deprives the property of its most beneficial use does not render it unconstitutional. * * *

This is not to say, however, that governmental action in the form of regulation cannot be so onerous as to constitute a taking which constitutionally requires compensation. * * * How far regulation may go before it becomes a taking we need not now decide, for there is no evidence in the present record which even remotely suggests that prohibition of further mining will reduce the value of the lot in question. Indulging in the usual presumption of constitutionality, * * * we find no indication that the prohibitory effect * * * is sufficient to render it an unconstitutional taking if it is otherwise a valid police regulation.

The question, therefore, narrows to whether the prohibition of further excavation below the water table is a valid exercise of the town's police power. The term "police power" connotes the time-tested conceptional limit of public encroachment upon private interests. Except for the substitution of the familiar standard of "reasonableness," this Court has generally refrained from announcing any specific criteria. The classic statement of the rule in Lawton v. Steele, * * * (1894), is still valid today:

"To justify the state in * * * interposing its authority in behalf of the public, it must appear—First, that the interests of the public * * * require such interference; and, second, that the means are reasonably necessary for the accomplishment of the purpose, and not unduly oppressive upon individuals."

Even this rule is not applied with strict precision, for this Court has often said that "debatable questions as to reasonableness are not for the courts but for the Legislature * * *." * * *

The ordinance in question was passed as a safety measure, and the town is attempting to uphold it on that basis. * * *

Although one could imagine that preventing further deepening of a pond already 25 feet deep would have a *de minimis* effect on public safety, we cannot say that such a conclusion is compelled by facts of which we can take notice. Even if we could draw such a conclusion, we would be unable to say the ordinance is unreasonable; for all we know, the ordinance may have a *de minimis* effect on appellants. Our past cases leave no doubt that appellants had the burden on "reasonableness." * * * This burden not having been met, the prohibition of excavation on the 20-acre-lake tract must stand as a valid police regulation.

* * *

Affirmed.

PROBLEMS

1. Plaintiffs, home owners residing in close proximity to an airport owned and operated by the defendant city, brought an action for money damages to compensate them for the decrease in the value

of their homes due to the noise and air pollution caused by jet aircraft which made use of the airport. What judgment?

2. Do persons who reside adjacent to an Atomic Energy Commission facility have standing to maintain a suit to enjoin the use by the Commission of a gas device which they claim presented a danger to their health and safety?

3. Can a taxpayer obtain an injunction prohibiting the use of DDT by farmers on the ground that DDT represented a danger to the health and safety of his fellow human beings?

4. The plaintiffs were residents of Chicago and users of the water supplied by the City of Chicago. They brought a suit to enjoin the City from fluoridating its water supply. Are they entitled to an injunction?

5. May a state agency be constitutionally empowered to designate particular geographic areas as "blighted" and to arrange for the taking over and "renewal" of such areas by cities, the "renewal" requiring the destruction of existing tenements and commercial structures?

6. Is a home owner entitled to recover damages for injuries caused to his property as a result of the vibration, dirt, and particles originating from the defendant's cement plant?

7. Is a statute which empowers a state commission to issue orders calling for corrective action when it finds persons are guilty of "air pollution" too vague and indefinite a standard of improper conduct to satisfy the due process requirement of the Constitution that persons must have notice of prohibited behavior?

8. Is a municipal housing authority regulation which bans the playing of musical instruments during the day for more than one and a half hours or after 8:00 p. m. arbitrary, unreasonable, and unenforceable?

9. A state's Open Space Act authorized individual towns to require, as a condition of approving a developer's plans to build one family homes, that a portion of the property owned by the developer be set aside for use as a park or playground. A builder challenged a town's requirement that he set aside a portion of his property for use as a park or playground on the ground that the requirement deprived him of his property without just compensation. What judgment?

Chapter 6

MIND-ALTERING DRUGS

Drugs affect human beings in a variety of ways. Some may be used to restore or enhance health. Others can have a deleterious effect on human beings, ranging from a brief period of emotional or physical discomfort to permanent mental or physical injury or death. Some drugs have beneficial effects when properly used and injurious effects when abused.

The extent to which mind-altering drugs influence one's emotional state, perception, and consciousness varies with the drug, the quantity used, and the duration of use. Some mind-altering drugs, when taken sparingly for a short term, may cause little if any harm. Some may even be harmless if used on a long term basis. If used in large quantities or for a long period of time an otherwise harmless drug may cause serious injury. Some mind-altering drugs present a grave hazard to human life even if consumed sparingly. At times, because of the setting in which consumption takes place, or what the user undertakes to do during the period of the drug's effectiveness, even the least dangerous of the mind-altering drugs can cause permanent injury or snuff out a life.

Increased use of mind-altering drugs during the last decade and a half has triggered a reappraisal of those laws which prohibit the importation, manufacture, sale, possession, and use of such drugs. Persons taking part in the study of these laws have carried their probing beyond the mere content of the law. They have explored such basic questions as the desirability of government interfering with the use of mind-altering drugs and how society should treat those who illegally use drugs.

The competence of government to control the trafficking in and the using of mind-altering drugs is based on its police power. Legislators have generally concluded that it is in the best interests of individuals and society that the use of particular mind-altering drugs be banned. This conclusion may be ascribed to several factors: (1) belief or evidence that such drugs may (a) injure the user or (b) result in the user causing injury to other persons or (c) cause the user to engage in antisocial behavior; (2) belief or evidence that those who use mind-altering drugs will follow a life style inconsistent with the best interests of society and contrary to society's values; and (3) belief that it is immoral to use mind-altering drugs.

Courts have recognized that the police power confers broad competence on legislative bodies to regulate the use, sale and possession of mind-altering drugs. Laws enacted by a legislature need not satisfy a scientific test of accuracy. To sustain legislative action a court need not find that the beliefs held by the legislators are valid, or that the evidence on which they based their conclusions is accurate, or that the correctness of their action is undebatable. A court will not interfere with a legislative decision even though it may disagree with it if it finds that there is a rational relationship between what the legislature has done and an objective toward which the legislature may properly direct its attention.

Generally outlawed are such mind-altering drugs as cannabis, commonly known as marijuana, pot or weed, LSD, heroin, morphine, cocaine, barbiturates, and amphetamines. Statutes provide that the latter four may be lawfully sold, bought, and used when prescribed by a physician for medicinal purposes.

The interaction of some of the mind-altering drugs with the human body produces a craving for the drug. This craving is referred to as addiction to the drug. Morphine, heroin, cocaine, and barbiturates are usually regarded as addictive. There is some disagreement as to whether or not amphetamines are addictive. Addiction can be the result of the demands of the body's chemistry following use of the drug or a psychological desire to once again experience the sensations and emotions which accompany the use of the drug. Cannabis does not appear to produce a craving by the body for its continued use. However, there are those who find that it does generate a form of addiction in the user. He manifests a desire to experience the emotions and sensations which accompany its use. This desire can bring one to repeatedly use cannabis. Often stated, but apparently as yet not corroborated, is the assertion that one who uses cannabis will ultimately proceed to use more disruptive and addictive drugs. Clouding the entire subject of drug addiction is the fact that not every person becomes addicted to generally addictive drugs.

Those who insist that the use of cannabis should be legalized compare it with alcohol. They insist that persons who use cannabis become no more addicted to it than persons who consume alcohol. The consumption of alcohol and alcoholism cause grave personal, family, and community problems. With minor exceptions state laws limit and regulate the use of alcohol rather than totally ban its sale or use. A like approach, goes the argument, should be employed in regard to cannabis. Regulation rather than outlawing its use, or, even better yet, leaving the decision to use or not to use it to the individual, would relieve society and its officials from the toils and frustrations of trying to enforce a needless and unenforceable policy.

Legislative response to legalizing the trafficking in and the use of cannabis has so far been negative. But some legislators have manifested a willingness to no longer treat those who use cannabis as criminals and to soften the penalties which may be imposed upon those who use this mind-altering drug. Recent legislative action has revealed a readiness to increase the penalties that may be imposed upon those who sell cannabis, especially if the purchaser is a minor.

Courts have rejected each of the following defenses raised by defendants charged with violating a statute which prohibited the possession or use of cannabis: (1) it is arbitrary, unreasonable, and a denial of equal protection of the laws to allow persons to buy and consume alcohol but not cannabis; (2) it is arbitrary and unreasonable to treat cannabis the same as other mind-altering drugs; (3) it violates one's right to information, intellectual pursuit, and the consuming of ideas to outlaw the possession and use of cannabis in the privacy of one's home; (4) one has a right to experience the euphoria and sensations which accompany the use of cannabis; (5) the use of cannabis is a matter of personal decision-making protected by one's constitutional right to privacy; and (6) one's right to practice his religion guarantees him a right to use cannabis if he believes its use is essential for the practice of his religion.

ROBINSON v. CALIFORNIA

Supreme Court of the United States, 1962.
82 S.Ct. 1417, 370 U.S. 660, 8 L.Ed.2d 758.

A California statute made it a crime for a person to "be addicted to the use of narcotics." Robinson was found guilty of having violated the statute. His conviction was based on the testimony of two police officers. One testified that four months prior to the trial he had examined the appellant's arms and at that time he observed "scar tissue and discoloration" and "what appeared to be numerous needle marks and a scab wound * * * below the crook of the elbow." The other officer testified that on the basis of ten years of experience with the police Narcotics Division he was of the opinion that the marks and discoloration "were the result of the injection of [unsterile] hypodermic needles." He told the jury that at the time he observed him Robinson "was neither under the influence of narcotics nor suffering withdrawal symptoms." Both officers testified that Robinson admitted to them that he had used narcotics in the past. A state appellate court affirmed the conviction. Robinson appealed.

MR. JUSTICE STEWART delivered the opinion of the Court.

* * *

This statute, * * * is not one which punishes a person for the use of narcotics, for their purchase, sale or possession, or for antisocial or disorderly behavior resulting from their administration. It is not a law which even purports to provide or require medical treatment. Rather, we deal with a statute which makes the "status" of narcotic addiction a criminal offense, for which the offender may be prosecuted "at any time before he reforms." California has said that a person can be continuously guilty of this offense, whether or not he has ever used or possessed any narcotics within the State, and whether or not he has been guilty of any antisocial behavior there.

It is unlikely that any State at this moment in history would attempt to make it a criminal offense for a person to be mentally ill, or a leper, or to be afflicted with a venereal disease. A State might determine that the general health and welfare require that the victims of these and other human afflictions be dealt with by compulsory treatment, involving quarantine, confinement, or sequestration. But, in the light of contemporary human knowledge, a law which made a criminal offense of such a disease would doubtless be universally thought to be an infliction of cruel and unusual punishment in violation of the Eighth and Fourteenth Amendments.   *   *   *

We cannot but consider the statute before us as of the same category. In this Court counsel for the State recognized that narcotic addiction is an illness. Indeed, it is apparently an illness which may be contracted innocently or involuntarily. We hold that a state law which imprisons a person thus afflicted as a criminal, even though he has never touched any narcotic drug within the State or been guilty of any irregular behavior there, inflicts a cruel and unusual punishment in violation of the Fourteenth Amendment. To be sure, imprisonment for ninety days is not, in the abstract, a punishment which is either cruel or unusual. But the question cannot be considered in the abstract. Even one day in prison would be a cruel and unusual punishment for the "crime" of having a common cold.

We are not unmindful that the vicious evils of the narcotics traffic have occasioned the grave concern of government. There are, as we have said, countless fronts on which those evils may be legitimately attacked. We deal in this case only with an individual provision of a particularized local law as it has so far been interpreted by the California courts.

Reversed.

COMMONWEALTH v. LEIS

Supreme Court of Massachusetts.
243 N.E.2d 898, 355 Mass. 189 (1969).

The defendants were charged with unlawfully having marijuana in their possession and illegally possessing marijuana with the intent to sell it unlawfully. They moved to dismiss the charges on the ground that the Massachusetts statute which made possession, use, or sale of marijuana a criminal offense was unconstitutional. The trial court, after holding a lengthy hearing at which eighteen experts testified as to the effect of marijuana on human beings, found the statute constitutional. The defendants appealed.

SPIEGEL, JUSTICE.

*   *   *

The defendants first argue that the law is "irrational and unreasonable" because the Legislature did not thoroughly investigate the available scientific and medical evidence concerning marihuana when enacting and revising the law.

We know of nothing that *compels* the Legislature to thoroughly investigate the available scientific and medical evidence when enacting a law. The test of whether an act of the Legislature is rational and reasonable is not whether the records of the Legislature contain a sufficient basis of fact to sustain that act. The Legislature is presumed to have acted rationally and reasonably. * * * "Unless the act of the Legislature cannot be supported upon any rational basis of fact that reasonably can be conceived to sustain it, the court has no power to strike it down as violative of the Constitution." * * *

The defendants then argue that the law is irrational and unreasonable and that it serves no legitimate State interest because there is no evidence that marihuana endangers the health, safety, welfare or morals of the community. * * *

The testimony of the experts fully justifies the conclusion that marihuana is a "mind-altering" drug. There was evidence that the effect of such a drug is "a complex interaction between the physical or pharmacological properties of that drug * * * and most importantly the personality or character structure of the person consuming that drug, and * * * the social setting or context in which the drug is taken, including expectations, attitudes, et cetera." The smoking of marihuana may cause a state of euphoria and hallucinations or mental confusion and acute panic. It tends to exacerbate an underlying mental condition and to accentuate the smoker's basic personality makeup. When used by persons who have personality disorders or who are predisposed to "psychotic breaks," it may contribute to the onset of a "psychotic break." The problem is magnified by the fact that persons having personality disorders and predispositions to "psychotic breaks" are more likely to experiment with marihuana and to become psychologically dependent upon it. Although the smoking of marihuana triggers only "acute [short-term] psychotic breaks" and does not apparently cause permanent psychotic injury or mental deterioration, an acute psychotic break, while it lasts, is as serious as a chronic mental disorder.

* * *

In an attempt to disprove the claim that the use of marihuana may cause automobile accidents, the defendants say that "no evidence [was] produced linking marihuana use with * * * [such] accidents." The evidence, however, showed there is no accurate, reliable scientific means of determining whether the operator of a motor vehicle has recently smoked marihuana. * * *

We do not think that the present unavailability of or inability to collect absolute, statistical and scientific proof that the smoking of marihuana (1) triggers "psychotic breaks," (2) leads to the use of more dangerous drugs and (3) causes automobile accidents prevents the Legislature from acting to prohibit its use. Surely the defendants would not contend, for example, that unless experiments absolutely establish that thalidomide causes birth defects the Legislature could not prevent the distribution of that drug. To prevent "psychotic breaks," to guard against the use of more dangerous drugs and to eliminate a cause of automobile accidents are valid State interests.

The defendants insist that the right to smoke marihuana is guaranteed by the Constitutions of the Commonwealth and of the United States and must be balanced against the interests of the State in prohibiting its use. No such right exists. It is not specifically preserved by either Constitution. The right to smoke marihuana is not "fundamental to the American scheme of justice * * * necessary to an Anglo-American regime of ordered liberty." * * * It is not within a "zone of privacy" formed by "penumbras" of the First, Third, Fourth and Fifth Amendments and the Ninth Amendment of the Constitution of the United States. * * * The defendants have no right, fundamental or otherwise, to become intoxicated by means of the smoking of marihuana. * * *

The defendants maintain that the Narcotic Drugs Law "has singled out for prohibition and punishment possessors of and possessors of with intent to sell, marihuana, while the laws permit the regulated use, sale and possession of substances far more harmful than marihuana * * * punish less harshly possession and sale of substances far more harmful than marihuana * * * and punish equally harshly substances far more harmful than marihuana." Therefore, they say that it violates art. 1 of the Declaration of Rights of the Constitution of the Commonwealth and the Equal Protection Clause of the Fourteenth Amendment of the Constitution of the United States.

* * *

They concede that the Legislature may select the kinds of behavior that it wishes to proscribe. They claim, however, that this "does not mean that a Legislature may actually proscribe behavior of one class of people (e. g., those who choose to obtain a mild state of intoxication with marihuana) and allow another class of people to freely indulge in behavior of an exactly similar nature (e. g., those who choose to obtain a mild state of intoxication with alcohol)."

We do not think that a statute which proscribes generally certain conduct can be said to be discriminatory simply because a certain group of persons tend to engage more often in that conduct than others. Such "de facto" discrimination does not violate the Equal Protection Clause. There are at least two distinctions between alcohol and the "mind-altering" intoxicants that are defined by the law to be narcotic drugs. First, alcohol is susceptible to a less restrictive alternative means of control. There are recognized, accurate means of determining its use and its abuse. Second, the effects of alcohol upon the user are known. We think that the Legislature is warranted in treating this known intoxicant differently from marihuana, LSD or heroin, the effects of which are largely still unknown and subject to extensive dispute. The Legislature is free to recognize degrees of harm and may confine its restrictions to instances where it determines the need for them is clearest. * * *

Finally, the defendants contend that the "penalties provided for offenses under the Narcotic Drugs Law, as applied to marihuana, constitute cruel and excessive punishment." * * *

* * * The defendants are not charged with having a "status" over which they have no control. See Robinson v. California, * * * "The basic concept underlying the Eighth Amendment is nothing less than the dignity of man. * * * Fines, imprisonment and even execution may be imposed depending upon the enormity of the crime." * * * Unless the punishment exceeds a constitutional limit, the task of assigning penalties is for the Legislature. * * *

Here the Legislature has seen fit to give the trial judge considerable leeway in sentencing. We have no reason to believe that a judge will not continue to exercise this discretion wisely and fail to distinguish between the youth who was experimenting with marihuana or even a constant user of the drug and the "pusher" or person trafficking in marihuana for financial gain.

* * * It is clear that the Legislature acted well within constitutional limitations.

————

PROBLEMS

1. The defendant was found guilty of unlawfully selling marijuana and was sentenced to prison for a term of five years to life. On appeal he argued that the state statute was unconstitutional since marijuana falls within "a zone of mental or sensory privacy" which the state may not invade. What judgment?

2. Can a husband's extended refusal to engage in sexual intercourse with his wife constitute a form of extreme cruelty so as to entitle the wife to a divorce if the abstention was due to the husband's addiction to heroin which had a dampening effect on his desire to have sexual relations?

3. Having reasonable grounds to believe that a student possessed marijuana a college administrator at a state college conducted a warrantless search of the student's dormitory residence. The search revealed that the student had stored a supply of marijuana in his room. The college thereupon indefinitely suspended him. He sues for reinstatement. What judgment?

4. Several college professors were served with subpoenas which directed that they appear before a grand jury to testify about student drug abuse on campus. The prosecutor announced that he planned to ask the professors, when they appeared before the grand jury, if they had ever used drugs in violation of law and if they advocated student use of mind-altering drugs. The professors moved to vacate the subpoenas on the ground that to require them to appear before the grand jury would be unconstitutional. What judgment?

5. A state statute made it unlawful to use peyote. Peyote affects individuals in essentially the same fashion as marijuana. The

defendants, members of an Indian tribe which for many generations had traditionally made use of peyote during religious ceremonies, were charged with violating the statute. They contended that the First Amendment's bar on government regulation of religion made it unconstitutional to punish them for their use of peyote because the charge against them was based on use which occurred during religious ceremonies. What judgment?

6. A federal statute provided that any "citizen * * * who * * * uses narcotic drugs" must register with a customs official on his or her entry into, or departure from, the United States. The defendant claimed that the statute was unconstitutional since it was so vague and indefinite as to violate the due process clause of the Fifth Amendment. What judgment?

7. The defendant was found guilty of unlawfully selling marijuana. He was sentenced to six months in jail. On appeal he contended that the sentence was excessive and constituted cruel and unusual punishment in violation of the Constitution. What judgment?

8. A 1909 federal statute made it a crime to unlawfully possess imported heroin. It also provided that if the government established that a defendant unlawfully possessed heroin a jury could presume it was imported. If a defendant wished he could offer evidence to rebut the presumption. The accused challenged the statute as unconstitutional. The government established that it was a fact that little heroin is grown in the United States and argued that therefore the presumption was constitutional. What judgment?

Chapter 7

ALCOHOLISM

The Twenty-first Amendment allows each state to use its police power to regulate the manufacture, transportation, sale, possession, and use of alcoholic beverages within its boundaries. Legislatures have exercised their power to control the consumption of alcoholic beverages on the basis of such beliefs as: (1) to drink alcohol is immoral; (2) imbibing can lead to immoral behavior; and (3) drinking can adversely affect society's values. Reasons for legislative action have been that consumption of alcohol can: (1) have a debilitating effect on the user; (2) harm the user's immediate family; (3) cause injury or death to innocent third persons; and (4) harm society.

Dram shop laws, in force in a large number of states, allow one injured by an intoxicated person to obtain money damages from the person who sold liquor to the inebriated party when he was already intoxicated. Generally, to recover, the plaintiff must show that the liquor sold was consumed but he need not prove that the sale in fact caused the behavior which produced the injury. A number of states permit a like result in the absence of a dram shop law. An intoxicated person who is sold liquor is usually not permitted to recover damages from the seller for the injuries he suffers following an unlawful sale.

Since one's mental, nervous, and physical processes may be so affected by the amount of alcohol in his body as to make it dangerous for him to operate a motor vehicle states have enacted laws making it a crime to operate an automobile while under the influence of liquor. A state statute may specify the kinds of tests and test results which may be used as evidence to establish that the accused was in fact under the influence of liquor in violation of law. Blood, breath, saliva, and urine tests may be authorized. To be admissible in evidence the test must be shown to be reliable and the results accurate. Courts may also consider the observations of those who saw the accused at the time he was supposedly under the influence of liquor to determine whether or not he operated a motor vehicle while under the influence of liquor.

The Constitution does not require a police officer to obtain the consent of one believed to have been driving while under the influence of liquor before performing a blood, breath, urine, or saliva test so long as the test is carried out in a reasonable, safe, and civilized manner. States have adopted "implied consent" statutes. Such statutes provide that one who operates an automobile is deemed to have consented to take a sobriety test if arrested and charged with having operated a motor vehicle while under the influence of liquor. If when requested one knowingly and wilfully refuses to submit to a test, for a reason other than permitted by law, and it is determined that there was probable cause to believe that he was under the influence of liquor while operating a motor vehicle, his driving license may be suspended or revoked.   Such a statute does not treat the refusal to take the test as an admission of criminal responsibility.

While the consumption and sale of alcoholic beverages are generally stringently regulated by laws drawn to promote temperance, if not abstinence, persons who deal in or consume such beverages are entitled to due process of law.   For example, the Supreme Court has ruled unconstitutional a state practice which authorized police officers to post in bars the names of persons they believed to be excessive drinkers without first notifying such persons of their planned action.   State law prohibited the sale of alcoholic beverages to those whose names were so listed.   The Court declared that the posting could not constitutionally take place unless it was preceded by notice to those persons the police planned to include in their list and such persons were given an opportunity to defend themselves against the charge.   At stake, in the Court's opinion, was a named person's "good name, reputation, honor or integrity."

In spite of the Twenty-first Amendment the federal government is not totally precluded from dealing with some aspects of the liquor business.   The Amendment does not deny Congress the power to place a tax on alcoholic beverages nor does it cancel the power of Congress over interstate commerce.   A state may not so deal with liquor that it infringes on the power of Congress to regulate interstate commerce nor may a state place an export tax on liquor to be exported from the state.

There are those who insist that alcoholism should be treated as a disease.   The Supreme Court, most lower courts, and legislatures have shunned this proposition.   If at some future time courts or legislatures elect to affix the label "disease" to alcoholism, public drunkenness would no longer be punishable as a crime.   Commission of an illegal act by an alcoholic while drunk might be excused.   Could persons suffering from this disease be forced to undergo treatment since so long as they were alcoholics and free they represented a danger to the health and safety of other persons?   If the view that alcoholism is a disease is accepted, this question will have to be answered.

SCHMERBER v. CALIFORNIA

Supreme Court of the United States, 1966.
86 S.Ct. 1826, 384 U.S. 757, 16 L.Ed.2d 908.

The petitioner was convicted of the crime of driving an automobile while under the influence of intoxicating liquor.   During the trial the state was allowed to use as evidence of intoxication the report of an analysis made of a sample of the petitioner's blood.   The sample had been taken at police direction, over the objection of the petitioner, after his attorney had advised him not to consent. The petitioner appealed.

MR. JUSTICE BRENNAN delivered the opinion of the Court.

* * *

I.

THE DUE PROCESS CLAUSE CLAIM

Breithaupt was also a case in which police officers caused blood to be withdrawn from the driver of an automobile involved in an accident, and in which there was ample justification for the officer's conclusion that the driver was under the influence of alcohol. There, as here, the extraction was made by a physician in a simple, medically acceptable manner in a hospital environment. There, however, the driver was unconscious at the time the blood was withdrawn and hence had no opportunity to object to the procedure. We affirmed the conviction there resulting from the use of the test in evidence, holding that under such circumstances the withdrawal did not offend "that 'sense of justice' of which we spoke in Rochin v. [People of] California, * * *. *Breithaupt* thus requires the rejection of petitioner's due process argument, and nothing in the circumstances of this case or in supervening events persuades us that this aspect of *Breithaupt* should be overruled.

II.

THE PRIVILEGE AGAINST SELF-INCRIMINATION CLAIM

* * *

We hold that the privilege protects an accused only from being compelled to testify against himself, or otherwise provide the State with evidence of a testimonial or communicative nature, and that the withdrawal of blood and use of the analysis in question in this case did not involve compulsion to these ends.

* * *

It is clear that the protection of the privilege reaches an accused's communications, whatever form they might take, and the compulsion of responses which are also communications, for example, compliance with a subpoena to produce one's papers. * * * On the other hand, both federal and state courts have usually held that it offers no protection against compulsion to submit to fingerprinting, photographing, or measurements, to write or speak for identification, to appear in court, to stand, to assume a stance, to walk, or to make a particular gesture. The distinction which has emerged, often expressed in different ways, is that the privilege is a bar against compelling "communications" or "testimony," but that compulsion which makes a suspect or accused the source of "real or physical evidence" does not violate it.

* * * There will be many cases in which such a distinction is not readily drawn. Some tests seemingly directed to obtain "physical evidence," for example, lie detector tests measuring changes in body function during interrogation, may actually be directed to eliciting responses which are essentially testimonial. To compel a person to submit to testing in which an effort will be made to determine his guilt or innocence on the basis of physiological responses, whether willed or not, is to evoke the spirit and history of the Fifth Amendment. * * *

In the present case, however, no such problem of application is presented. Not even a shadow of testimonial compulsion upon or enforced communication by the accused was involved either in the extraction or in the chemical analysis. Petitioner's testimonial capacities were in no way implicated; indeed, his participation, except as a donor, was irrelevant to the results of the test, which depend on chemical analysis and on that alone. Since the blood test evidence, although an incriminating product of compulsion, was neither petitioner's testimony nor evidence relating to some communicative act or writing by the petitioner, it was not inadmissible on privilege grounds.

III.

THE RIGHT TO COUNSEL CLAIM

This conclusion also answers petitioner's claim that, in compelling him to submit to the test in face of the fact that his objection was made on the advice of counsel, he was denied his Sixth Amendment right to the assistance of counsel. Since petitioner was not entitled to assert the privilege, he has no greater right because counsel erroneously advised him that he could assert it. His claim is strictly limited to the failure of the police to respect his wish, reinforced by counsel's advice, to be left inviolate. * * *

IV.

THE SEARCH AND SEIZURE CLAIM

* * *

The question is squarely presented * * * whether the chemical analysis introduced in evidence in this case should have been excluded as the product of an unconstitutional search and seizure.

The overriding function of the Fourth Amendment is to protect personal privacy and dignity against unwarranted intrusion by the State. * * *

We begin with the assumption that once the privilege against self-incrimination has been found not to bar compelled intrusions into the body for blood to be analyzed for alcohol content, the Fourth Amendment's proper function is to constrain, not against all intrusions as such, but against intrusions which are not justified in the circumstances, or which are made in an improper manner. In other words, the questions we must decide in this case are whether the police were justified in requiring petitioner to submit to the blood test, and whether the means and procedures employed in taking his blood respected relevant Fourth Amendment standards of reasonableness.

In this case, as will often be true when charges of driving under the influence of alcohol are pressed, these questions arise in the context of an arrest made by an officer without a warrant. Here, there was plainly probable cause for the officer to arrest petitioner and charge him with driving an automobile while under the influence of intoxicating liquor. * * * The interests in human dignity and privacy which the Fourth Amendment protects forbid any such intrusions on the mere chance that desired evidence might be obtained. In the absence of a clear indication that in fact such evidence will be found, these fundamental human interests require law officers to suffer the risk that such evidence may disappear unless there is an immediate search.

* * *

The officer in the present case, however, might reasonably have believed that he was confronted with an emergency, in which the delay necessary to obtain a warrant, under the circumstances, threatened "the destruction of evidence," * * *. We are told that the percentage of alcohol in the blood begins to diminish shortly after drinking stops, as the body functions to eliminate it from the system. Particularly in a case such as this, where time had to be taken to bring the accused to a hospital and to investigate the scene of the accident, there was no time to seek out a magistrate and secure a warrant. Given these special facts, we conclude that the attempt to secure evidence of blood-alcohol content in this case was an appropriate incident to petitioner's arrest.

Similarly, we are satisfied that the test chosen to measure petitioner's blood-alcohol level was a reasonable one. Extraction of blood samples for testing is a highly effective means of determining the degree to which a person is under the influence of alcohol. * * * Such tests are a commonplace in these days of periodic physical examinations and experience with them teaches that the quantity of blood extracted is minimal, and that for most people the procedure involves virtually no risk, trauma, or pain. Petitioner is not one of the few who on grounds of fear, concern for health, or religious scruple might prefer some other means of testing, such as the "breathalyzer" test petitioner refused, * * *. We need not decide whether such wishes would have to be respected.

Finally, the record shows that the test was performed in a reasonable manner. Petitioner's blood was taken by a physician in a hospital environment according to accepted medical practices. We are thus not presented with the serious questions which would arise if a search involving use of a medical technique, even of the most rudimentary sort, were made by other than medical personnel or in other than a medical environment—for example, if it were administered by police in the privacy of the stationhouse. To tolerate searches under these conditions might be to invite an unjustified element of personal risk of infection and pain.

We thus conclude that the present record shows no violation of petitioner's right under the Fourth and Fourteenth Amendments to be free of unreasonable searches and seizures. It bears repeating, however, that we reach this judgment only on the facts of the present record. The integrity of an individual's person is a cherished value of our society. That we today hold that the Constitution does not forbid the States minor intrusions into an individual's body under stringently limited conditions in no way indicates that it permits more substantial intrusions, or intrusions under other conditions.

Affirmed.

———

POWELL v. TEXAS

Supreme Court of the United States, 1968.
88 S.Ct. 2145, 392 U.S. 514, 20 L.Ed.2d 1254.

The defendant was charged with the crime of public drunkenness. He contended that since he was "afflicted with the disease of chronic alcoholism" the state could not punish him. If it did it would violate the Eighth Amendment's prohibition on "cruel and unusual punishment." The trial judge ruled as a matter of law that chronic alcoholism was not a defense to the charge. He found the defendant guilty and fined him $50.00. The defendant appealed.

MR. JUSTICE MARSHALL announced the judgment of the Court and delivered an opinion in which THE CHIEF JUSTICE, MR. JUSTICE BLACK, and MR. JUSTICE HARLAN join.

   *   *   *

There is as yet no known generally effective method for treating the vast number of alcoholics in our society. Some individual alcoholics have responded to particular forms of therapy with remissions of their symptomatic dependence upon the drug. But just as there is no agreement among doctors and social workers with respect to the causes of alcoholism, there is no consensus as to why particular treatments have been effective in particular cases and there is no generally agreed-upon approach to the problem of treatment on a large scale.
*   *   *

Thus it is entirely possible that, even were the manpower and facilities available for a full-scale attack upon chronic alcoholism, we would find ourselves unable to help the vast bulk of our "visible"—let alone our "invisible"—alcoholic population.

However, facilities for the attempted treatment of indigent alcoholics are woefully lacking throughout the country. It would be tragic to return large numbers of helpless, sometimes dangerous and frequently unsanitary inebriates to the streets of our cities without even the opportunity to sober up adequately which a brief jail term provides. Presumably no State or city will tolerate such a state of affairs. Yet the medical profession cannot, and does not, tell us with any assurance that, even if the buildings, equipment and trained personnel were made available, it could provide anything more than slightly higher-class jails for our indigent habitual inebriates. Thus we run the grave risk that nothing will be accomplished beyond the hanging of a new sign—reading "hospital"—over one wing of the jailhouse.

One virtue of the criminal process is, at least, that the duration of penal incarceration typically has some outside statutory limit; this is universally true in the case of petty offenses, such as public drunkenness, where jail terms are quite short on the whole. "Therapeutic civil commitment" lacks this feature; one is typically committed until one is "cured." Thus, to do otherwise than affirm might subject indigent alcoholics to the risk that they may be locked up for an indefinite period of time under the same conditions as before, with no more hope than before of receiving effective treatment and no prospect of periodic "freedom."

Faced with this unpleasant reality, we are unable to assert that the use of the criminal process as a means of dealing with the public aspects of problem drinking can never be defended as rational. * * *

Obviously, chronic alcoholics have not been deterred from drinking to excess by the existence of criminal sanctions against public drunkenness. But all those who violate penal laws of any kind are by definition undeterred. The longstanding and still raging debate over the validity of the deterrence justification for penal sanctions has not reached any sufficiently clear conclusions to permit it to be said that such sanctions are ineffective in any particular context or for any particular group of people who are able to appreciate the consequences of their acts. * * *

Appellant, however, seeks to come within the application of the Cruel and Unusual Punishment Clause announced in Robinson v. State of California, * * * which involved a state statute making it a crime to "be addicted to the use of narcotics." This Court held there that "a state law which imprisons a person thus afflicted [with narcotic addiction] as a criminal, even though he has never touched any narcotic drug within the State or been guilty of any irregular behavior there, inflicts a cruel and unusual punishment * * *." * * *

On its face the present case does not fall within that holding, since appellant was convicted, not for being a chronic alcoholic, but for being in public while drunk on a particular occasion. The State of Texas thus has not sought to punish a mere status, as California did in *Robinson*; nor has it attempted to regulate appellant's behavior in the privacy of his own home. Rather, it has imposed upon appellant a criminal sanction for public behavior which may create substantial health and safety hazards, both for appellant and for members of the general public, and which offends the moral and esthetic sensibilities of a large segment of the community. This seems a far cry from convicting one for being an addict, being a chronic alcoholic, being "mentally ill, or a leper * * *." * * *

Traditional common-law concepts of personal accountability and essential considerations of federalism lead us to disagree with appellant. We are unable to conclude, on the state of this record or on the current state of medical knowledge, that chronic alcoholics in general, and Leroy Powell in particular, suffer from such an irresistible compulsion to drink and to get drunk in public that they are utterly unable to control their performance of either or both of these acts and thus cannot be deterred at all from public intoxication. And in any event this Court has never articulated a general constitutional doctrine of *mens rea*.

*   *   *

Affirmed.

PROBLEMS

1.   A police officer had good reason to believe that the defendant, who had just been involved in an automobile accident, was intoxicated. Fearful that the evidence of alcoholism would disappear before competent medical assistance could be obtained, the police officer removed a sample of blood from the defendant's arm while two other officers restrained the defendant who kept shouting: "No, no. Not my blood. I said no." The officer who removed the blood had done so only on one previous occasion and later stated: "I was not too sure what had to be done and I was a little concerned since I did not know if the needle was sterile." A report of the analysis of the sample indicated that the defendant had been intoxicated. Could the report be used as evidence of intoxication in a criminal proceeding?

2.   The defendant was arrested and charged with driving a vehicle while intoxicated. Immediately after his arrest he insisted that he wanted to speak with a lawyer. A police officer told him: "That comes later, for the present, let's talk." After several hours of questioning, he admitted that he had been drinking heavily just before he decided to drive to his uncle's home. He had been driving for only five minutes before he was stopped and arrested. During the defendant's trial the state sought to make use of the confession. The defendant objected. Is the confession admissible?

3.   May a state treat a defendant's refusal to take a sobriety test as an admission of his guilt in a proceeding which charged him with driving a motor vehicle while under the influence of an intoxicating beverage?

4.   The defendant was arrested for a minor traffic violation. The police officer asked him to open the trunk of his car so he could see what was inside. The defendant refused. The police officer told him he would use force if necessary to take the key to the trunk from him. "I'm opening that trunk one way or another," the officer said. The defendant opened the trunk. It contained several cases of liquor, none of which bore a required state tax stamp. In a proceeding brought against the defendant could the unstamped liquor containers be used as evidence against him to establish that he had violated state law?

5.   The defendant sold liquor to the plaintiff in violation of the state's dram shop law. The plaintiff brought suit against the defend-

ant for injuries he suffered after he had been served liquor by the defendant. The evidence established that because of the plaintiff's intoxicated condition he had injured himself. Is the plaintiff entitled to a judgment in his favor?

6. May a State Liquor Commission treat the congregation of well-behaved apparent homosexuals at a tavern as a nuisance and therefore terminate the license of the tavern operator to sell alcoholic beverages?

Part Three

PERSONAL LIBERTIES

Chapter 8

ACTIVISM

Activists resort to action to effect change. When in disagreement with some aspect of governmental, social, political, theological, educational, or economic policy the activist turns to speech or some other form of behavior to put an end to the objected to state of affairs. The Constitution encourages activism by limiting the power of government to regulate speech, press, and public assembly, and by granting persons the right to associate with one another and to undertake diverse forms of group action.

Courts look with suspicion upon federal, state, or municipal laws intended to regulate public assembly, speech, press, the association of individuals, or group action. But all such laws are not unconstitutional. Activists are not free to say or to print whatever they desire, or to publicly assemble, or to band together wherever, however, or whenever they wish. Under the Constitution an activist's freedom to speak, to publish, to take part in a public assembly, to associate with other persons, or to take part in organized group activities is protected from governmental interference so long as he or she exercises such freedoms within the framework of "liberty under law." The right to challenge, to criticize, to dissent, and to press for change do not imbue one with a right to engage in any and all kinds of conduct under the protection of the Constitution.

An activist is not free to destroy human life, cause physical injury to other persons, or to take or destroy public or private property. The Constitution does not authorize the use of violence to attain one's ends however beneficent they may be. One does not have a constitutional right to carry on an armed revolution. It has been said that the Constitution is not a "suicide pact." Government may pass reasonable laws and take reasonable steps to prevent its destruction and to protect and preserve the well-being of society and each of its members. Neither nobility of purpose, nor the high moral quality of an activist's motives, shield him from constitutional governmental action.

The Constitution is said to decree a standard of "ordered liberty" or "liberty under law." Under this directive both anarchy and the regimen of a police state are barred. When called upon to adjudicate the constitutional rights and legal responsibilities of an activist vis-à-vis the rights and responsibilities of government, society, and other persons a judge must engage in a formidable and delicate task. He must take into account the at times conflicting demands of individual liberty and an orderly society. Carefully, he must balance rights and responsibilities. When asked to rule on the rights of activists a court must treat them as members of a democratic society which guarantees a broad array of constitutional liberties to every one of its citizens. But, like all other persons, activists are obliged to abide by such restraints as society, acting through its established machinery of government, may lawfully impose on its members.

Various forms of activist activities carried on in schools and colleges have compelled courts to speak out on the rights and responsibilities of students, faculty members, and administrators. A number of courts have found that the rights and duties of activists attending or working at private institutions are exclusively governed by relevant federal and state statutes and the contract between the activist and the institution. Contractual terms are to be found in the school's catalog and its published regulations. Other courts have taken the position that the relationship between an activist and a private institution is not governed solely by contract and statute. These courts have asserted that even a private institution may not act arbitrarily or unfairly when it undertakes to suspend or oust an activist. They have found that constitutional demands play a part in the relationship between the institution and the activist. Uniformly courts have ruled that receipt by a private institution of financial assistance from the government does not subject that institution to the same restraints the Constitution places on public schools, colleges, and universities.

Public educational institutions are treated as akin to other forms of governmental activity. The behavior of school officials must satisfy the same general demands the Constitution places on all governmental officers. The precise content of these demands is determined by the unique role assigned to such institutions. Courts acknowledge that (1) school administrators must be free to invoke fair and reasonable procedures so that the school may fulfill its assigned tasks, (2) schools do not stand in strict *in loco parentis* with their students, (3) each student has rights and responsibilities vis-à-vis his or her fellow students, and (4) in contemporary society the loss of an educational opportunity is not to be taken lightly. It is within the framework of these assumptions that courts have proceeded to balance the rights and responsibilities of students, faculty, and school officers.

A student or faculty activist does not have a constitutional right to prevent a school from carrying out its assigned functions. Activists are not free to deprive their fellow students of their right to take part in the educational process. An activist charged with having gone beyond the limits of his or her constitutional liberties may not be denied equal protection of the laws nor be suspended or ousted without being accorded due process. Ordinarily due process requires (1) notification of the charges, (2) a hearing, (3) an opportunity to defend, (4) knowledge of adverse evidence, (5) names of adverse witnesses, and (6) the disciplinary action taken be supported by substantial evidence.

Courts view public educational institutions as market places of ideas. The Constitution protects a teacher's academic freedom to speak out and to explore the subject area in which he is teaching. He is free to take unpopular positions. His employment may not be conditioned on the surrender of constitutional rights. Administrators may not demand uniformity of thought or expression. However, they do have a legitimate interest in the competency and fitness of faculty members and in their conduct in the educational milieu. If a teacher's behavior is such that it renders him unfit to take part in the educational process, or it makes learning by students impossible, or is destructive of the institution, he may be suspended or discharged.

The Hatch Political Activities Act prohibits certain federal employees from taking an "active part in political management or in political campaigns." A like restraint is placed on certain state and municipal employees who are employed by an agency which receives federal financial assistance. An employee's violation of the Act can result in his dismissal. In 1940 the Supreme Court sustained the Act, finding that Congress could subordinate some form of individual political activity in the interest of hoped for employee efficiency.

In several recent decisions dealing with state and local laws which in broad terms barred state or municipal employees from taking part in political campaigns courts have looked favorably on political involvement by governmental employees. They have placed greater emphasis on the constitutional rights to speak out and engage in political activities than on the presumption that efficiency will be promoted by prohibiting employee involvement in political campaigns. But even under this point of view courts have sustained laws which prohibit political activity by governmental employees when such activity would patently disrupt public service. For example, a state may prohibit its employees from seeking election to public office in contests which pit them against their immediate superiors.

Educational and political activism are but two aspects of activism but the principles governing these forms of activism apply to other kinds of activism. In subsequent chapters, such as those focusing on freedom of speech, press, and public assembly, issues intimately related to activism are considered. The rights of activists cannot be compartmentalized. When one thinks of the rights of an activist he or she must think in terms of a variety of constitutional and statutory rights which are intended to recognize individual freedom to dissent and to work for change.

ANDERSON v. SILLS

Supreme Court of New Jersey, 1970.
265 A.2d 678, 56 N.J. 210.

The defendant, the Attorney General of New Jersey, sent a memorandum and prescribed forms to all county and local police units, asking that they use the forms to supply information to the Security Unit of the State Police. The requested information pertained to organizations and individuals involved in such incidents as civil disorders, riots, rallies, protests, demonstrations, marches, and confrontations. Plaintiffs, a branch of the NAACP and several individuals who had been involved in sit-ins, marches, rallies, and protests in opposition to the Viet Nam War, racism, and the draft, brought an action asking the court to adjudge the Attorney General's action unconstitutional. The trial court, finding that the Attorney General's scheme violated the constitutional guarantees of freedom of speech and association, granted the plaintiffs' motion for summary judgment. The defendant appealed.

WEINTRAUB, C. J.

*   *   *

We are not dealing with a statute imposing criminal liability for its violation, * * * or a statute which affects the right to public employment, * * * or to pursue a profession, * * *. Where a statute thus affects an individual, it may on its face invite the question whether because of vagueness or overbreadth it unnecessarily deters an individual from speech or activity protected by the First Amendment.

Here, the Memorandum imposes no liability or obligation or restriction whatever upon the citizen. Nor does it order the policeman to take action against a citizen upon the pain of discipline if the policeman does not comply. It is no more than a communication to law enforcement agencies about their respective powers and duties. It is wholly informative and advisory. It does not command; it merely encourages cooperation among all agencies concerned with the problem of civil disorders.

*   *   *   There have been serious disorders involving heavy losses of life and property. The police function is pervasive. It is not limited to the detection of past criminal events. Of at least equal importance is the responsibility to prevent crime. * * * In the current scene, the preventive role requires an awareness of group tensions and preparations to head off disasters as well as to deal with them if they appear. To that end the police must know what forces exist, what groups or organizations could be enmeshed in public disorders. This is not to ask the police to decide which are "good" and which are "bad." In terms of civil disorders, their respective virtues are irrelevant, for a group is of equal concern to the police whether it is potentially the victim or the aggressor. * * *

In the summer of 1967 there were serious riots. Both the President of the United States and the Governor of this State appointed commissions to study the problem and to make recommendations. The Report of the National Advisory Commission on Civil Disorders (March 1, 1968) in its "Supplement on Control of Disorders" encouraged the preparations which the Memorandum here involved seeks to achieve. It reads (p. 269):

Intelligence—The absence of accurate information both before and during a disorder has created special control problems for police. Police departments must develop means to obtain adequate intelligence for planning purposes, as well as on-the-scene information for use in police operations during a disorder.

An intelligence unit staffed with full-time personnel should be established to gather, evaluate, analyze, and disseminate information on potential as well as actual civil disorders. It should provide police administrators and commanders with reliable information essential for assessment and decisionmaking. It should use undercover police personnel and informants but it should also draw on community leaders, agencies, and organizations in the ghetto.

* * *

It is a serious matter for the judiciary to interfere with the preventive measures devised by the executive branch of government in response to its constitutional obligation to protect all the citizens. Surely, such interference may not rest upon a hypothetical exposition of what could happen under a set of forms in the hands of an officer indifferent to the restraints upon his office. Rather the premise must be accepted, absent proof the other way, that the Memorandum assumed a lawful exercise of the judgment and discretion vested in the local police. The Memorandum did not originate the duty of the local police unit to decide what situations harbor the potential of disaster and what data should be gathered for responsible performance in office. The forms do not enlarge upon that power and responsibility. Rather, being designed for many situations, the forms are necessarily comprehensive, leaving it to the local authorities to decide in their judgment what incidents are worthy of note and what information should be obtained as to the individuals concerned or involved.

* * *

Here we are dealing with the critical power of government to gather intelligence to enable it to satisfy the very reason for its being—to protect the individual in his person and things. * * * The First Amendment itself would be meaningless if there were no constituted authority to protect the individual from suppression by others who disapprove of him or the company he keeps. Hence the First Amendment rights must be weighed against the competing interests of the citizen. If there is no intent to control the content of speech, an overriding public need may be met even though the measure adopted to that end operates incidentally to limit the unfettered exercise of the First Amendment right. * * *

The power to investigate is basic. So the cases recognize a vast power to investigate in the legislative branch so long as the inquiry is relevant to the legislative function. * * * An administrative agency may on its own initiative investigate to see that there is compliance with law within the ambit of its responsibility. * * * So, too, a grand jury may inquire as to whether a crime occurred and who was the culprit, and its power to compel testimony does not depend upon the existence of "probable cause" either as to the fact of a crime or the culpability of the suspect. * * *

The investigatory obligation of the police is surely no less extensive than the grand jury's. Indeed, the preventive role of the police necessarily implies a duty to gather data along a still wider range. * * * There is the power of surveillance. It includes even the deceptive use of undercover agents to infiltrate situations in which criminal events have occurred or may be anticipated. * * * And electronic surveillance of a public meeting has been sustained. * * *

The basic approach must be that the executive branch may gather whatever information it reasonably believes to be necessary to enable it to perform the police roles, detectional and preventive. A court should not interfere in the absence of proof of bad faith or arbitrariness. * * *

We are not unmindful of the unfortunate polarization within our society, and we can understand how in that light some may fear that officials will unlawfully take sides. Yet, to deny to government, on that account, the authority it must have to fulfill its mission would heighten that fear or even make it a reality. Lawlessness has a tyranny of its own, and it would be folly to deprive government of its power to deal with that tyranny merely because of a figment of a fear that government itself may run amuck. * * *

The judgment is reversed and the matter remanded for further proceedings not inconsistent with this opinion.

TINKER v. DES MOINES INDEPENDENT COMMUNITY SCHOOL DISTRICT

Supreme Court of the United States, 1969.
89 S.Ct. 733, 393 U.S. 503, 21 L.Ed.2d 731.

The petitioners, 15, 16 and 13 years of age, students in the public school system operated by the defendant, in violation of a school regulation, wore black arm bands while in school to publicize their objection to the Viet Nam War. They were suspended from school for the period during which they planned to wear the arm bands. The petitioners brought an action to enjoin the defendant from disciplining them. After a hearing, the District Court dismissed the complaint.

An equally divided Court of Appeals, sitting *en banc,* affirmed. The Supreme Court granted certiorari.

MR. JUSTICE FORTAS delivered the opinion of the Court.

* * *

* * * As we shall discuss, the wearing of armbands in the circumstances of this case was entirely divorced from actually or potentially disruptive conduct by those participating in it. It was closely akin to "pure speech" which, we have repeatedly held, is entitled to comprehensive protection under the First Amendment. * * *

First Amendment rights, applied in light of the special characteristics of the school environment, are available to teachers and students. It can hardly be argued that either students or teachers shed their constitutional rights to freedom of speech or expression at the schoolhouse gate. * * *

Our problem involves direct, primary First Amendment rights akin to "pure speech."

The school officials banned and sought to punish petitioners for a silent, passive expression of opinion, unaccompanied by any disorder or disturbance on the part of petitioners. There is here no evidence whatever of petitioners' interference, actual or nascent, with the schools' work or of collision with the rights of other students to be secure and to be let alone. Accordingly, this case does not concern speech or action that intrudes upon the work of the schools or the rights of other students.

* * *

The District Court concluded that the action of the school authorities was reasonable because it was based upon their fear of a disturbance from the wearing of the armbands. But, in our system, undifferentiated fear or apprehension of disturbance is not enough to overcome the right to freedom of expression. Any departure from absolute regimentation may cause trouble. Any variation from the majority's opinion may inspire fear. Any word spoken, in class, in the lunchroom, or on the campus, that deviates from the views of another person may start an argument or cause a disturbance. But our Constitution says we must take this risk, * * * and our history says that it is this sort of hazardous freedom—this kind of openness—that is the basis of our national strength and of the independence and vigor of Americans who grow up and live in this relatively permissive, often disputatious, society.

In order for the State in the person of school officials to justify prohibition of a particular expression of opinion, it must be able to show that its action was caused by something more than a mere desire to avoid the discomfort and unpleasantness that always accompany an unpopular viewpoint. Certainly where there is no finding and no showing that engaging in the forbidden conduct would "materially and substantially interfere with the requirements of appropriate discipline in the operation of the school," the prohibition cannot be sustained. * * *

In the present case, the District Court made no such finding, and our independent examination of the record fails to yield evidence that the school authorities had reason to anticipate that the wearing of the armbands would substantially interfere with the work of the school or impinge upon the rights of other students. * * *

In our system, state-operated schools may not be enclaves of totalitarianism. School officials do not possess absolute authority over their students. Students in school as well as out of school are "persons" under our Constitution. They are possessed of fundamental rights which the State must respect, just as they themselves must respect their obligations to the State. In our system, students may not be regarded as closed-circuit recipients of only that which the State chooses to communicate. They may not be confined to the expression of those sentiments that are officially approved. In the absence of a specific showing of constitutionally valid reasons to regulate their speech, students are entitled to freedom of expression of their views. As Judge Gewin, speaking for the Fifth Circuit, said, school officials cannot suppress "expressions of feelings with which they do not wish to contend." * * *

* * * A student's rights, * * *, do not embrace merely the classroom hours. When he is in the cafeteria, or on the playing field, or on the campus during the authorized hours, he may express his opinions, even on controversial subjects like the conflict in Vietnam, if he does so without "materially and substantially interfer[ing] with the requirements of appropriate discipline in the operation of the school" and without colliding with the rights of others. * * * But conduct by the student, in class or out of it, which for any reason—whether it stems from time, place, or type of behavior—materially disrupts classwork or involves substantial disorder or invasion of the rights of others is, of course, not immunized by the constitutional guarantee of freedom of speech. * * *

If a regulation were adopted by school officials forbidding discussion of the Vietnam conflict, or the expression by any student of opposition to it anywhere on school property except as part of a prescribed classroom exercise, it would be obvious that the regulation would violate the constitutional rights of students, at least if it could not be justified by a showing that the students' activities would materially and substantially disrupt the work and discipline of the school. * * * In the circumstances of the present case, the prohibition of the silent, passive "witness of the armbands," as one of the children called it, is no less offensive to the constitution's guarantees.

* * *

Reversed and remanded.

PROBLEMS

1. The House Internal Security Committee prepared a report which contained a list of sixty-five persons it described as radical campus speakers. Several persons named in the report brought an

action to enjoin the publication of the Committee report by the United States Government Printing Office. The plaintiffs contended that publication would violate their constitutional right to freedom of speech. What judgment?

2. A federal court was asked by one who had been arrested, but not convicted of a crime, to order that his arrest record, fingerprints, and mug shots be destroyed. The F.B.I. insisted that it had a right to keep such records and opposed their destruction. What judgment?

3. To show his support of Viet Nam moratorium activities, a public school teacher wore a black armband to class. The State Education Commission ruled that a local school board had acted properly in dismissing him for such action. The Commission stated: "symbolic speech in the classroom is a form of teaching * * *. Free public education, if faithful to the ideal of secular instruction and political neutrality, * * * [must] not be partisan or enemy of any class, creed, party or faction." Does the dismissal violate the teacher's constitutional right to free speech?

4. May Congress empower the United States Post Office to delay delivery in the United States of mail which originates in a foreign country until the addressee indicates a "desire to receive it" if in the opinion of the postal authorities such mail contains "communist propaganda?"

5. May a probationary public employee be denied continued employment on the ground that he was a member of an activist anti-discrimination group?

6. A local draft board terminated a student's draft deferment because he took part in an anti-Viet Nam protest rally. He was then classified 1–A. Is such action permissible under the First Amendment?

7. May an applicant for admission to the bar, who has otherwise met all of the other qualifications the state demands of persons wishing to be licensed to practice law, be denied admission on the ground that he had taken part in a number of non-violent acts of civil disobedience?

8. May a state university deny readmission to a student it had previously granted permission to resume his studies on the ground that he had taken part in a peaceful demonstration?

9. The dean of a state college barred students from establishing an organization on the campus which in his opinion would be identified with a national organization and would support acts of violence and disruption on the campus. The dean had no evidence to support his beliefs. Was his action constitutional?

10. May a state require persons who wish to be admitted to the bar to state the names and addresses of the activist organizations, if any, to which they belonged to at the time of their application, or within five years prior to their application?

Chapter 9

CRITICISM OF PUBLIC OFFICIALS

Individuals have a right to be free from unprivileged false statements which are harmful to their reputation. If the false statement is in writing it is known as libel and if it is oral it is known as slander. Libel and slander come under the general category of the law known as defamation.

The First and Fourteenth Amendments prohibit government from regulating speech or press. If these Amendments were literally construed they would bar all lawsuits based on libel or slander. But not all such lawsuits are barred. Courts have concluded that in most cases it is in society's best interest to protect persons from unprivileged libel or slander than to deny them a right to recover damages from the party who defamed them. A notable exception to this general rule is found in the scanty protection from defamation the law recognizes on behalf of public officials. Courts envision the right to criticize government as central to a democratic society. They see the First and Fourteenth Amendments as embodying the directive that as few barriers as possible should be allowed to stand in the way of citizens criticizing their government. If one is to criticize government often he must criticize public officials. If the rules of law which govern the right of private persons to be free from defamation were applied to public officials they might be too insulated from challenges to their behavior. When speaking out against a public official a critic might, because of an excess of ardor or in the heat of outrage make a false defamatory statement. Fear of crossing the line between truth and falsity could effectively stifle public disapproval. Too much of what government does or does not do might go unchallenged. But a totally unbridled approach in favor of the citizenry could also be detrimental. Unlimited freedom to speak and write falsehoods about public officials could result in persons refusing to accept or remain in the employ of government. Some officials might feel compelled to devote more time to rehabilitating their reputation than to their official duties.

To protect the citizen's right to find fault with governmental action and yet not leave totally unprotected the reputation of public officials the Supreme Court has adopted the following standard. Only when a public official can establish that the false defamatory statement directed at him was made with malice may he recover damages for the harm done to his reputation. A false defamatory statement is made with malice if it was made either with knowledge that it was false or with reckless disregard for its truth or falsity.

Simple failure to take reasonable steps to determine whether or not a statement is true prior to making it does not constitute malice nor does bare negligence constitute reckless disregard for truth or falsity. One is said to be guilty of reckless disregard for the truth or falsity of a statement if, aware of the likelihood or probability that what he was about to circulate was false, he failed to take reasonable steps to determine its truth or falsity. For the trier of fact to find that the defendant acted with reckless disregard there "must be sufficient evidence to permit the conclusion that the defendant in fact entertained serious doubts as to the truth of" the statement. It is the making of the statement "with such doubts [that] shows reckless disregard for truth or falsity and demonstrates actual malice." Recklessness may also "be found where there are obvious reasons [for the defendant] to doubt the veracity . . . or the accuracy" of the source from which he obtained the information.[1]

The test approved by the Supreme Court is based on the Court's interpretation of the First and Fourteenth Amendments. This means that the question of whether or not one is a public official must be determined by the Court's interpretation of these two Amendments. Neither federal nor state statutory definitions of who or who is not a public official would necessarily satisfy the constitutional standard. For the purpose of these Amendments a public official is a person who is "in a position significantly to influence the resolution" of "public issues." A person may be treated as a public official if he is "among the hierarchy of government employees who have, or appear to the public to have, substantial responsibility for or control over the conduct of government affairs."[2]

Denying recovery to a public official unless he can establish that the false statement assailing his reputation was made with malice affords significant protection to individuals who speak or write critically about public officials. However this qualified immunity, conditioned on the absence of malice, falls short of the absolute immunity conferred on many public officials. As pointed out in Chapter 1 various public officials enjoy complete immunity from suit. So while a private person who falsely defames a public official is immune from suit only if he is not guilty of malice, those public officials who possess absolute immunity are immune from suit even when, with malice, they make a false defamatory statement.

Federal, state, and local governmental employees may not be punished, discriminated against, denied renewal of employment, or be discharged simply because they exercise their constitutional right to criticize government or governmental officials. This freedom to speak and to write extends to employees who criticize their superiors unless their behavior is such that it makes it impossible for them to thereafter efficiently perform their assigned tasks. What an employee has said or written may reveal that he is not competent to carry on the duties demanded by the position he holds or seeks. Because of his incompetence he may be denied employment or promotion. Governmental action founded on an employee's incompetence is not unconstitutional.

1. St. Amant v. Thompson, 88 S.Ct. 1323, 390 U.S. 727, 20 L.Ed.2d 262 (1968).   2. Rosenblatt v. Baer, 86 S.Ct. 669, 383 U.S. 75, 15 L.Ed.2d 597 (1966).

The Constitution does not deny government the power to take such reasonable steps as may be necessary to insure that its employees efficiently go about their tasks and fulfill the duties entrusted to them.

NEW YORK TIMES CO. v. SULLIVAN

Supreme Court of the United States, 1964.
84 S.Ct. 710, 376 U.S. 254, 11 L.Ed.2d 686.

The *New York Times* published an "editorial" advertisement which attacked Sullivan, an elected official, claiming he and other persons were engaged in a "wave of terror" against Negroes, seeking to deny them their constitutional rights. Readers were asked to contribute funds to help Negroes in their fight to enjoy their constitutional rights. Sullivan claimed that the advertisement contained false defamatory statements. He sued the *New York Times* and those persons who had paid for the advertisement. The trial court rejected the defendants' contention that they were shielded from a libel suit by the constitutional guarantees of freedom of speech and of the press. The jury returned a verdict in favor of Sullivan for $500,000. The Supreme Court of Alabama affirmed. Certiorari was granted.

MR. JUSTICE BRENNAN delivered the opinion of the Court.

 * * *

The publication here * * * communicated information, expressed opinion, recited grievances, protested claimed abuses, and sought financial support on behalf of a movement whose existence and objectives are matters of the highest public interest and concern. * * * That the Times was paid for publishing the advertisement is as immaterial in this connection as is the fact that newspapers and books are sold. * * * Any other conclusion would discourage newspapers from carrying "editorial advertisements" of this type, and so might shut off an important outlet for the promulgation of information and ideas by persons who do not themselves have access to publishing facilities—who wish to exercise their freedom of speech even though they are not members of the press. * * * The effect would be to shackle the First Amendment in its attempt to secure "the widest possible dissemination of information from diverse and antagonistic sources." * * * To avoid placing such a handicap upon the freedoms of expression, we hold that if the allegedly libelous statements would otherwise be constitutionally protected from the present judgment, they do not forfeit that protection because they were published in the form of a paid advertisement.

 * * *

The general proposition that freedom of expression upon public questions is secured by the First Amendment has long been settled by our decisions. The constitutional safeguard, we have said, "was fashioned to assure unfettered interchange of ideas for the bringing about of political and social changes desired by the people." * * * "The maintenance of the opportunity for free political discussion to the end that government may be responsive to the will of the people and that changes may be obtained by lawful means, an opportunity essential to the security of the Republic, is a fundamental principle of our constitutional system." * * * "[I]t is a prized American privilege to speak one's mind, although not always with perfect good taste, on all public institutions," * * * and this opportunity is to be afforded for "vigorous advocacy" no less than "abstract discussion." * * * The First Amendment, said Judge Learned Hand, "presupposes that right conclusions are more likely to be gathered out of a multitude of tongues, than through any kind of authoritative selection. To many this is, and always will be, folly; but we have staked upon it our all." * * *

Thus we consider this case against the background of a profound national commitment to the principle that debate on public issues should be uninhibited, robust, and wide-open, and that it may well include vehement, caustic, and sometimes unpleasantly sharp attacks on government and public officials. * * * The present advertisement, as an expression of grievance and protest on one of the major public issues of our time, would seem clearly to qualify for the constitutional protection. The question is whether it forfeits that protection by the falsity of some of its factual statements and by its alleged defamation of respondent.

Authoritative interpretations of the First Amendment guarantees have consistently refused to recognize an exception for any test of truth—whether administered by judges, juries, or administrative officials—and especially one that puts the burden of proving truth on the speaker. * * * The constitutional protection does not turn upon "the truth, popularity, or social utility of the ideas and beliefs which are offered." * * * As Madison said, "Some degree of abuse is inseparable from the proper use of every thing; and in no instance is this more true than in that of the press." * * * That erroneous statement is inevitable in free debate, and that it must be protected if the freedoms of expression are to have the "breathing space" that they "need * * * to survive," * * *.

Injury to official reputation error affords no more warrant for repressing speech that would otherwise be free than does factual error. * * * Criticism of their official conduct does not lose its constitutional protection merely because it is effective criticism and hence diminishes their official reputations.

If neither factual error nor defamatory content suffices to remove the constitutional shield from criticism of official conduct, the combination of the two elements is no less inadequate. * * *

The constitutional guarantees require, we think, a federal rule that prohibits a public official from recovering damages for a defamatory falsehood relating to his official conduct unless he proves that the statement was made with "actual malice"—that is, with knowledge that it was false or with reckless disregard of whether it was false or not. * * *

Reversed and remanded.

———

PICKERING v. BOARD OF EDUCATION

Supreme Court of the United States, 1968.
88 S.Ct. 1731, 391 U.S. 563, 20 L.Ed.2d 811.

The plaintiff, a teacher employed by the defendant, sent a letter to a local newspaper in which he criticized the defendant's proposal to increase taxes. The letter contained some false information. The defendant held a hearing and thereafter discharged the plaintiff. The defendant found that the publication of the letter was "detrimental to the efficient operation and administration of the schools of the district." The plaintiff sued to be reinstated, claiming that the defendant's action was unconstitutional. From a decision in the state supreme court in favor of the defendant, the plaintiff appealed.

MR. JUSTICE MARSHALL delivered the opinion of the Court.
* * *

To the extent that the Illinois Supreme Court's opinion may be read to suggest that teachers may constitutionally be compelled to relinquish the First Amendment rights they would otherwise enjoy as citizens to comment on matters of public interest in connection with the operation of the public schools in which they work, it proceeds on a premise that has been unequivocally rejected in numerous prior decisions of this Court. * * * "[T]he theory that public employment which may be denied altogether may be subjected to any conditions, regardless of how unreasonable, has been uniformly rejected." * * * At the same time it cannot be gainsaid that the State has interests as an employer in regulating the speech of its employees that differ significantly from those it possesses in connection with regulation of the speech of the citizenry in general. The problem in any case is to arrive at a balance between the interests of the teacher, as a citizen, in commenting upon matters of public concern and the interest of the State, as an employer, in promoting the efficiency of the public services it performs through its employees.
* * *

An examination of the statements in appellant's letter objected to by the Board reveals that they, like the letter as a whole, consist essentially of criticism of the Board's allocation of school funds between educational and athletic programs, and of both the Board's and the superintendent's methods of informing, or preventing the informing of, the district's taxpayers of the real reasons why additional tax revenues were being sought for the schools. The statements are in no way directed towards any person with whom appellant would normally be in contact in the course of his daily work as a teacher. Thus no question of maintaining either discipline by immediate superiors or harmony among coworkers is presented here. * * *

What we do have before us is a case in which a teacher has made erroneous public statements upon issues then currently the subject of public attention, which are critical of his ultimate employer but which are neither shown nor can be presumed to have in any way either impeded the teacher's proper performance of his daily duties in the classroom or to have interfered with the regular operation of the schools generally. In these circumstances we conclude that the interest of the school administration in limiting teachers' opportunities to contribute to public debate is not significantly greater than its interest in limiting a similar contribution by any member of the general public.

The public interest in having free and unhindered debate on matters of public importance—the core value of the Free Speech Clause of the First Amendment—is so great that it has been held that a State cannot authorize the recovery of damages by a public official for defamatory statements directed at him except when such statements are shown to have been made either with knowledge of their falsity or with reckless disregard for their truth or falsity. * * * The same test has been applied to suits for invasion of privacy based on false statements where a "matter of public interest" is involved. * * * It is * * * perfectly clear that, were appellant a member of the general public, the State's power to afford the appellee Board of Education or its members any legal right to sue him for writing the letter at issue here would be limited by the requirement that the letter be judged by the standard laid down in New York Times.

This Court has also indicated, in more general terms, that statements by public officials on matters of public concern must be accorded First Amendment protection despite the fact that the statements are directed at their nominal superiors. * * *

In sum, we hold that, in a case such as this, absent proof of false statements knowingly or recklessly made by him, a teacher's exercise of his right to speak on issues of public importance may not furnish the basis for his dismissal from public employment. Since no such showing has been made in this case regarding appellant's letter * * * his dismissal for writing it cannot be upheld and the judgment of the Illinois Supreme Court must, accordingly, be reversed and the case remanded for further proceedings not inconsistent with this opinion. It is so ordered.

PROBLEMS

1. The plaintiff was president of the student senate at a private college. A student senator charged him with embezzling senate funds. The senator informed a local radio station that the plaintiff was an "embezzler." The radio station thereafter reported that the plaintiff was guilty of embezzlement. No formal charges were ever made against the plaintiff by the student senate or law enforcement authorities. The plaintiff brought a defamation action against the sen-

ator and the local radio station. What judgment as to each defendant?

2. The defendant was the officer in charge of security at a United States Post Office building. Several days after the building had been burglarized he arrested the plaintiff. He told a friend of his, a reporter, that "beyond a doubt, this is our man." The following day the defendant's remark was reported in a local newspaper. A grand jury failed to charge the plaintiff with the burglary. When sued, the defendant moved to dismiss the complaint on the ground that he was immune from suit because he was a public official. What judgment?

3. The defendant, a nationally respected newspaper published in New York City, erroneously reported that the plaintiffs, police officers, had permitted a number of suspects to escape from a police truck because they had failed to lock the truck's front door. The article appeared on the front page of the newspaper and carried the headline "Dice Raid in Stamford Follows the Script of a Keystone Comedy." The story was written in a humorous fashion, with the reporter having concocted the conversations contained in the article. The reporter had no personal information as to what did or did not happen. He relied on a single telephone call for his information. The plaintiffs sued for libel. What judgment?

4. The plaintiff, a governmental employee, in a letter he wrote to the commander of the shipyard at which he worked, criticized several supervisory personnel. He charged them with favoritism and wrongdoing. He failed to take advantage of an opportunity to prove that what he had written was true. Shortly thereafter he was discharged for having made "unfounded statements." He sued for reinstatement. What judgment?

5. A judge, prior to sentencing the plaintiff, adversely commented on his past conduct. The plaintiff claimed that the judge's statements were false and defamatory. He brought a defamation action against the judge. What judgment?

Chapter 10

FREEDOM OF SPEECH AND ASSOCIATION

The First and Fourteenth Amendments prohibit government from abridging freedom of speech. They withhold from federal, state, and local governments the power to prevent persons from speaking out in favor of, or against, popular or unpopular, acceptable or unacceptable, beliefs, opinions, and ideas. No branch of government may punish or retaliate against one who has chosen to exercise his constitutionally guaranteed right to speak.

The Supreme Court has classified freedom of speech as a "preferred" constitutional right. It has placed this liberty in the same category as such other First Amendment rights as freedom of religion, press, and public assembly. When reviewing a restraint government has placed on the exercise of this right the Court, with great sensitivity and concern, most carefully scrutinizes the nature of the challenged governmental action. Conscious of the possibility that governmental officials may resort to devious and unlawful means to stifle criticism and debate the Supreme Court has espoused the "chilling effect" doctrine. This doctrine allows a court to probe beneath the surface of governmental action and see if in fact what governmental officers have done will have a dampening effect on the readiness of individuals to exercise their right to speak freely. If the court finds that official action has such an effect, it will strike it down.

Ordinarily Federal District Courts abstain from interpreting and ruling upon the constitutionality of a state's criminal statute until the state courts have had the opportunity to do so. This principle is consistent with a concept of federalism which entrusts states with a broad power to pass and enforce legislation with federal intrusion being the last resort of a dissatisfied litigant. The need to await completion of state action before challenging the constitutionality of a state statute in a federal forum may "chill" one's desire to speak or to act in violation of state legislation even if it is clearly unconstitutional. The "chilling effect" doctrine permits a Federal District Court to intervene and enjoin enforcement of an obviously unconstitutional statute which curbs speech or the liberty of individuals to engage in various sorts of relationships before a state criminal proceeding is begun or even contemplated. But this doctrine may only be invoked by a District Court in "exceptional circumstances," such as when it appears that state officials are acting in bad faith and are harassing the complainant or are acting in bad faith and will, if not stopped, cause the complainant irreparable injury. When the Federal Court intervenes, strikes down the state statute, and enjoins its enforcement, the complainant no longer need fear harassment or injury by state officials. With the uncertainty abated he is free to enjoy his constitutional rights.

The liberty to express one's point of view includes the freedom to communicate with others. The use of a loud speaker, for instance, in a heavily traveled and densely populated area may be necessary if the speaker is to have an opportunity to communicate with persons who walk, live, or work in the area. A statute which prohibits any and all use of any sort of speech amplifier or outlaws the use of all sound trucks unless they are in constant motion is unconstitutional. It denies one the liberty to express himself in such a way as to permit him to actually communicate with his sought after audience.

The Constitution protects more than bare speech. Individuals have a right to use media of communication other than pure speech. The means and behavior entitled to the protection of the First and Fourteenth Amendments to the same extent as pure speech are categorized as "symbolic" free speech. The symbols and symbolic action chosen to express and to communicate thoughts, beliefs, and ideas may take a variety of forms. Examples of non-verbal expression and media of communication include music, painting, dance, photographs, sculpture, hair cut short or not cut at all, dirty clothes, overall physical uncleanliness, refusal to salute the American flag, the carrying of a foreign flag, and picketing. Each of these are generally treated as a form of speech, entitled to the protection accorded speech under the Constitution.

Non-verbal forms of expression and communication at times raise problems not fomented by pure speech. Some effects of symbolic speech may permit government to impose regulations on the selected form of expression in order to protect some other vital societal interest or value. For example, when dirty clothes and overall uncleanliness become a hazard to the health and safety of other persons they may be dealt with by reasonable governmental action. If one wished to express and communicate his objection to some federal or state policy by driving his automobile through red traffic signals at heavily traveled intersections he is not at liberty to do so. In each of these cases the symbol chosen by the individual, because of its impact on other persons, is distinguishable from pure speech and may therefore be regulated.

If interpreted literally the Constitution's directive that government not abridge freedom of speech would bar any form of governmental control of speech. Those jurists who have taken this position insist that government may regulate speech only when it is "brigaded with action." This would mean that only when some form of action of legitimate concern to the government accompanies speech may government regulate what one says. A majority of the Supreme Court has rejected the "brigaded with action" approach. Instead, the Court has chosen to follow the "clear and present danger" test whenever it is called upon to decide whether or not a restraint on speech is or is not constitutional.

The "clear and present danger" test is predicated on acceptance of several propositions. (1) Federal, state, and local governments have a right to survive. They may pass and enforce laws reasonably necessary to prevent their destruction. (2) Government need not wait until persons who are determined and ready to overthrow the established order as soon as the opportunity presents itself actually begin their *putsch*. (3) Government possesses the power to regulate speech at some point before speech becomes action, which action may be banned by government because its prevention is of legitimate interest to a democratic form of government. (4) Among the legitimate interests of concern to the government are national security, the prevention of armed revolution, violence, disorder, the protection of public property and essential governmental functions, and the life, safety, health, well-being, and privacy of individual members of society, and guarding the legitimate interests of those who own private property.

The "clear and present danger" test requires a court to take into account the nature of the interest which government is empowered to protect and the probability that the interest was in danger because of the contents of the challenged speech and the conditions prevailing in the milieu in which the speech was delivered. If the court finds that what was said constituted a clear and present danger to a legitimate interest of government, then the speech is not immune from control. One who makes such a speech can be punished. The delivery of a speech which falls outside the protection of the Constitution on account of the "clear and present danger" test can be halted. To decide if governmental action can pass muster under this test it has been said that a court must "ask whether the gravity of the 'evil' [the wrong which government has a legitimate interest in preventing from taking place or protecting from interference] discounted by its improbability, justifies such an invasion of free speech as is necessary to avoid the danger." [1] This test, the Supreme Court has said, takes into account "those factors which" the court deems "relevant, and relates to their significance." [2]

The "clear and present danger" test is fact-based. When a tribunal is asked to decide whether or not what was said by the defendant was protected by the First or Fourteenth Amendments the judges must engage in a critical analysis and appraisal of (1) what was said, (2) the setting in which it was said, and (3) the nature of the government's interest. They must predict the probable effect of the speech on the interest which the government undertook to protect. In a setting in which tempers were flaring, where there had already been a history of violence, where tension had been mounting, and the summer day's temperature and humidity were high, a court might properly find that a speech intended to arouse immediate, violent, and destructive behavior did warrant official reaction. The very same speech, made in a different setting, could very well lead a court to conclude that the Constitution prohibited governmental interference.

1. United States v. Dennis, (2d Cir., 1950) 183 F.2d 201.

2. Dennis v. United States, 71 S.Ct. 857, 341 U.S. 494, 95 L.Ed. 1137 (1951).

Censorship requires that before one may lawfully speak he obtain official permission. Governments resort to censorship to enforce thought control. Censorship and thought control are prohibited by the Constitution. Yet not every statute which requires one to obtain a license before he speaks is unconstitutional. When considering whether or not such a law is valid courts invoke the "clear and present danger" test. The nature and depth of government's legitimate interest is examined. Attention is paid to the objectives of the statute, its wording, how it is administered, and what one must do to obtain a license. For example, a licensing statute is constitutional if its purpose is to allow the government to make suitable arrangements to accommodate the speaker's needs, it does not place an unconstitutional test on what the speaker may say, its prescribed procedures are simple and speedy, it is administered fairly and in a non-discriminatory fashion, it sets forth precisely the type of conduct which requires a license, and the criteria to be followed by the official who is responsible to rule on license applications are clearly stated.

Persons may wish to band together to promote the attainment of mutually shared goals. Group action may permit them to most effectively carry their message to other persons. The act of persons associating with one another in order to have a united voice is treated as a form of speech and is protected as such.

Officials, opposed to the position taken by an association, might wish to learn the names of those who belong to the association. If government possessed the power to obtain such information whenever it wished individuals might decide not to take part in group activities. They might fear harassment or recrimination by government or private persons once their membership was disclosed. The Supreme Court, insisting that speech must have "breathing space" and not be "chilled," has ruled that in the absence of some legitimate governmental interest officials may not obtain association membership lists. They are to be treated as a private affair, of interest only to the association and its members. Similarly, unless it appears that there is a legitimate need for it, government may not compel an individual to disclose the names of the associations to which he belongs. Whether the request for association affiliation information is made of an individual or an association, the "clear and present danger" test is used to determine whether or not otherwise private information must be revealed.

UNITED STATES v. O'BRIEN

Supreme Court of the United States, 1968.
88 S.Ct. 1673, 391 U.S. 367, 20 L.Ed.2d 672.

The defendant publicly burned his Selective Service Registration Certificate. The Federal District Court found him guilty of violating a 1965 Amendment to the Selective Service Act which made it a crime to knowingly destroy, knowingly mutilate, or in any manner change a registration certificate. He was sentenced to the custody of the Attorney General for a maximum period of six years for supervision and treatment. The Court of Appeals declared the 1965 Amendment unconstitutional on the ground that it infringed on the defendant's right to freedom of speech. But the Court affirmed his conviction on the ground that the defendant had violated another section of the Selective Service Act which made it a crime for a man of his age not to possess a registration certificate. The United States and the defendant each petitioned for certiorari. Their petitions were granted.

MR. CHIEF JUSTICE WARREN delivered the opinion of the Court. * * *

* * * We note at the outset that the 1965 Amendment plainly does not abridge free speech on its face, and we do not understand O'Brien to argue otherwise. * * * A law prohibiting destruction of Selective Service certificates no more abridges free speech on its face than a motor vehicle law prohibiting the destruction of drivers' licenses, or a tax law prohibiting the destruction of books and records.

O'Brien nonetheless argues that the 1965 Amendment is unconstitutional in its application to him, and is unconstitutional as enacted because what he calls the "purpose" of Congress was "to suppress freedom of speech." We consider these arguments separately.

O'Brien first argues that the 1965 Amendment is unconstitutional as applied to him because his act of burning his registration certificate was protected "symbolic speech" within the First Amendment. His argument is that the freedom of expression which the First Amendment guarantees includes all modes of "communication of ideas by conduct," and that his conduct is within this definition because he did it in "demonstration against the war and against the draft."

We cannot accept the view that an apparently limitless variety of conduct can be labeled "speech" whenever the person engaging in the conduct intends thereby to express an idea. However, even on the assumption that the alleged communicative element in O'Brien's conduct is sufficient to bring into play the First Amendment, it does not necessarily follow that the destruction of a registration certificate is constitutionally protected activity. This Court has held that when "speech" and "nonspeech" elements are combined in the same course of conduct, a sufficiently important governmental interest in regulating the nonspeech element can justify incidental limitations on First Amendment freedoms. To characterize the quality of the governmental interest which must appear, the Court has employed a variety of descriptive terms: compelling; substantial; subordinating; paramount; cogent; strong. Whatever imprecision inheres in these terms, we think it clear that a government regulation is sufficiently justified if it is within the constitutional power of the Government; if it furthers an important or substantial governmental interest; if the governmental interest is unrelated to the suppression of free expression; and if the incidental restriction on alleged First Amendment freedoms is no greater than is essential to the furtherance of that interest. We find that the 1965 Amendment * * * meets all of these requirements, and consequently that O'Brien can be constitutionally convicted for violating it.

The constitutional power of Congress to raise and support armies and to make all laws necessary and proper to that end is broad and sweeping. * * * The power of Congress to classify and conscript manpower for military service is "beyond question." * * * Pursuant to this power, Congress may establish a system of registration for individuals liable for training and service, and may require such individuals within reason to cooperate in the registration system. The issuance of certificates indicating the registration and eligibility classification of individuals is a legitimate and substantial administrative aid in the functioning of this system. And legislation to insure the continuing availability of issued certificates serves a legitimate and substantial purpose in the system's administration.

* * *

The many functions performed by Selective Service certificates establish beyond doubt that Congress has a legitimate and substantial interest in preventing their wanton and unrestrained destruction and assuring their continuing availability by punishing people who knowingly and wilfully destroy or mutilate them. * * *

It is equally clear that the 1965 Amendment specifically protects this substantial governmental interest. We perceive no alternative means that would more precisely and narrowly assure the continuing availability of issued Selective Service certificates than a law which prohibits their wilful mutilation or destruction. * * * When O'Brien deliberately rendered unavailable his registration certificate, he wilfully frustrated this governmental interest. For this noncommunicative impact of his conduct, and for nothing else, he was convicted.

* * *

In conclusion, we find that because of the Government's substantial interest in assuring the continuing availability of issued Selective Service certificates, because * * * [the Amendment] is an appropriately narrow means of protecting this interest and condemns only the independent noncommunicative impact of conduct within its reach, and because the noncommunicative impact of O'Brien's act of burning his registration certificate frustrated the Government's interest, a sufficient governmental interest has been shown to justify O'Brien's conviction.

O'Brien finally argues that the 1965 Amendment is unconstitutional as enacted because what he calls the "purpose" of Congress was "to suppress freedom of speech." We reject this argument because under settled principles the purpose of Congress, as O'Brien uses that term, is not a basis for declaring this legislation unconstitutional.

It is a familiar principle of constitutional law that this Court will not strike down an otherwise constitutional statute on the basis of an alleged illicit legislative motive.   *   *   *

Since the 1965 Amendment   *   *   *   is constitutional as enacted and as applied, the Court of Appeals should have affirmed the judgment of conviction entered by the District Court.   Accordingly, we vacate the judgment of the Court of Appeals, and reinstate the judgment and sentence of the District Court.   This disposition makes unnecessary consideration of O'Brien's claim that the Court of Appeals erred in affirming his conviction on the basis of the nonpossession regulation.

BRANDENBURG v. OHIO

Supreme Court of the United States.
89 S.Ct. 1827, 395 U.S. 444, 23 L.Ed.2d 430 (1969).

The Ohio Criminal Syndicalism Act made it a crime to advocate the duty or propriety of crime, sabotage, or unlawful methods of terrorism as a means of accomplishing industrial or political reform or to voluntarily assemble with any group or assemblage of persons formed to teach or advocate doctrines which called for the use of terrorism, sabotage, violence, or criminal acts to accomplish such reform.   The defendant took part in a Ku Klux Klan rally.   Some of the hooded figures who took part in the rally carried firearms.   The participants gathered around, and then burned, a large wooden cross.   Derogatory statements were made about black persons and Jews.   One speaker stated that if the President, Congress or the Supreme Court continued to suppress the white race "it's possible that there might have to be some revengeance [sic] taken."   A speaker stated: "We are marching on Congress July 4th, 400,000 strong."   The defendant was found guilty of violating the statute, was fined $1,000 and was sentenced to 1 to 10 years imprisonment.   The state appellate court affirmed.   He appealed.

PER CURIAM.

*   *   *

The Ohio Criminal Syndicalism Statute was enacted in 1919. From 1917 to 1920, identical or quite similar laws were adopted by 20 States and two territories.   *   *   *   In 1927, this Court sustained the constitutionality of California's Criminal Syndicalism Act,   *   *   * the text of which is quite similar to that of the laws of Ohio.   Whitney v. California,   *   *   *.   The Court upheld the statute on the ground that, without more, "advocating" violent means to effect political and economic change involves such danger to the security of the State that the State may outlaw it.   *   *   *   But *Whitney* has been thoroughly discredited by later decisions.   See Dennis v. United States,   *   *   * (1951).   These later decisions have fashioned the principle that the constitutional guarantees of free speech and free press do not permit a State to forbid or proscribe advocacy of the use of force or of law violation except where such advocacy is directed to inciting or pro-ducing imminent lawless action and is likely to incite or produce such action. As we said in Noto v. United States, * * * (1961), "the mere abstract teaching * * * of the moral propriety or even moral necessity for a resort to force and violence, is not the same as pre-paring a group for violent action and steeling it to such action." * * * A statute which fails to draw this distinction impermissibly intrudes upon the freedoms guaranteed by the First and Fourteenth Amendments. It sweeps within its condemnation speech which our Constitution has immunized from governmental control. * * *

Measured by this test, Ohio's Criminal Syndicalism Act cannot be sustained. The Act punishes persons who "advocate or teach the duty, necessity, or propriety" of violence "as a means of accomplish-ing industrial or political reform"; or who publish or circulate or display any book or paper containing such advocacy; or who "justify" the commission of violent acts "with intent to exemplify, spread or advocate the propriety of the doctrines of criminal syndicalism"; or who "voluntarily assemble" with a group formed "to teach or advocate the doctrines of criminal syndicalism." Neither the indictment nor the trial judge's instructions to the jury in any way refined the statute's bald definition of the crime in terms of mere advocacy not distin-guished from incitement to imminent lawless action.

Accordingly, we are here confronted with a statute which, by its own words and as applied, purports to punish mere advocacy and to forbid, on pain of criminal punishment, assembly with others merely to advocate the described type of action. Such a statute falls within the condemnation of the First and Fourteenth Amendments. The contrary teaching of Whitney v. California, *supra*, cannot be supported, and that decision is therefore overruled.

Reversed.

PROBLEMS

1. The defendant, during a state legislative investigation held in the early 1960's, answered questions posed to him about his rela-tionship with the Communist party after 1957 but refused to answer questions pertaining to his relationship with the party prior to 1957. Prosecution for any pre-1957 criminal activities was barred by the statute of limitations. He refused to answer on the ground that he enjoyed a constitutional right to political and associational privacy, that what was being sought was historical information which was of no present need to the state, and that there was lacking an overriding and compelling state interest such as a present danger of sedition against the state to require him to forego his constitutional right. May the defendant be punished for contempt for his refusal to an-swer?

2.   The petitioner sought admission to the state bar.   The Chairman on the Committee of Bar Admissions asked him if he was a member of the Communist Party.   He refused to answer the question. The Committee thereafter reported that due to his refusal to answer it was unable to complete its study of the applicant's moral character and hence could not certify him as fit to practice law.   The petitioner claimed he had a constitutional right not to respond since to require him to do so would violate his right to freedom of speech and association.   The Committee argued that freedom of speech and association are not "absolutes" and in this instance there was a sufficient state interest to allow the inquiry to be made since the state had a right to exclude from the practice of law applicants who might resort to illegal means to change the form of the state or the federal governments.   Is the Committee or the petitioner correct?

3.   The Federal Communications Commission adopted a rule which required all licensed broadcast stations within one week after broadcasting a personal attack on any person or group to notify that person or group of the attack, specify the broadcast, provide a copy of the script or a tape of the broadcast, and offer the person or group a reasonable opportunity to respond by making use of the licensee's facilities.   The plaintiff, a licensee, challenged the rule as a violation of freedom of speech and press claiming that it imposed an unreasonable burden on communications?   What judgment?

4.   A state statute made it a misdemeanor to intentionally encourage persons to riot or to engage in group activities which encouraged persons to engage in acts of force, violence, or destruction under circumstances which produce a clear, present, and immediate danger of acts of force, violence, or destruction.   The statute excluded otherwise lawful activities engaged in by, or on behalf of, labor organizations.   The defendant, not involved in labor activities, was found guilty of violating the statute.   Is the statute constitutional?

5.   A state legislative committee demanded that a NAACP chapter reveal the names of persons who had contributed funds to its operations.   The committee said it sought this information so that it could investigate whether or not taxpayers had falsely declared that they had donated funds to the chapter.   A state tax official had heard of one taxpayer having submitted a false claim.   Is the committee entitled to a list of the names of those persons who had made contributions to the chapter?

Tucker, Adjudication Social Issues Pamph. MCB—7

Chapter 11

PUBLIC ASSEMBLY AND THE RIGHT TO PETITION

The First Amendment bars Congress from passing laws abridging the two intimately related rights of "peaceable" assembly and petitioning government "for redress of grievances." The due process clause of the Fourteenth Amendment makes these two prohibitions applicable to state and local governments. Like the freedoms of speech and press these two rights are conceived as fundamental rights. Each is treated as an integral part of our political framework in which a broad-based electorate has a constitutional right to select and replace their most important public officials.

When individuals make use of their rights to assemble and to petition governmental officials can readily learn of the beliefs, desires, displeasures, ideas, opinions, and wishes of their constituents. When alerted to the thinking of the populace officials have an opportunity to bring about change within the framework of ordered liberty. Sensitive and responsive reaction by public officials to the voice of the citizenry makes highly unattractive resort to violence and destruction to alter the *status quo*.

Constitutional rights do not exist, and are not exercised, in vacuo. They exist to be exercised in a live and often tumultuous environment. When persons assemble to communicate their ideas or petition they usually do so in a milieu in which their behavior affects at least the senses, if not the physical comfort, of other persons in addition to impinging on the psyche of governmental officials. One who claims that he has a right to make loud and raucous noises to effectively exercise his right to peaceably assemble and to petition government is at the same time saying that he has a right to deprive others of a right to be free from such noises. When one group is permitted to assemble at a particular time and place another group perforce must be denied the same opportunity. When persons insist they have a right to assemble in the office of a public official to petition him for redress of their grievances they are also saying that they have a right to bring the official's work to a halt and thereby deny other persons the benefit of his services.

Courts have the task of balancing conflicting claims and rights of individuals to assemble and petition and the claims and rights of other persons and the constitutional powers and duties of government. Persons are not free to assemble and to petition wherever, however, and whenever they wish. For instance, government has the power to place limits on the free exercise of these rights when a failure to do so would likely result in a breach of the peace, a riot, or violence. If a once peaceful assembly becomes a tool for inciting a breach of the

88

peace, a riot, or violence, the assembly may be dispersed by police action.

In the following two cases the Supreme Court found that the power of the state to bar an assembly was paramount to the rights of the participants to assemble. In each case the Court found that the assembly had interfered with a vital function of government and accordingly was not protected by the Fourteenth Amendment. In one case an assembly was held on jail grounds to express dissatisfaction with governmental policies unrelated to the jail. The Court was of the opinion that it was not appropriate to hold an assembly on jail grounds because of the purpose for which a jail is operated. In the other case the assembly took place near a courthouse and was intended to effect the release of persons who were awaiting trial. The Court spoke of the possibility of such behavior intimidating the judge, jurors, and court officials. It feared that even if these persons were not intimidated still if those awaiting trial were released there would be persons who would believe that the result was due to the pressure placed on the court by those assembled outside. It found that the state might take reasonable steps to insure that a mob does not control the outcome of a judicial proceeding or otherwise interfere with the orderly and fair administration of justice. The motive of the members of the mob, good or bad, was said to be irrelevant.

Traditionally streets and public parks have been places where people can come to speak out and call upon government to respond to their demands. Here orators, good and bad, have beckoned the throngs, large or small, to follow them. But even in these settings government, under certain circumstances and for particular purposes, may place restrictions on the right of assembly and to petition for redress of grievances. For example, government may enforce rules designed to keep streets open so that traffic can pass and to safeguard the well-being of those who use the streets and highways. One does not have a right to demand that government cordon off a public street or highway so that he can exercise his First and Fourteenth Amendment rights. A speaker does not have a constitutional right to cordon off a public or private building and refuse to allow persons to enter the building unless they first agree with what he has to say. In each case public officials are empowered to act since their failure to do so would prevent use of public or private property for the lawful purposes to which it had been dedicated.

SHUTTLESWORTH v. CITY OF BIRMINGHAM, ALABAMA

Supreme Court of the United States, 1969.
89 S.Ct. 935, 394 U.S. 147, 22 L.Ed.2d 162.

An ordinance made it an offense to participate in any "parade or procession or other public demonstration" without first obtaining a permit from the City Commission. The defendant was one of 52 black persons who walked in an orderly non-obstructive fashion, two abreast, for four blocks to protest the alleged denial of civil rights to blacks. Some spectators joined the march. The defendant was convicted of violating the ordinance and sentenced to 90 days at hard labor, an additional 48 days or $75, and was charged $24 costs. The state appellate courts affirmed. Certiorari was granted.

MR. JUSTICE STEWART delivered the opinion of the Court.

*   *   *

There can be no doubt that the Birmingham ordinance, as it was written, conferred upon the City Commission virtually unbridled and absolute power to prohibit any "parade," "procession," or "demonstration" on the city's streets or public ways. For in deciding whether or not to withhold a permit, the members of the Commission were to be guided only by their own ideas of "public welfare, peace, safety, health, decency, good order, morals or convenience." This ordinance as it was written, therefore, fell squarely within the ambit of the many decisions of this Court over the last 30 years, holding that a law subjecting the exercise of First Amendment freedoms to the prior restraint of a license, without narrow, objective, and definite standards to guide the licensing authority, is unconstitutional. "It is settled by a long line of recent decisions of this Court that an ordinance which, like this one, makes the peaceful enjoyment of freedoms which the Constitution guarantees contingent upon the uncontrolled will of an official—as by requiring a permit or license which may be granted or withheld in the discretion of such official—is an unconstitutional censorship or prior restraint upon the enjoyment of those freedoms." *   *   *   And our decisions have made clear that a person faced with such an unconstitutional licensing law may ignore it and engage with impunity in the exercise of the right of free expression for which the law purports to require a license. "The Constitution can hardly be thought to deny to one subjected to the restraints of such an ordinance the right to attack its constitutionality, because he has not yielded to its demands." *   *   *

It is argued, however, that what was involved here was not "pure speech," but the use of public streets and sidewalks, over which a municipality must rightfully exercise a great deal of control in the interest of traffic regulation and public safety. That, of course, is true. We have emphasized before this that "the First and Fourteenth Amendments [do not] afford the same kind of freedom to those who would communicate ideas by conduct such as patrolling, marching, and picketing on streets and highways, as these amendments afford to those who communicate ideas by pure speech." *   *   *   "Governmental authorities have the duty and responsibility to keep their streets open and available for movement." *   *   *

But our decisions have also made clear that picketing and parading may nonetheless constitute methods of expression, entitled to First Amendment protection. *   *   *   "Wherever the title of streets and parks may rest, they have immemorially been held in trust for the use of the public and, time out of mind, have been used for purposes of assembly, communicating thoughts between citizens, and discussing public questions. Such use of the streets and public places has, from ancient times, been a part of the privileges, immunities, rights, and liberties of citizens. The privilege of a citizen of the United States to use the streets and parks for communication of views on national questions may be regulated in the interest of all; it is not absolute, but relative, and must be exercised in subordination to the general comfort and convenience, and in consonance with peace and good order; but it must not, in the guise of regulation, be abridged or denied." *   *   *

Accordingly, "[a]lthough this Court has recognized that a statute may be enacted which prevents serious interference with normal usage of streets and parks, *   *   * we have consistently condemned licensing systems which vest in an administrative official discretion to grant or withhold a permit upon broad criteria unrelated to proper regulation of public places." *   *   * Even when the use of its public streets and sidewalks is involved, therefore, a municipality may not empower its licensing officials to roam essentially at will, dispensing or withholding permission to speak, assemble, picket, or parade according to their own opinions regarding the potential effect of the activity in question on the "welfare," "decency," or "morals" of the community.

*   *   *

Reversed.

UNITED STATES v. SPOCK

United States Court of Appeals, First Circuit, 1969.
416 F.2d 165.

Spock was one of four defendants convicted of conspiring to counsel, aid, and abet Selective Service registrants to neglect, fail, refuse, and evade service in the armed forces and to fail and refuse to have in their personal possession Selective Services Registration Certificates. The four opposed United States involvement in Viet Nam. Spock helped draft a statement which was entitled "A Call to Resist Illegitimate Authority." It spoke of the legal right of young men to resist the war and summoned its readers to resist military service. Spock signed the statement. At a press conference, at which Spock was present, one of the other defendants announced that there was a plan to conduct a nationwide collection of Selection Service Registration Certificates. This was to be followed by a ceremonial surrender of the certificates to the Attorney General. Two of the other defendants arranged for a registration certificate turn-in to be followed by the burning of the certificates. The four defendants attended a demonstration in Washington, D.C. during which an unsuccessful attempt was made to turn over a number of collected certificates to the Attorney General. Spock and the three other defendants appealed.

ALDRICH, CHIEF JUDGE.

*   *   *

We approach the constitutional problem on the assumption, which we will later support, that the ultimate objective of defendants' alleged agreement, viz., the expression of opposition to the war and the draft, was legal, but that the means or intermediate objectives encompassed both legal and illegal activity without any clear indication, initially, as to who intended what. This intertwining of legal and illegal aspects, the public setting of the agreement and its political purposes, and the loose confederation of possibly innocent and possibly guilty participants raise the most serious First Amendment problems.   *   *   *

As the defendants point out, most conspiracies are secret. To argue from this, however, that illegality presupposes secrecy is to confuse means with ends. Illegality normally seeks cover, but conspirators may act openly or not, as best suits their purpose. Here the defendants' primary object was publicity, and their conduct was designedly open. No one before has suggested that this fact, or the concomitant warning to the government of impending danger, requires that the government's hand be stayed until the substantive offense is committed. Contrary to the defendants' position, many "public" conspiracies have been successfully prosecuted.   *   *   *

Admittedly, the First Amendment rights of free speech and free association,   *   *   *   are of such importance that they must prevail if the government's interest in deterring substantive crimes before they take place is insubstantial, or there is a "less restrictive alternative" by which the substantive evil may be prevented.   *   *   *   This calls for a weighing.   *   *   *

In comparing the present private and public interests we start with the assumption that the defendants were not to be prevented from vigorous criticism of the government's program merely because the natural consequences might be to interfere with it, or even to lead to unlawful action.   *   *   *   The defendants here are not charged, however, with expressions of sympathy and moral support, but with conspiring to counsel, aid and abet Selective Service registrants to disobey various duties imposed by the Selective Service Act. The maintenance of an army in peacetime is a valid, in fact vital, governmental function.   *   *   *   If a registrant may be convicted for violation of the draft laws, surely "[a] man may be punished for encouraging the commission of [the] crime."   *   *   *

The government's ability to deter and punish those who increase the likelihood of crime by concerted action has long been established. *   *   *   When the alleged agreement is both bifarious and political within the shadow of the First Amendment, we hold that an individual's specific intent to adhere to the illegal portions may be shown in one of three ways: by the individual defendant's prior or subsequent unambiguous statements; by the individual defendant's subsequent commission of the very illegal act contemplated by the agreement; or by the individual defendant's subsequent legal act if that act is "clearly undertaken for the specific purpose of rendering effective the later illegal activity which is advocated."   *   *   *

Application of such a standard should forcefully answer the defendants' protests that conviction of any of them would establish criminal responsibility of all of the many hundreds of persons who signed the Call. Even if the Call included illegal objectives, there is a wide gap between signing a document such as the Call and demonstrating one's personal attachment to illegality. * * *

At the same time, this principle demonstrates a fundamental error in the government's approach. Adopting the panoply of rules applicable to a conspiracy having purely illegal purposes, the government introduced numerous statements of third parties alleged to be co-conspirators. This was improper. The specific intent of one defendant in a case such as this is not ascertained by reference to the conduct or statements of another even though he has knowledge thereof. * * *

Spock argues that there was no "agreement among leaders of an integrated political group * * *. [T]his case presents no more than the publicly expressed coincidence of views on public affairs." No merit, however, lies in the suggestion that there must be a cohesiveness in the group beyond the confines of the agreement itself. * * * In the light of all the circumstances the jury was not obliged, in considering the question of agreement, to find a mere coincidence in the appearance of several speakers on the same platform. * * *

The defendants contend that nothing in the record would justify a finding of unlawful purpose in their agreement. Spock puts this succinctly: "There is nothing in the Call to Resist * * * which suggests the objective of counseling, aiding and abetting anyone to resist induction." Rather, he contends the only action contemplated was "simply moral support and financial aid for young men and their families who in good conscience are unable to participate in the war." * * *

Examination of the Call shows nothing suggesting it sought to distinguish between "resistance" and "refusal."

* * * The Call had "a double aspect: in part it was a denunciation of governmental policy and, in part, it involved a public call to resist the duties imposed by the Act."

* * *

There remains the question whether it could have been found, within the strict test laid down by the cases *supra*, that the individual defendants personally agreed to employ the illegal means contemplated by the agreement including counselling unlawful refusal to be drafted or other violations of the Selective Service Act. * * *

The principle of *strictissimi juris* requires the acquittal of Spock. It is true that he was one of the drafters of the Call, but this does not evidence the necessary intent to adhere to its illegal aspects. Nor does his admission to a government agent that he was willing to do "anything" asked to further opposition to the war. Specific intent is not established by such a generalization. Whatever the reason the fact is that his speech was limited to condemnation of the war and the draft, and lacked any words or content of counselling. The jury could not find proscribed advocacy from the mere fact, which he freely admitted, that he hoped the frequent stating of his views might give young men "courage to take active steps in draft resistance." This is a natural consequence of vigorous speech.

Similarly, Spock's actions lacked the clear character necessary to imply specific intent under the First Amendment standard. He was not at the Arlington Street Church meeting; in fact he knew nothing of it until afterwards. Although he was at the Washington demonstration he had, unlike Goodman and Coffin, no part in its planning. He contributed nothing, even by his presence, to the turning in of cards. Nor, finally, did his statements in the course of the Washington demonstration extend at all beyond the general anti-war, anti-draft remarks he had made before. His attendance is as consistent with a desire to repeat this speech as it is to aid a violation of the act.

* * *

[Judgment to be entered for Spock.]

PROBLEMS

1. The evidence established that the defendants, city officials, took advantage of every opportunity, serious or trivial, to break up demonstration protests directed against racial discrimination by arresting the participants. Many of the arrests had no other motive and some had no justification whatsoever. The plaintiff, a chapter of NAACP, asked the court to enjoin the defendants from arresting persons engaged in peaceful demonstrations. What judgment?

2. Would a statute, intended to regulate mass gatherings, by requiring promoters to make special arrangements with a state official before staging a public event expected to attract more than 5,000 people for more than 24 hours be constitutional?

3. The petitioners, accompanied by police and the assistant city attorney, marched in a peaceful and orderly procession from city hall to the mayor's office to press for public school desegregation. While they behaved in a lawful fashion the number of bystanders increased and some of the onlookers became unruly. The police, to prevent what they regarded as an impending civil disorder, ordered the petitioners to disperse. When they failed to do so, they were arrested, charged, and convicted of disorderly conduct. They appealed. What judgment?

4. City officials obtained a temporary injunction which ordered that persons refrain from participating in planned sit-ins, kneel-ins, and street parades. The petitioners, aware of the injunction, but of the opinion that it was illegal, violated it by taking part in a parade. When arrested and charged with violating the injunction they claimed that they were not obliged to obey it since it was unlawful. The petitioners could have followed established court procedures and could have requested the court to set aside the injunction. They failed to do so. The city officials argued that the petitioners could not judge the

merits of their own case and simply "carry their battle to the streets." The trial court found the petitioners guilty of knowingly violating the injunction and sentenced each petitioner to five days in jail and fined each $50. They appealed. What judgment?

5. The defendants, opponents of the policies of the Russian Government, gathered together on the sidewalk in front of the Russian Embassy in Washington, D. C. Loudly they shouted: "Communists Go Home." At times they sang out "Let Our People Go." At the request of the Russian Ambassador local police, using a loud speaker, directed that those taking part in the gathering disperse. The participants shouted back at the police: "No, never!" After several minutes, as more protestors arrived, the police arrested several of the protesters and charged them with disorderly conduct. Were the arrests lawful?

6. The petitioner asked that policemen be assigned to protect him and 100 of his friends who planned to meet on the town common and stage a rally in favor of legalizing abortion. The last time the petitioner spoke at the common in favor of legalizing abortions he was assaulted and hospitalized. Police officials denied his request. He petitioned the court for an order directing that police be assigned to protect him. What judgment?

Chapter 12

FREEDOM OF THE PRESS

The First and Fourteenth Amendments mark out a broad area of immunity from civil and criminal liability on behalf of those who make use of written media to express and communicate their points of view. Courts employ the same constitutional criteria when passing on a publication sold to earn a profit as when passing on a publication distributed free of charge by a group of persons devoted to promoting a charitable cause. The Constitution protects the preparation and dissemination of written communications rather than any particular kind of setting in which a publication is produced. A distinction may not be drawn solely on the basis of who publishes or sponsors a publication. Courts pay no attention to whether an individual, political party, or business enterprise prepared, printed, or distributed the publication. The freedom to publish enjoyed by persons urging the conservation of natural resources is the same as that guaranteed to the publishers of the *Harvard Law Review, Time,* or *Playboy.*

Liberty to publish includes the liberty to use any type of physical format. Handbills, leaflets, pamphlets, newspapers, magazines, paperback books, and hardcover books each enjoy the same protection. Inexpensive publications of poor design, poor print, or poor scholarship are entitled to the same constitutional protection as expensive, artistically designed, excellently printed hardcover books embodying a display of exemplary scholarship. The Constitution knows no favorites.

Freedom of the press is a vital base point of our political framework. Responsive and responsible representative government cannot exist without all persons having the liberty to press their views by making use of written media. Our nation's political institutions require that those seeking public office vie for support. It is essential that all persons be free to present all aspects of political issues. Freedom to publish must not be simply freedom to publish what is generally acceptable. The Constitution requires that government allow those who laud the present state of affairs and wish to perpetuate the current order, as well as those who dissent and deride present policies and advocate change, to be heard.

Courts assume that competition and conflict in the market place of ideas can help individuals and society come to grip with and solve problems and advance truth, science, morality, and the arts. Judges are guided by the philosophy that more harm can come to individuals and society by following a restrictive rather than a non-restrictive policy. It is far better that written materials of little worth be available to the public than to entrust to governmental officials the power to appraise the worth of what is written and conclusively decide whether or not a particular publication may or may not be distributed.

Like other constitutional rights freedom of the press is not an absolute right. One does not have an unlimited right to publish whatever he wants, however he wishes, whenever he wishes. The "clear and present danger" test applies to written expression and communication. So, when there is a high present degree of likelihood that a written communication will bring to pass an evil which government has the right to prevent it may bar its distribution. Government has an interest in preventing disorder, violence, and revolution; protecting life and private and public property; guarding the privacy of individuals; seeing to it that essential functions of government are carried on; having justice administered in an orderly and fair way; protecting persons from fraudulent practices; enforcing the antitrust laws; and helping employees to enjoy the rights guaranteed to them by the Labor Management Relations Act. Each of these interests may serve as a basis for reasonable governmental regulation of those engaged in any of the facets involved with any form of written communication.

In every case in which a publication is challenged the court has the difficult task of weighing the conflicting interests of the right to publish and the government's interest in regulating the press. For example, one is free to express his dissatisfaction with the judicial process and court officers. If the only impact of a publication attacking the legal system or a judicial officer is to stir up hostility and instigate change the publication is entitled to the protection of the First or Fourteenth Amendments. But, if the content of a publication is such that it constitutes a clear and present danger to the orderly and fair administration of justice it can be regulated. The need to protect the integrity of the judicial process and the interests of the parties before the court outweighs the urgency that one enjoy the liberty to write and distribute his opinions about the judicial process.

Courts insist that freedom of the press have "breathing space." Government may place no greater restraint on freedom of the press than is absolutely necessary to protect an area in which it has a legitimate interest. When reviewing a restriction on the press courts ask the question: "Is this restriction absolutely necessary or could the government, to secure a legitimate objective, have used some other means to accomplish its purpose?" When it appears that there was a suitable alternative the restraint placed on the liberty to publish is unconstitutional.

Courts are especially alert to the fact that governmental officials may use devious means to make the outpouring of dissent unattractive. For example, legislation which prohibits the distribution of any publication unless it contains the name of the person or organization distributing it is unconstitutional. By protecting the right of persons to publish anonymously the courts guarantee freedom of the press to those who prefer that others not know that they hold a particular philosophy or favor or oppose a particular cause.

One who is accused of a crime or is a party to a civil suit is entitled to a fair trial. Due process requires that a trial proceed in an orderly fashion. The result arrived at by the court must be based on evidence introduced during the proceeding. Trial by mob, or trial by press, or a result attributable to aroused emotions is inconsistent with due process. When persons reporting a court proceeding behave in such a way that it becomes apparent that if their conduct is not altered it is improbable that one accused of a crime or is a party to a civil suit will receive a fair trial, it is the duty of the trial judge to act. The Constitution requires that he place reasonable restraints on the press when it is apparent that his failure to do so would prevent a fair trial. The conflicting demands of due process and freedom of the press require a court to judiciously accommodate the right of the press and the rights of the litigants. The press must have the right to communicate what is taking place but not at the expense of the litigants' rights to a fair trial.

A public figure is a person who has called himself to the attention of the public. Perhaps by what he has said or done he has "projected himself into the arena of public controversy" or due to his chosen calling what he does or does not do is of legitimate concern to the public. A person who repeatedly speaks out on public issues or is a television or motion picture star has invited the public to pay attention to him. By so doing, he has surrendered his right to demand the same sort of protection from false defamatory statements as persons whose behavior is of no interest to the public. The right to be free from false defamatory statements recognized on behalf of public figures is narrower than the right of nonpublic figures but broader than the already considered right of public officials. A public figure may recover damages "for a defamatory falsehood whose substance makes substantial danger to reputation * * * apparent, on a showing of highly unreasonable conduct, constituting an extreme departure from the standards of investigation and reporting ordinarily adhered to by responsible publishers." [1] This test recognizes that even responsible reporters make mistakes and investigations carried on by responsible publishers do not always reveal that what is to be published about a public figure is in fact false. Falsehoods which defame a public figure but pass the test of responsible journalism may not serve as the basis for a lawsuit brought by the public figure who has been injured as a result of the publication of a falsehood. On the other hand, should it appear that one who published a false defamatory statement about a public figure acted in an irresponsible fashion, the public figure is entitled to damages from the guilty party.

The law of libel protects those who are neither public officials nor public figures from false defamatory statements but not from publi-

---

1. Curtis Publishing Co. v. Butts, 87 S. Ct. 1975, 388 U.S. 130, 18 L.Ed.2d 1094 (1967).

cation of the truth. The principle of technical tort permits a person to recover compensatory damages from one who made a true statement about him but with the intention of causing him injury. Here the wrong is not due to the falsity of the publication but the reason for the publication. The Constitution does not protect persons who make use of the truth in order to cause another injury.

MILLS v. ALABAMA

Supreme Court of the United States, 1966.
86 S.Ct. 1434, 384 U.S. 214, 16 L.Ed.2d 484.

The complaint filed against the defendant charged him with violating a state law which made it a crime to publish an editorial on election day urging people to vote in a particular fashion on any of the questions placed before them in the election. The trial court sustained a demurrer to the complaint on the ground that the statute was an unconstitutional abridgement of freedom of speech and press. The state supreme court reversed. It found the statute reasonable and therefore proper under the state's police power. The defendant appealed.

MR. JUSTICE BLACK delivered the opinion of the Court.

* * *

Whatever differences may exist about interpretations of the First Amendment, there is practically universal agreement that a major purpose of that Amendment was to protect the free discussion of governmental affairs. This of course includes discussions of candidates, structures and forms of government, the manner in which government is operated or should be operated, and all such matters relating to political processes. The Constitution specifically selected the press, which includes not only newspapers, books, and magazines, but also humble leaflets and circulars, * * * to play an important role in the discussion of public affairs. Thus the press serves and was designed to serve as a powerful antidote to any abuses of power by governmental officials and as a constitutionally chosen means for keeping officials elected by the people responsible to all the people whom they were selected to serve. Suppression of the right of the press to praise or criticize governmental agents and to clamor and contend for or against change, which is all that this editorial did, muzzles one of the very agencies the Framers of our Constitution thoughtfully and deliberately selected to improve our society and keep it free. The Alabama Corrupt Practices Act by providing criminal penalties for publishing editorials such as the one here silences the press at a time when it can be most effective. It is difficult to conceive of a more obvious and flagrant abridgment of the constitutionally guaranteed freedom of the press.

* * *

The state statute leaves people free to hurl their campaign charges up to the last minute of the day before election. The law held valid by the Alabama Supreme Court then goes on to make it a crime to answer those "last-minute" charges on election day, the only time they can be effectively answered. Because the law prevents any adequate reply to these charges, it is wholly ineffective in protecting the electorate "from confusive last-minute charges and countercharges." We hold that no test of reasonableness can save a state law from invalidation as a violation of the First Amendment when that law makes it a crime for a newspaper editor to do no more than urge people to vote one way or another in a publicly held election.

     *   *   *

Judgment reversed and case remanded.

SHEPPARD v. MAXWELL

Supreme Court of the United States, 1966.
86 S.Ct. 1507, 384 U.S. 333, 16 L.Ed.2d 600.

The defendant's pregnant wife was bludgeoned to death in her bedroom. Three days later a local newspaper reported that the defendant had been criticized by an Assistant County Attorney for his non-cooperation with the police. Later newspaper headlines called attention to his lack of cooperation and his refusal to take a lie detector test. Editorials criticized the lack of action by law officers. Many photographs were taken at the coroner's hearing which was broadcast live on television and radio. The coroner did not recommend that the defendant be held for grand jury action. Newspapers emphasized that the evidence incriminated the defendant. Reporters commented extensively on his personal behavior. There were stories about his alleged involvements with other women. Articles spoke of smart lawyers protecting him from prosecution. After the defendant was formally charged with the murder of his wife the publicity grew more intense. The three local newspapers printed the names and addresses of prospective jurors, some of whom were in turn contacted by interested persons. The chief prosecutor was a candidate for judicial office and the presiding judge was a candidate for re-election. During the trial twenty representatives from newspapers and wire services had courtroom seats assigned to them. At times the courtroom was so noisy that it was difficult to hear counsel or the witnesses. When the lawyers spoke to the judge in his chambers media representatives were also present. They reported what they heard to the newspapers. Their reports were published. Such publications were available to the jurors. Private telephone and telegraphic lines were installed in the courtroom. One radio station was allowed to set up broadcast facilities in the courthouse from which newscasts were made during the trial. Outside the courthouse and in the courthouse corridors photographers and television and newsreel cameramen photographed the judge, the jurors, counsel, and the defendant. During the trial newspapers criticized defense counsel, charging him with throwing roadblocks in the way of the prosecution. The newspapers called attention to the deceased and queried who would protect her interests. One radio commentator announced that the defendant had fathered an illegitimate child. Two of the jurors heard the report but told the judge it would not affect their judgment. After receiving their instructions from the judge the jurors deliberated for five days. During this period they were allowed to telephone home. The jury returned a verdict of guilty. The defendant filed a petition for habeas corpus in the Federal District Court, claiming that he had been denied a fair trial because the trial judge had failed to protect him sufficiently from massive, pervasive, and prejudicial publicity. The District Court ruled that he had been denied a fair trial and ordered his release unless the state granted him a new trial. The Court of Appeals, by a divided vote, reversed. Certiorari was granted.

MR. JUSTICE CLARK delivered the opinion of the Court.

* * *

The principle that justice cannot survive behind walls of silence has long been reflected in the "Anglo-American distrust for secret trials." * * * A responsible press has always been regarded as the handmaiden of effective judicial administration, especially in the criminal field. * * * The press does not simply publish information about trials but guards against the miscarriage of justice by subjecting the police, prosecutors, and judicial processes to extensive public scrutiny and criticism. This Court has, therefore, been unwilling to place any direct limitations on the freedom traditionally exercised by the news media for "[w]hat transpires in the court room is public property." * * *

But the Court has also pointed out that "[l]egal trials are not like elections, to be won through the use of the meeting-hall, the radio, and the newspaper." * * * And the Court has insisted that no one be punished for a crime without "a charge fairly made and fairly tried in a public tribunal free of prejudice, passion, excitement, and tyrannical power." * * * "Freedom of discussion should be given the widest range compatible with the essential requirement of the fair and orderly administration of justice." * * * But it must not be allowed to divert the trial from the "very purpose of a court system * * * to adjudicate controversies, both criminal and civil, in the calmness and solemnity of the courtroom according to legal procedures."

The undeviating rule of this Court was expressed by Mr. Justice Holmes over half a century ago * * *: "The theory of our system is that the conclusions to be reached in a case will be induced only by evidence and argument in open court, and not by any outside influence, whether of private talk or public print."

* * *

Only last Term in Estes v. State of Texas, * * * we set aside a conviction despite the absence of any showing of prejudice. We said there:

"It is true that in most cases involving claims of due process deprivations we require a showing of identifiable prejudice to the accused. Nevertheless, at times a procedure employed by the State involves such a probability that prejudice will result that it is deemed inherently lacking in due process."

* * *

It is clear that the totality of circumstances in this case also warrants such an approach. * * *

While we cannot say that Sheppard was denied due process by the judge's refusal to take precautions against the influence of pretrial publicity alone, the court's later rulings must be considered against the setting in which the trial was held. In light of this background, we believe that the arrangements made by the judge with the news media caused Sheppard to be deprived of that "judicial serenity and calm to which [he] was entitled." * * * The fact is that bedlam reigned at the courthouse during the trial and newsmen took over practically the entire courtroom, hounding most of the participants in the trial, especially Sheppard. * * *

The court's fundamental error is compounded by the holding that it lacked power to control the publicity about the trial. From the very inception of the proceedings the judge announced that neither he nor anyone else could restrict prejudicial news accounts. And he reiterated this view on numerous occasions. * * *

The carnival atmosphere at trial could easily have been avoided since the courtroom and courthouse premises are subject to the control of the court. As we stressed in *Estes*, the presence of the press at judicial proceedings must be limited when it is apparent that the accused might otherwise be prejudiced or disadvantaged. * * *

The fact that many of the prejudicial news items can be traced to the prosecution, as well as the defense, aggravates the judge's failure to take any action. * * * Effective control of these sources— concededly within the court's power—might well have prevented the divulgence of inaccurate information, rumors, and accusations that made up much of the inflammatory publicity, at least after Sheppard's indictment.

More specifically, the trial court might well have proscribed extrajudicial statements by any lawyer, party, witness, or court official which divulged prejudicial matters, such as the refusal of Sheppard to submit to interrogation or take any lie detector tests; any statement made by Sheppard to officials; the identity of prospective witnesses or their probable testimony; any belief in guilt or innocence; or like statements concerning the merits of the case. * * *

* * * Due process requires that the accused receive a trial by an impartial jury free from outside influences. Given the pervasiveness

of modern communications and the difficulty of effacing prejudicial publicity from the minds of the jurors, the trial courts must take strong measures to ensure that the balance is never weighed against the accused. And appellate tribunals have the duty to make an independent evaluation of the circumstances. Of course, there is nothing that proscribes the press from reporting events that transpire in the courtroom. But where there is a reasonable likelihood that prejudicial news prior to trial will prevent a fair trial, the judge should continue the case until the threat abates, or transfer it to another county not so permeated with publicity. * * *

Since the state trial judge did not fulfill his duty to protect Sheppard from the inherently prejudicial publicity which saturated the community and to control disruptive influences in the courtroom, we must reverse the denial of the habeas petition. The case is remanded to the District Court with instructions to issue the writ and order that Sheppard be released from custody unless the State puts him to its charges again within a reasonable time.

PROBLEMS

1. The plaintiff was a licensed osteopathic physician. The defendant published three articles about her professional practice. He derided her and labeled her a "quack." She sued the defendant for libel, asking for compensatory damages for the injury caused to her practice. She also asked for punitive damages. The trial judge refused to charge, as requested by the plaintiff, that the only defense available to the defendant was truth and then only if the publication had been made with good motives and for justifiable ends. He took the position that since the plaintiff was a public figure she was not entitled to such a charge. Was the trial judge correct?

2. A newspaper published the defendant's critical remarks about the charge given by three judges to a grand jury which was investigating possible election law violations. He objected to the judges' direction that the jury investigate "Negro block voting." He took issue with the judges "singling out the Negro people for particular investigation." Because of his remarks he was charged with the use of contemptuous language, ridiculing the investigation, and hampering, hindering, interfering with, and obstructing the grand jury investigation. He contended that he could not be punished for what he had said because he had a constitutional right to state his points of view. It was the state's position that the defendant's behavior represented a clear and present danger to the fair administration of justice and could therefore be punished. Is the state correct?

3. The plaintiff was convicted of murdering a college coed. The state supreme court reversed his conviction on the ground that pre-trial publicity had made a fair trial impossible. The plaintiff thereafter brought a suit for money damages against the defendant newspaper which the supreme court had cited as having been in-

volved in the objectionable publicity. He asked for money damages to compensate him for his imprisonment and for his loss of family, friends, and all of the natural pleasures free men enjoy and which were denied him during his imprisonment. What judgment?

4. The defendant, a newspaper reporter, was served with a subpoena which directed that he appear before a grand jury to testify about information given to him by Black Panther leaders and to make available to the grand jury tape recordings and notes of his interviews with such leaders. The reporter refused to appear before the grand jury on the ground that he enjoyed a unique relationship of trust and confidence with these leaders, had obtained sensitive information from them, and to require him to disclose the sought after information would impair his ability to gather news in violation of his constitutional right to freedom of the press. Is he correct?

5. On the eve of the trial of several Black Panther Party members who were charged with murder and kidnapping, the trial judge signed an order prohibiting cameras, sound equipment, sketching, and demonstrations in and around the courthouse. He also prohibited lawyers and witnesses from making prejudicial statements to newsmen. Is such an order constitutional?

Part Four

INDIVIDUALISM

Chapter 13

CONSCIENTIOUS OBJECTORS

Should a legal system allow each individual to be governed solely by the dictates of his conscience? Should one be excused whenever he disobeys a law if his conscience directed such disobedience?

If one's conscience were paramount to society's laws every person would be free to pass final judgment on the propriety or applicability of each of the law's directives. Each person would be his own law-maker and the exclusive and final judge of his behavior. He alone could decide if he should or should not act and if his actions were right or wrong. Law would have relevance to one's behavior only if his conscience approved. One could never be called upon to defend the validity of any of the dictates of his conscience. No one could demand protection from any action which affected him if the action to which he objected was dictated by the actor's conscience. Society could not punish a person for his conduct, whatever it might be, so long as it did not violate his personal standard of what constituted proper behavior.

Should a legal system completely and unrelentlessly refuse to pay heed to any of the demands of an individual's conscience? Should law be treated as a body of directives distinct from all moral and ethical considerations which play a part in determining why individuals think and behave as they do? A legal system which failed to take into account any of the demands of the individual and collective conscience of the persons it was supposed to serve could become unrelated and insensitive to critical human needs. It might formulate and enforce principles which failed to take due cognizance of bona fide human needs and values. New individual and societal needs could go unanswered. Isolated from those human values and goals which distinguish the human being from all other living creatures and mechanical devices the legal system could demand obedience to a body of rules totally irrelevant to the contemporary human predicament. The use of brute force to effect compliance with legislative, executive, judicial, and administrative directives would be commonplace. This sort of legal system is unthinkable in a society which emphasizes individual liberty under a Constitution which places stringent limits on the powers of government over individual behavior and protects and promotes dissent.

In a variety of ways our legal system accommodates the at times conflicting demands of group and individual conscience. To varying degrees those who make, enforce, and administer the law take into account the consensus of society's standard of suitable morality and ethical behavior. At times lawmakers make special provision for the demands of individual conscience. For example, persons who satisfy the specific criteria provided for by Congress may be excused from service in the armed forces on the basis of the dictates of their conscience. A state law which prohibits persons from engaging in particular types of business activities on Sunday may allow persons who observe Saturday as their holy day to carry on otherwise prohibited business activities on Sunday. If a person's conscience dictates that he not take an oath prior to testifying at a trial he may, if he prefers, affirm rather than swear that he will tell the truth. Under the Uniform Commercial Code a court may deny enforcement of a sales contract it finds to be unconscionable. In various areas of the law courts insist that persons are obliged to act in good faith in their dealings with other persons.

Many matters of conscience have their origin in one's religious beliefs. Religious liberty, as guaranteed by the First and Fourteenth Amendments, requires that government be neutral in religious matters and show neither favor nor disfavor toward any form of religion. Except as pointed out in the paragraph which follows, government may not interfere with one's practice of his religion. This means that demands of conscience, founded on religious tenets, are free from governmental control. For example, the Supreme Court has held that a state may not refuse to pay unemployment insurance to a person who, because of religious scruples, will not accept employment which requires that he work on Saturday, his Sabbath Day. The state's refusal to make payment on the ground of his unwillingness to take employment requiring him to work on Saturday was condemned as an unconstitutional intrusion on the applicant's right to practice his religion.

Governmental action directed at religious beliefs and practices may take several forms. Governmental officials might wish to promote or prohibit particular forms of religious beliefs. This they may not do. Government may not challenge the truth or accuracy of one's faith. A demand a religion makes on a believer may require of him behavior which does not conflict with a compelling interest of government. Even if such behavior is unusual or unpopular government may not bar it. An example of this kind of behavior is found in the cited case of the Saturday observer. A religious practice may conflict with a compelling interest of government. Such a practice may be regulated or prohibited. For instance, a religious tenet may require its followers to periodically make human sacrifices or practice polygamy. Government may outlaw these forms of behavior. They conflict with a compelling interest of government. In one case government is seeking to protect human life and in the other to prevent a practice society regards as violative of "social duties and subversive of good order."

The Constitution directs that persons be accorded due process and equal protection of the laws. Much of what is demanded by these two clauses is predicated on the dictates of conscience, but it is the collective rather than the individual conscience to which courts usually look for guidance. When speaking of due process courts often refer to the demands of fundamental fairness. By following a test of fundamental fairness courts frequently arrive at a result consistent with the demands of the conscience of a majority of the citizenry. At times courts prefer to be in the forefront, imposing standards of moral and ethical behavior which go beyond contemporary mores. When the court has acted wisely and intelligently, it usually sets a tone with which society in general soon agrees. At other times courts lag behind the consensus of what is right and what is wrong. On such occasions the failure of the courts to bring their standards into line with those of a majority of the citizens can injure litigants as well as the legal process. On a long run basis our legal system has proved to be viable and dynamic, keeping in close contact with the dictates of conscience shared by most Americans.

The Supreme Court has recognized that the power of Congress to require individuals to serve in the armed forces and take part in warfare to defend the United States is paramount to the dictates of one's conscience that he not serve in the armed forces or participate in warfare. Aware of its power, yet sensitive to the demands of individual conscience, Congress has provided for the exemption of individuals who, because of the dictates of their conscience, must refuse to serve in the armed forces or take part in warfare. Congress has also provided that individuals may, on the basis of the dictates of their conscience, be exempted from general military service but still be obliged to engage in some other form of involuntary activity.

The Supreme Court has ruled that one is not entitled to conscientious objector status unless his conscience dictates that he not take part in all wars. A selective approach to war, with one's conscience approving of some wars and disapproving of others, is not recognized as a basis for exemption from service in the armed forces under the present Selective Service Act.

To qualify for conscientious objector status one must establish that his objection to service is based on the dictates of conscience. The local board must decide if one who requests conscientious objector status is sincere and if he otherwise satisfies the criteria Congress has stated must be met if a Selective Service registrant is to be excused from military service. If the board finds that the applicant is not sincere in his assertion that because of the dictates of his conscience he qualifies for an exemption, his request must be denied. A later refusal to serve in the armed forces can result in fine or imprisonment or both.

A board's decision as to whether or not one should receive a conscientious objector classification must be based on the evidence contained in its files. It would be unlawful for a board to find that one was not sincere in his beliefs merely on the basis of speculation. If an applicant establishes a *prima facie* case that he is entitled to conscientious objector status, but the board refuses to grant him such status, the board must set forth in its records the reasons for its decision. Draft board action which fails to meet the requirements of due process of law can be vacated.

A person may not be denied conscientious objector status simply because he failed to claim it when he first registered with his draft board. He may do so at a later time. If one qualifies for such status it may not be denied because of what he says or does unless his speech or behavior refutes the sincerity of his contention. A draft board may not use its power to order one to enter the armed forces to punish him for his views or for his having committed an illegal act unrelated to his claim that he is a conscientious objector. A board's failure to comply with statutory directives, judicial interpretation of such directives, or Selective Service Regulations entitles a registrant to have the board's action reversed. Board action which is the result of the board lawlessly wielding its power, if challenged in a judicial proceeding, will not be allowed to stand.

Individuals who are on active duty in the armed forces may, under Defense Department Regulations, demand conscientious objector status. The fact that one first arrived at his beliefs after he entered the armed forces does not bar him from seeking or obtaining such status.

UNITED STATES v. SEEGER

Supreme Court of the United States, 1965.
85 S.Ct. 850, 380 U.S. 163, 13 L.Ed.2d 733.

The Selective Service Act exempts from combat training and service in the armed forces persons who by reason of their "religious training and belief" are conscientiously opposed to participation in war in any form. In § 6(j) of the Act "religious training and belief" is defined as "an individual's belief in a relation to a Supreme Being involving duties superior to those arising from any human relation, but [not including] essentially political, sociological, or philosophical views or a merely personal moral code." Seeger requested conscientious objector status. In his request he failed to indicate whether or not he believed in a Supreme Being, but he would not say he had "lack of faith in anything whatsoever." He based his request on "belief in and devotion to goodness and virtue for their own sakes, and a religious faith in a purely ethical creed." Seeger cited "Plato, Aristotle and Spinoza for support of his ethical belief in intellectual and moral integrity 'without belief in God, except in the remotest sense.' His belief was found to be sincere, honest and made in good faith." His draft board denied his request because "it was not based upon a 'belief in a relation to a Supreme Being.' " Seeger was classified 1–A and ordered to report for induction. He refused. He was tried and convicted for having violated the Selective Service Act. The Court of Appeals reversed. Certiorari was granted.

MR. JUSTICE CLARK delivered the opinion of the Court.

* * *

The crux of the problem lies in the phrase "religious training and belief" which Congress has defined as "belief in a relation to a Supreme Being involving duties superior to those arising from any human relation." * * * Our question, therefore, is the narrow one: Does the term "Supreme Being" as used in § 6(j) mean the orthodox God or the broader concept of a power or being, or a faith, "to which all else is subordinate or upon which all else is ultimately dependent"? * * * In considering this question we resolve it solely in relation to the language of § 6(j) and not otherwise.

* * *

In spite of the elusive nature of the inquiry, we are not without certain guidelines. In amending the 1940 Act, Congress adopted almost intact the language of Chief Justice Hughes in United States v. Macintosh, * * *:

"The essence of religion is belief in a relation to *God* involving duties superior to those arising from any human relation." * * * (Emphasis supplied.)

By comparing the statutory definition with those words, however, it becomes readily apparent that the Congress deliberately broadened them by substituting the phrase "Supreme Being" for the appellation "God." And in so doing it is also significant that Congress did not elaborate on the form or nature of this higher authority which it chose to designate as "Supreme Being." * * *

Moreover, the Senate Report on the bill specifically states that § 6(j) was intended to re-enact "substantially the same provisions as were found" in the 1940 Act. That statute, of course, refers to "religious training and belief" without more. Admittedly, all of the parties here purport to base their objection on religious belief. It appears, therefore, that we need only look to this clear statement of congressional intent as set out in the report. Under the 1940 Act it was necessary only to have a conviction based upon religious training and belief; we believe that is all that is required here. Within that phrase would come all sincere religious beliefs which are based upon a power or being, or upon a faith, to which all else is subordinate or upon which all else is ultimately dependent. The test might be stated in these words: A sincere and meaningful belief which occupies in the life of its possessor a place parallel to that filled by the God of those admittedly qualifying for the exemption comes within the statutory definition. This construction avoids imputing to Congress an intent to classify different religious beliefs, exempting some and excluding others, and is in accord with the well-established congresssional policy of equal treatment for those whose opposition to service is grounded in their religious tenets.

*   *   *

Moreover, we believe this construction embraces the ever-broadening understanding of the modern religious community. The eminent Protestant theologian, Dr. Paul Tillich, whose views the Government concedes would come within the statute, identifies God not as a projection "out there" or beyond the skies but as the ground of our very being. *   *   *

We recognize the difficulties that have always faced the trier of fact in these cases. We hope that the test that we lay down proves less onerous. The examiner is furnished a standard that permits consideration of criteria with which he has had considerable experience. While the applicant's words may differ, the test is simple of application. It is essentially an objective one, namely, does the claimed belief occupy the same place in the life of the objector as an orthodox belief in God holds in the life of one clearly qualified for exemption?

Moreover, it must be remembered that in resolving these exemption problems one deals with the beliefs of different individuals who will articulate them in a multitude of ways. In such an intensely personal area, of course, the claim of the registrant that his belief is an essential part of a religious faith must be given great weight. *   *   * The validity of what he believes cannot be questioned. Some theologians, and indeed some examiners, might be tempted to question the existence of the registrant's "Supreme Being" or the truth of his concepts. But these are inquiries foreclosed to Government. *   *   * "Men may believe what they cannot prove. They may not be put to the proof of their religious doctrines or beliefs. Religious experiences which are as real as life to some may be incomprehensible to others." Local boards and courts in this sense are not free to reject beliefs because they consider them "incomprehensible." Their task is to decide whether the beliefs professed by a registrant are sincerely held and whether they are, in his own scheme of things, religious.

But we hasten to emphasize that while the "truth" of a belief is not open to question, there remains the significant question whether it is "truly held." This is the threshold question of sincerity which must be resolved in every case. It is, of course, a question of fact—a prime consideration to the validity of every claim for exemption as a conscientious objector. *   *   *

In summary, Seeger professed "religious belief" and "religious faith." He did not disavow any belief "in a relation to a Supreme Being"; indeed he stated that "the cosmic order does, perhaps, suggest a creative intelligence." He decried the tremendous "spiritual" price man must pay for his willingness to destroy human life. In light of his beliefs and the unquestioned sincerity with which he held them, we think the Board, had it applied the test we propose today, would have granted him the exemption. We think it clear that the beliefs which prompted his objection occupy the same place in his life as the belief

in a traditional deity holds in the lives of his friends, the Quakers.
* * *

It may be that Seeger did not clearly demonstrate what his beliefs were
with regard to the usual understanding of the term "Supreme Being."
But as we have said Congress did not intend that to be the test. We
therefore affirm the judgment * * *.

WELSH v. UNITED STATES

Supreme Court of the United States, 1970.
90 S.Ct. 1792, 398 U.S. 333, 26 L.Ed.2d 308.

Welsh applied to his local draft board for conscientious objector
status. He informed the board that he was "conscientiously opposed
to participation in war in any form." The board did not question the
sincerity and depth of his convictions nor was there any doubt that
the beliefs he held were "held with the strength of more traditional religious convictions". Welsh's request was denied on the ground that
there was no "religious" basis for "his belief, opinions, and convictions." He refused to be inducted and was convicted for violating the
Selective Service Act. The Court of Appeals affirmed. Certiorari
was granted.

MR. JUSTICE BLACK announced the judgment of the Court and
delivered an opinion in which MR. JUSTICE DOUGLAS, MR. JUSTICE
BRENNAN, and MR. JUSTICE MARSHALL join.

* * *

The controlling facts in this case are strikingly similar to those
in *Seeger*. * * * In filling out their exemption applications both
Seeger and Welsh were unable to sign the statement which, as printed
in the Selective Service form, stated "I am, by reason of my religious
training and belief, conscientiously opposed to participation in war in
any form." Seeger could sign only after striking the words "training
and" putting quotations marks around the word "religious." Welsh
could sign only after striking the words "religious training and." On
those same applications, neither could definitely affirm or deny that
he believed in a "Supreme Being," both stating that they preferred to
leave the question open. But both Seeger and Welsh affirmed on those
applications that they held deep conscientious scruples against taking
part in wars where people were killed. Both strongly believed that
killing in war was wrong, unethical, and immoral, and their consciences forbade them to take part in such an evil practice. Their
objection to participating in war in any form could not be said to come
from a "still, soft voice of conscience"; rather, for them that voice
was so loud and insistent that both men preferred to go to jail rather
than serve in the Armed Forces. There was never any question about
the sincerity and depth of Seeger's convictions as a conscientious
objector, and the same is true of Welsh. In this regard the Court of
Appeals noted, "[t]he government concedes that (Welsh's) beliefs are

held with the strength of more traditional religious convictions."
* * * But in both cases the Selective Service System concluded that
the beliefs of these men were in some sense insufficiently "religious"
to qualify them for conscientious objector exemptions under the terms
of § 6(j). Seeger's conscientious objector claim was denied "solely
because it was not based upon a 'belief in a relation to a Supreme
Being' as required by § 6(j) of the Act." * * * while Welsh was
denied the exemption because his Appeal Board and the Department
of Justice hearing officer "could find no religious basis for the registrant's belief, opinions, and convictions." * * *

In the case before us the Government seeks to distinguish our
holding in *Seeger* on basically two grounds, both of which were relied
upon by the Court of Appeals in affirming Welsh's conviction. First,
it is stressed that Welsh was far more insistent and explicit than
Seeger in denying that his views were religious. For example, in filling out their conscientious objector applications, Seeger put quotation
marks around the word "religious," but Welsh struck the word "religious" entirely and later characterized his beliefs as having been
formed "by reading in the fields of history and sociology." * * *
The Court of Appeals found that Welsh had "denied that his objection
to war was premised on religious belief" and concluded that "the Appeal Board was entitled to take him at his word." * * * We think
this attempt to distinguish *Seeger* fails for the reason that it places undue emphasis on the registrant's interpretation of his own beliefs.
The Court's statement in *Seeger* that a registrant's characterization
of his own belief as "religious" should carry great weight, * * *
does not imply that his declaration that his views are nonreligious
should be treated similarly. When a registrant states that his objections to war are "religious," that information is highly relevant to
the question of the function his beliefs have in his life. But very few
registrants are fully aware of the broad scope of the word "religious"
as used in § 6(j), and accordingly a registrant's statement that his
beliefs are nonreligious is a highly unreliable guide for those charged
with administering the exemption. Welsh himself presents a case in
point. Although he originally characterized his beliefs as nonreligious, he later upon reflection wrote a long and thoughtful letter to
his Appeal Board in which he declared that his beliefs were "certainly religious in the ethical sense of that word." He explained:

"I believe I mentioned taking of life as not being, for me, a religious wrong. Again, I assumed Mr. Bradley (the Department of
Justice hearing officer) was using the word 'religious' in the conven-
tional sense, and, in order to be perfectly honest did not characterize
my belief as 'religious.' * * * "

The Government also seeks to distinguish *Seeger* on the ground
that Welsh's views, unlike Seeger's, were "essentially political, sociological, or philosophical or a merely personal moral code." * * *
In this case, Welsh's conscientious objection to war was undeniably
based in part on his perception of world politics. In a letter to his local board, he wrote:

"I can only act according to what I am and what I see. And I see that the military complex wastes both human and material resources, that it fosters disregard for (what I consider a paramount concern) human needs and ends; I see that the means we employ to 'defend' our 'way of life' profoundly change that way of life. I see that in our failure to recognize the political, social, and economic realities of the world, we, *as a nation*, fail our responsibility *as a nation*." * * *

We certainly do not think that § 6(j)'s exclusion of those persons with "essentially political, sociological, or philosophical views or a merely personal moral code" should be read to exclude those who hold strong beliefs about our domestic and foreign affairs or even those whose conscientious objection to participation in all wars is founded to a substantial extent upon considerations of public policy. The two groups of registrants which obviously do fall within these exclusions from the exemption are those whose beliefs are not deeply held and those whose objection to war does not rest at all upon moral, ethical, or religious principle but instead rests solely upon considerations of policy, pragmatism, or expediency. In applying § 6(j)'s exclusion of those whose views are "essentially political, etc.," it should be remembered that these exclusions are definitional and do not therefore restrict the category of persons who are conscientious objectors "by religious training and belief." Once the Selective Service System has taken the first step and determined under the standards set out here and in *Seeger* that the registrant is a "religious" conscientious objector, it follows that his views cannot be "essentially political, sociological or philosophical." Nor can they be a "merely personal moral code." * * *

Welsh stated that he "believe[d] the taking of life—anyone's life —to be morally wrong." * * * In his original conscientious objector application he wrote the following:

> "I believe that human life is valuable in and of itself; in its living; therefore I will not injure or kill another human being. This belief (and the corresponding 'duty' to abstain from violence toward another person) is not 'superior to those arising from any human relation.' On the contrary: *it is essential to every human relation*. I cannot, therefore, conscientiously comply with the Government's insistence that I assume duties which I feel are immoral and totally repugnant." * * *

Welsh elaborated his beliefs in later communications with Selective Service officials. On the basis of these beliefs and the conclusion of the Court of Appeals that he held them "with the strength of more traditional religious convictions," * * * we think Welsh was clearly entitled to a conscientious objector exemption. Section 6(j) requires no more. That section exempts from military service all those whose consciences, spurred by deeply held moral, ethical, or religious beliefs, would give them no rest or peace if they allowed themselves to become a part of an instrument of war.

* * *

Reversed.

PROBLEMS

1.   The defendant refused to be inducted.   When tried for violating the Selective Service Act he claimed that he had erroneously been denied conscientious objector status.   He had informed his draft board that he believed the Viet Nam conflict to be immoral and for this reason he could not serve in the armed forces.   He told the board that he did not believe all wars to be immoral.   After the jury returned a verdict of guilty he asked the trial judge to set the verdict aside. He argued that it was unconstitutional to punish him simply because he chose to abide by the dictates of his conscience.   What judgment?

2.   The defendant, a poor person, was ordered to report for induction.   He refused.   He defended his behavior on the ground that the Selective Service Act was unconstitutional.   He argued that the Act invidiously discriminated against poor persons since it exempted persons because of their ethical or religious beliefs.   The defendant pointed out that (1) the ability to establish that one's ethical or religious beliefs entitled him to be exempted from service was intimately tied to education and training of the type commonly not available to poor persons and (2) legal counsel was available to persons with financial resources to assist them to intelligently and persuasively present and support their position.   He claimed that poor persons were denied sufficient training or legal assistance to prepare requests for exemption based on their ethical and religious beliefs.   What judgment?

3.   The local board, instead of classifying the registrant a conscientious objector, classified him 1–A and ordered him to report for civilian work at one of three hospitals instead of reporting for induction.   The Selective Service Act permitted local draft boards to follow such a procedure. He refused to accept any work whatsoever.   He was charged with violating the Selective Service Act.   He defended his action on the ground that he could not be forced to work in any civilian task because the Constitution prohibited involuntary servitude.   What judgment?

4.   The appellant was denied unemployment compensation on the ground that the act prohibited payments to persons who refused available employment.   He had refused to accept a job because he would be required to join a union.   He insisted that he was entitled to compensation even though he refused the job because he was a "conscientious objector" to union membership.   The lower court ruled against the appellant.   He appealed.   What judgment?

5.   The local board denied the registrant conscientious objector status because of the adverse information it had in its files.   The board failed to inform the registrant that it possessed such information.   When tried for his refusal to report for induction the defendant contended that the board's procedure denied him due process of law since it had failed to afford him an opportunity to rebut the information it used to arrive at its decision.   Is the defendant correct?

6. A Selective Service Regulation provided that when an application form for conscientious objector status is mailed by a local draft board to a registrant who requests one it is conclusively presumed that the registrant received it. The defendant's board claimed that it had mailed such a form to him. He claimed he did not receive the form. The local board refused to accept his statement, classified him 1–A, and ordered that he proceed to a pre-induction physical examination. He challenged the regulation, claiming that it denied him due process of law. Is he correct?

————————

Chapter 14

PRIVACY

Privacy has been described as the right of an individual to enjoy "a private enclave where he may lead a private life." Courts commonly refer to the right to privacy as the right "to be let alone." [1]

There are forms of personal behavior which men and women engage in which they do not wish to be observed, be interfered with, or be reported. A civilized free society recognizes that there are aspects of human conduct which fall beyond the legitimate concern of other persons and government. Respect for the dignity of the individual and for his emotional and intellectual needs requires that some of what he says or does be shielded from outside interference, intrusion, detection, or knowledge.

The Constitution does not explicitly provide for a right to privacy. However, it does contain a number of provisions which direct that government abstain from controlling or intruding upon several categories of human behavior. We have already seen that the First Amendment places limits on governmental interference with speech, press, assembly, petitioning government for the redress of grievances, and religious practices. The Third Amendment outlaws governmental action calling for the involuntary quartering of soldiers in homes in time of peace and in time of war except as "prescribed by law." The Fourth Amendment provides that persons have a right "to be secure in their persons, houses, papers, and effects, against unreasonable searches and seizures * * * and no Warrants shall issue, but upon probable cause, supported by Oath or affirmation, and particularly describing the place to be searched, and the persons or things to be seized." The Fifth Amendment denies government the power to compel a person to incriminate himself. The Ninth Amendment recognizes that individuals possess rights in addition to those expressly set forth in the Constitution. It declares that "the enumeration" of "certain rights, shall not be construed to deny or disparage others retained by the people."

As pointed out in the chapter on Family Planning the Supreme Court has found that the aforementioned Amendments "have penumbras, formed by emanations from those guarantees that help give them life and substance." It is the penumbras cast by these Amendments which serve as the basis for the constitutional principle that individuals have a right to privacy. By treating the Amendments as casting shadows of liberty and immunity from various kinds of governmental interference with individual behavior the Supreme Court has

1. For a discussion of the desirability of the law recognizing a right of persons "to be let alone" see Warren and Brandeis, "The Right to Privacy," 4 Harvard Law Review 193 (1890).

entrusted the judiciary with a most flexible instrument. Judges, under the penumbra concept, have a broad latitude of competence to decide whether or not particular sorts of individual behavior are beyond the eye or ear of governmental officials. Since the due process clause of the Fourteenth Amendment, as interpreted, imposes restraints found in the First, Fourth, and Fifth Amendments on state and local governments they too are required to respect an individual's right "to be let alone" under a variety of circumstances.

The right to privacy from governmental intrusion protects people, not places. This means that wherever one may be, because of his right to privacy, he has a right to be free from certain kinds of governmental action. For example, governmental officials have no greater right to eavesdrop on a telephone conversation originating from a public telephone than from one's home. In each case the constitutional standard of freedom from unreasonable searches must be satisfied.

We have already seen that (1) government may not require an individual to disclose the names of associations to which he belongs or require an association to disclose the names of its members unless it is apparent that the request for such information is necessary to protect an interest which is of legitimate concern to the government and (2) government may not prohibit the dissemination of birth control information or birth control devices since the decision to have or not have children is a matter of private personal choice. Similarly, government may not (1) treat as criminals married persons or unmarried adults who have engaged in an act or acts of sodomy, in private, if each voluntarily agreed to take part in such an act or acts; (2) deny employment to either an unmarried man or woman because he or she has engaged in extra-marital sexual intercourse in private unless there is a rational nexus between the fact that the man or woman engaged in such acts and the demands of his or her employment; or (3) treat homosexual or lesbian tendencies or behavior as a basis for the refusal or termination of employment unless the governmental position sought or held is of such a sensitive nature that such activity could impede the proper performance of his or her duties or the nature of the sexual activity is such that it would adversely affect the individual's efficiency and performance.

Courts frequently call attention to the danger modern technology presents to the dignity of the individual in a mass, often too impersonal, society. They emphasize the urgency that courts act as stalwart defenders of each individual's right "to be let alone." Courts time and again express fear that if judges are lax rather than vigilant official use of scientific and technological techniques will ultimately decimate the right to privacy and put an end to "enclaves" which are free from governmental intrusion. This apprehension has led the Supreme Court to conclude that the Fourth Amendment bars unlawful snooping rather than any particular method of snooping. This means that the Amendment bans general searches of persons, their homes, and their papers, outlaws indiscriminate seizures, and prohibits general governmental use of electronic eavesdropping and wiretapping devices.

Ordinarily, prior to a governmental official making a search, a seizure, or in any fashion spying upon a person who is within an "enclave" of privacy, be it his home, his office, his home away from home, or any other place which he has not indicated he invites persons to come and see and listen to what he says and does, the official must request a court to issue a search warrant. Before issuing a warrant a judge must be reasonably satisfied that a crime is probably being committed, or has probably been committed, and the search, or seizure, or snooping is essential to enforce the law. Only in exceptional cases, such as when a police officer is in hot pursuit of a suspect leaving the scene of a crime, or when a police officer observes one committing a crime, or when delay would probably result in the loss of evidence, may a police officer proceed to carry on a search or make a seizure without first obtaining a warrant. In every case in which a search or seizure is challenged on the ground that the warrant relied upon by the officer should not have been issued, or that it was improper to carry on the challenged search without a warrant, or that the search went beyond the limits specified by the warrant, and incriminating evidence was found, the court must answer this question: "On balancing the individual's right to privacy and the legitimate interest of society to bring criminals to justice, was the government's conduct reasonable?" If under all of the circumstances what took place was reasonable then the search or seizure was lawful. Should the court conclude that the search or seizure was unreasonable then any evidence obtained as a result of the search cannot be used against the accused.

The right to privacy embraces more than simply the right to be free from various types of governmental action. The right "to be let alone" includes a right of privacy of each individual vis-à-vis all other persons. But, like the right to be insulated from a governmental sponsored intrusion, it is not absolute. It is circumscribed by the demands of yet other rights which are enjoyed by all members of society. The right to privacy is limited by the constitutional rights of freedom of speech and press as well as the right of all persons in a free society to know what public officials and public figures have done, are doing, or plan to do.

At times it is more consistent with the tenets of a free, humane, orderly, and civilized society to permit a person's "enclave of privacy" to be penetrated than to protect it from intrusion, scrutiny, or exposure. There are facets of human behavior which, for one or more policy reasons, should not be kept from the public at large. The position one holds within the societal framework or what one has said or done may entitle other persons to learn about his behavior even though he would prefer that it went unobserved and unreported. When a court finds that freedom of speech, or freedom of the press, or society's right to know is a more weightier demand than the right to privacy, it will treat that right as paramount and refuse to protect an individual's right "to be let alone." In order to determine which of the rights in question should be respected at the expense of the other right a court must examine the context in which the challenged behavior took place and evaluate which of the competing rights, under the circumstances, merits protection and which does not.

States disagree as to the precise nature of the right of privacy. Some see it as a right to be free from intrusion. Under this standard whether or not the intruder communicates what he learned or observed is not determinative of whether or not one's right to privacy has been violated. The intrusion or observation constitutes the wrong. Other states define the right as a right to be free from the reporting of behavior which is of no legitimate concern to the public. Under this test the truth or falsity of the publication is of no consequence. The wrong is the act of reporting what did or did not take place and not the inaccuracy of the report. A true presentation of behavior which is of no legitimate interest to the public is a violation of one's right to privacy. There is general agreement that the right, whichever way defined, is a personal one, entitling only that person whose privacy has been invaded to recover damages. A disclosure of conduct which is of no concern to the public about a person already deceased does not give any surviving relatives of the deceased a right to sue for money damages.

Judicial acceptance of the proposition that it is necessary in a free society to make available to its members information about public officials and public figures means that these persons have no right to privacy in regard to what they do or say unless it falls outside of society's legitimate interest in their activities.

When one's right to privacy has been violated he may recover money damages in an amount sufficient to compensate him at least for the outrage, mental suffering, shame, or humiliation the defendant's wrongful conduct caused him. In the event the defendant's conduct was carried on for the very purpose of injuring the plaintiff, the court may in addition award punitive damages. An invasion of privacy has been found in each of the following cases: (1) A photograph of an arrested woman's naked body, the photograph having been taken at the direction of police officers, was distributed to members of the police force. (2) A photograph of a physician, taken without his permission, by one who entered the physician's home without his consent, was later published in a magazine. (3) Defendants were found guilty of "overzealous" shadowing, wiretapping, and bugging.

BUCHANAN v. BATCHELOR

United States District Court, N.D. Texas, Dallas Division, 1970.
308 F.Supp. 729.

The plaintiff, an admitted homosexual, was twice arrested by state police and charged with violating Article 524 of the Texas Penal Code which made sodomy a crime. Each of the plaintiff's alleged acts of sodomy took place in a public rest room. He asked the court to enjoin both state prosecutions and to declare Article 524 unconstitutional. After the plaintiff commenced the suit three other persons asked permission to intervene in the suit. Two were a husband and wife who claimed that the plaintiff did not fairly and adequately protect the interest of married persons who feared future prosecution for private acts of sodomy. The third alleged that the plaintiff did not protect the interests of homosexuals who committed private rather than public acts of sodomy. Each of the three intervenors challenged the constitutionality of the statute.

HUGHES, DISTRICT JUDGE.

* * *

It is defendants' contention that as a matter of comity this court should abstain from deciding whether or not the Texas Statute is unconstitutional until the Texas courts have had an opportunity to construe the statute and rule on its constitutionality. We disagree, first, because there is no prospect of the immediate availability of a state forum where the questions raised here could be litigated which is particularly significant given the operation of an alleged overbroad statute on First Amendment rights, * * * and, second, because there exists in Article 524 no question of statutory interpretation for which the courts of this State would be of assistance in resolving.

Article 524 makes no distinction whether acts it describes as sodomy are committed in public or in private, whether they are committed homosexually, or whether by married or unmarried persons. Indeed it plainly appears that Article 524 applies to private consensual acts between married persons and private acts of sodomy between homosexuals.

There have been no prosecutions under the Act of married persons for private acts of sodomy. As to whether there have been prosecutions of homosexuals for private acts of sodomy is unclear. To require such persons to await a state court's disposition of the prosecution of an offense of sodomy committed by either of these classes of persons would result in an unfair delay in determination of their rights and a substantial impairment of freedom of action for reasons appearing subsequently in this opinion.

* * *

In the case before us it is clear that the statute applies to married persons and to homosexuals practicing acts of sodomy in private. There is no need for the state courts to interpret its provisions. Abstention is unwarranted. * * *

For the reasons stated we hold that we should not abstain but that this Court should determine the constitutionality of Article 524, Texas Penal Code.

An examination of the statute reveals that it operates directly on an intimate relation of husband and wife. While this relationship is not mentioned in the Constitution nor its amendments, it has been held by the Supreme Court to be included in the First Amendment.

It was said in Griswold v. Connecticut, * * * that "the First Amendment has a penumbra where privacy is protected from governmental intrusion."

* * *

The State, in defense of Article 524, points out that sodomy was an offense under the common law and has been a statutory offense in Texas for more than a hundred years. We agree that it is not the function of the Court to determine the policy of the state as it relates to morals. The State has regulated sexual relations by the passage of laws prohibiting what it considers immoral acts, such as adultery and fornication and we believe that it has that right with reference to sodomy. The Court's holding today, "in no way interferes with a State's proper regulation of sexual promiscuity or misconduct." * * * We hold simply as stated in Griswold:

"Such a law cannot stand in light of the familiar principle, so often applied by this Court, that a 'governmental purpose to control or prevent activities constitutionally subject to state regulation may not be achieved by means which sweep unnecessarily broadly and thereby invade the area of protected freedoms'. * * * "

Sodomy is not an act which has the approval of the majority of the people. In fact such conduct is probably offensive to the vast majority, but such opinion is not sufficient reason for the State to encroach upon the liberty of married persons in their private conduct. Absent some demonstrable necessity, matters of (good or bad) taste are to be protected from regulation. * * *

In conclusion, Article 524 is void on its face for unconstitutional over-breadth insofar as it reaches the private, consensual acts of married couples. * * *

HAMBERGER v. EASTMAN

Supreme Court of New Hampshire (1965).
206 A.2d 239, 106 N.H. 107, 11 A.L.R.3d 1288.

The plaintiffs, husband and wife, alleged that the defendant, without their knowledge or consent, installed and concealed "a listening and recording device" in their bedroom near their bed, which device recorded as well as transmitted to the defendant's residence "any sound and voices originating in the bedroom." The plaintiffs asked money damages for the defendant's invasion of their privacy and the mental suffering, distress, humiliation, and embarassment they suffered upon learning of what he had done. The defendant moved to dismiss the complaint on the ground that it did not state a cause of action. As permitted by local practice, the trial court refused to rule on the motion and transferred it to this court for a decision.

KENISON, CHIEF JUSTICE.

* * *

The four kinds of invasion comprising the law of privacy include: (1) intrusion upon the plaintiff's physical and mental solitude or seclusion; (2) public disclosure of private facts; (3) publicity which places the plaintiff in a false light in the public eye; (4) appropriation, for the defendant's benefit or advantage, of the plaintiff's name or likeness. In the present case, we are concerned only with the tort of intrusion upon the plaintiffs' solitude or seclusion. * * *

"It is evident that these four forms of invasion of privacy are distinct, and based on different elements. It is the failure to recognize this which has been responsible for much of the apparent confusion in the decisions. Taking them in order—intrusion, disclosure, false light, and appropriation—the first and second require the invasion of something secret, secluded or private pertaining to the plaintiff; the third and fourth do not. The second and third depend upon publicity, while the first does not, nor does the fourth, although it usually involves it. The third requires falsity or fiction; the other three do not. The fourth involves a use for the defendant's advantage, which is not true of the rest." * * *

The tort of intrusion upon the plaintiff's solitude or seclusion is not limited to a physical invasion of his home or his room or his quarters. * * * the principle has been carried beyond such physical intrusion "and extended to eavesdropping upon private conversations by means of wire tapping and microphones." * * * The right of privacy has been upheld in situations where microphones have been planted to overhear private conversations. * * *

We have not searched for cases where the bedroom of husband and wife has been "bugged" but it should not be necessary—by way of understatement—to observe that this is the type of intrusion that would be offensive to any person of ordinary sensibilities. What married "people do in the privacy of their bedroom is their own business so long as they are not hurting anyone else." * * * The Restatement, Torts s. 867 provides that "a person who unreasonably and seriously interferes with another's interest is not having his affairs known to others * * * is liable to the other." As is pointed out in *comment* d "liability exists only if the defendant's conduct was such that he should have realized that it would be offensive to persons of ordinary sensibilities. It is only where the intrusion has gone beyond the limits of decency that liability accrues. These limits are exceeded where intimate details of the life of one who has never manifested a desire to have publicity are exposed to the public * * *."

The defendant contends that the right of privacy should not be recognized on the facts of the present case as they appear in the pleadings because there are no allegations that anyone listened or overheard any sounds or voices originating from the plaintiffs' bedroom. The tort of intrusion on the plaintiffs' solitude or seclusion does not require publicity and communication to third persons although this would affect the amount of damages, * * *. The defendant also contends that the right of privacy is not violated unless something has been published, written or printed and that oral publicity is not sufficient. Recent cases make it clear that this is not a requirement. * * *

If the peeping Tom, the big ear and the electronic eavesdropper (whether ingenious or ingenuous) have a place in the hierarchy of social values, it ought not to be at the expense of a married couple minding their own business in the seclusion of their bedroom who have never asked for or by their conduct deserved a potential projection of their private conversations and actions to their landlord or to others. Whether actual or potential such "publicity with respect to private matters of purely personal concern is an injury to personality. It impairs the mental peace and comfort of the individual and may produce suffering more acute than that produced by a mere bodily injury." * * * The use of parabolic microphones and sonic wave devices designed to pick up conversations in a room without entering it and at a considerable distance away makes the problem far from fanciful. * * *

It is unnecessary to determine the extent to which the right of privacy is protected as a constitutional matter without the benefit of statute. * * * For the purposes of the present case it is sufficient to hold that the invasion of the plaintiffs' solitude or seclusion, as alleged in the pleadings, was a violation of their right of privacy and constituted a tort for which the plaintiffs may recover damages to the extent that they can prove them. "Certainly, no right deserves greater protection, for, as Emerson has well said, 'solitude, the safeguard of mediocrity, is to genius the stern friend.'" * * *

The motion to dismiss should be denied.

PROBLEMS

1. The state commissioner of motor vehicles sold to business organizations lists containing the names and addresses of all persons who were owners of automobiles registered with the state. The plaintiff, the owner of a registered automobile, brought an action against the commissioner, asking the court to enjoin any future sale of such lists. He claimed that those who purchased the lists used them to solicit business. As a result he had received, and would probably continue to receive, mail from those who used the lists. The sale of the lists, the plaintiff insisted, violated his right to privacy. Is he correct?

2. The defendant, a private detective, was employed by an insurance company to investigate the validity of the plaintiff's claim for disability benefit payments. The plaintiff claimed that she had become physically disabled due to an accident. For a period of time the defendant conducted a surveillance of the plaintiff, trailing her wherever she went. He also took photographs of her when she took part in various sorts of physical activities. The plaintiff contended that the de-

fendant's behavior invaded her privacy. Is she entitled to a judgment in her favor?

3. When a woman attorney refused to replace the miniskirt she was wearing with a longer dress she was convicted of contempt of court. The appellate court noted that the wearing of the miniskirt did not shock one's sense of propriety and did not create a distraction nor disrupt the lower court's proceedings. The judge who charged the attorney with contempt did not assert that her wearing the miniskirt produced such results. Was the lower court judge's action proper?

4. When a vigorous crusader for consumers' rights made charges against an automobile manufacturer the manufacturer employed detectives to trail him. The detectives engaged in prolonged and zealous surveillance of the crusader. They also made use of electronic equipment to overhear his conversations with other persons. Would the manufacturer's conduct constitute an invasion of the crusader's right to privacy?

5. Without the plaintiff's consent, the defendant used the plaintiff's name and photographs in a sales brochure and in advertisements. Is the plaintiff entitled to damages on the ground that the defendant invaded his right to privacy?

6. Plaintiff, born a male, underwent "conversive" surgery. Thereafter the plaintiff demanded that the local board of health change "his" birth certificate from male to female. Is the plaintiff entitled to such relief?

7. A motion picture was made of various events which took place inside a state mental institution. In several scenes a number of the inmates were nude. Neither the inmates nor their guardians had consented to the making or showing of the film. An action was brought to enjoin the public showing of the film on the ground that such showing violated the nude inmates' rights to privacy. What judgment?

8. May a state require the employees of stock exchange member firms be fingerprinted?

9. The plaintiff, a teacher, was transferred from one school to another because he wore a beard. He brought an action to cancel the transfer on the ground that this action taken by the school board violated his constitutional right to privacy. What judgment?

10. The plaintiff, a United States Senator, brought an action against a newspaper reporter who made use of materials stolen from the Senator's Washington, D. C. office by the Senator's secretary. The material contained information pertaining to the Senator's use of campaign funds. He claimed that the reporter's use of the material in stories which he wrote violated his right to privacy. Is he correct?

Chapter 15

OBSCENITY

The First Amendment does not expressly exclude obscene oral and written communications from the full scope of its protection. Yet only a small minority of the Supreme Court has concluded that this Amendment protects obscene speech and written materials from governmental control. Under this view the power of government over obscenity would be confined to those cases in which the obscene speech or writing appeared in a context of "action" and the "clear and present danger" test was satisfied.

A majority of the Court takes the position that for constitutional purposes obscene oral and written communications are to be treated as a distinct form of expression. This approach originated in a 1942 decision in which the Court said that there were "certain well-defined and narrowly limited classes of speech, the prevention and punishment of which have never been thought to raise any constitutional problem." The Court included among the mentioned examples of such classes of speech "the lewd and obscene, the profane, the libelous, and the insulting or 'fighting' words." These forms of speech were described as not essential to the "exposition of ideas" and "of such slight value as a step to truth that any benefit that may be derived from them is clearly outweighed by the social interest in order and morality." [1] In a later decision the Court asserted that "the social interest in order and morality" requires that little concern be shown for oral or written communications which are "lewd or obscene." [2]

While the Supreme Court continues to hold that the First and Fourteenth Amendments do not require obscene speech and publications to be treated in the same fashion as any other form of oral or written expression it has progressively limited the extent to which government may regulate obscenity by (1) very narrowly defining "obscene," (2) making the judiciary rather than any other governmental officers the final judges of whether or not what was said or published meets the constitutional test of "obscene," (3) giving judges rather than jurors the final power to decide if a challenged form of oral or written expression is "obscene," and (4) by so broadly insulating speech and press from governmental regulation that only the most objectionable forms of obscenity can be prohibited and only then if the action taken by the government represents no danger to constitutionally protected speech or press.

The present definition of obscene which usually musters the support of more Supreme Court Justices than any other definition denies

1. Chaplinsky v. New Hampshire, 62 S. Ct. 766, 315 U.S. 568, 86 L.Ed. 1031 (1942).

2. Winters v. New York, 68 S.Ct. 665, 333 U.S. 507, 92 L.Ed. 840 (1948).

protection to oral or written expression if it deals with sex in a manner that (1) "to the average person," (2) "applying contemporary community standards" [a majority of the Court uses "community" to connote the nation rather than a state or smaller geographic area], (3) "the dominant theme of the material taken as a whole appeals to prurient interest," (4) is "patently offensive on its face," and (5) is "utterly without redeeming social importance."[3] Judicial sensitivity and responsiveness to individual taste is reflected in (1) and to societal taste in (2). Requisites (3), (4), and (5) patently call for the exercise of individual judgment by each jurist. At present, a majority of the Justices see their obligation to be one which requires them to personally examine the challenged material and to then decide, on the basis of the stated criteria, if it is or is not obscene.

One member of the Court who in individual cases might agree with the result called for by making use of the five stated requirements refuses to treat (5) as a distinct test.[4] He sees it as part of the Court's overall test of what is and what is not obscene. Another Justice believes that the Constitution allows government to regulate nothing less than hard-core pornography.[5] To decide if what is said or depicted constitutes hard-core pornography he uses an intuitive test. This test requires each jurist to take a look at the challenged form of expression and to then decide if it is hard-core pornography. While this Justice acknowledges that he may not be able to succinctly verbalize what he means by hard-core pornography he insists that he knows "it" when he sees "it." He has approved of definitions of hard-core pornography which describe it as material which "focuses predominantly upon what is sexually morbid, grossly perverse and bizarre, without any artistic or scientific purpose or justification * * *. Depicting dirt for dirt's sake * * *. It smacks, at times, of fantasy and unreality, of sexual perversion and sickness and represents, according to one thoughtful scholar, 'a debauchery of the sexual faculty.' " It "cannot conceivably be characterized as embodying communication of ideas or artistic values." [6]

At least two members of the Court would distinguish between the powers of the federal and the state governments to deal with obscenity. They see the First Amendment as limiting the power of the federal government to control nothing less than hard-core pornography. States, on the other hand, bound by the Fourteenth Amendment, would be held to a standard of "ordered liberty" which, in essence, would be satisfied by a test which makes use of the five stated requisites. So long as the result arrived at under state law made use of "criteria rationally related to the accepted notion of obscenity" and the results

3. A Book Named "John Cleland's Memoirs of a Woman of Pleasure" v. Attorney General, 86 S.Ct. 975, 383 U.S. 413, 16 L.Ed.2d 1 (1966).

4. Justice White, dissenting in Memoirs v. Attorney General, *supra*.

5. Justice Stewart in Jacobellis v. Ohio, 84 S.Ct. 1676, 378 U.S. 184, 12 L.Ed.2d 793 (1964).

6. Justice Stewart in Ginzburg v. United States, 86 S.Ct. 942, 383 U.S. 463, 16 L.Ed.2d 31 (1966).

reached by the state were "not wholly out of step with current American standards" these Justices would treat the state's action as constitutional.[7]

Each of the following principles of obscenity law has the support of a majority of the Justices now sitting on the Supreme Court. (1) A state may follow a "variable concept of obscenity." Materials dealing with sex and sexual behavior which may not constitutionally be kept from adults may be kept from children. A state may make use of "reasonable" legislation to protect infants from what the state rationally sees as "harmful" to them. For example, a state may bar the knowing sale of nude photos to persons under seventeen, if such photos, taken as a whole, are "harmful to minors." (2) Government may protect a person's right to privacy by giving him the right to decide what materials are obscene and to allow him to demand that such materials be kept out of his home. The power of government to protect persons in their homes from unwanted obscene materials is distinct from its power to protect one from being exposed, against his wishes, to obscene material in a public place. In a public place an individual's right to privacy is severely limited, with the Court paying more attention to the right of those who wish to see and to display materials than the right of those who wish to be in a public place which is free from such displays. For example, one need not accept into his home pictures of men or women, scantily clad, in sexually arousing poses, but he may not object to a display of such pictures in front of a motion picture theater. There are those who wish to see motion pictures which include such scenes and they have a right to know where they are being shown. Those who operate motion picture theaters have a right to inform the public of their wares. (3) The Supreme Court will not reverse a lower court determination that material is obscene, even if such material could not ordinarily constitutionally be so classified, if the defendant charged with unlawfully trafficking in such material was guilty of pandering. To pander is to solicit the purchase of materials which pervasively treat or describe "sexual matters" in a fashion calculated to exploit individual interest "in titillation by pornography." For constitutional purposes, in the area of obscenity law, pandering can take place only if the material in question lends itself "to such exploitation." This test requires the Court to consider the merchandising techniques used by the defendant as well as the nature of his offering.

In the absence of a "clear and present danger" to some vital interest which the state has a right to protect, individuals have a constitutional right to privately enjoy such emotional experiences as obscene material may incite. Government may not censor what a person, out of the view of others, may write, read, see, or listen to. Similarly persons who have an intimate personal relationship with one another may privately communicate between themselves orally or in writing

7. Justice Harlan in Roth v. United States, 77 S.Ct. 1304, 354 U.S. 476, 1 L.Ed.2d 1498 (1957).

their thoughts or comments about sex, in such language or in such fashion as they may choose, free from governmental interference.

When searching for obscene materials governmental officials must comply with the Fourth Amendment's prohibition against unreasonable searches and seizures. Obscene material obtained in violation of the Amendment may not be used to convict one charged with unlawfully trafficking in obscene matter.

To protect publications which are not obscene officials are prohibited from seizing any publications by use of a general warrant or on the basis of their own opinions. Before seizing any publication an official must obtain a warrant which specifies the publication to be seized. Prior to issuing a warrant a court must take reasonable steps to determine if the challenged material is obscene. It has been held that there must be a hearing at which the possessor of the supposedly obscene material has an opportunity to refute the charge. If after the hearing the court decides that the materials are obscene then a warrant may be issued. This procedure is intended to protect the free flow of published material. The same objective is served by the principle that before a court may convict a person of unlawfully dealing in obscene material there must be evidence that he knew the material in his possession contained obscene matter. If such knowledge were not required persons might be deterred from dealing in printed materials which, while suspicious, did not in fact contain obscene matter.

Motion pictures are treated as a form of speech. But the same stringent demands the Constitution makes on government in regard to speech are not precisely applicable to this medium. The characteristics which differentiate motion pictures from speech may under particular circumstances allow for different treatment. A state may prohibit the display of obscene films so long as the prohibiting legislation clearly sets forth what is prohibited and contains a constitutionally acceptable definition of obscene. Legislation may require that a license be obtained before a film may be shown to the public. Such legislation (1) must clearly indicate what may and may not be exhibited, (2) the constitutional definition of obscene must be satisfied, and (3) there must be available to one dissatisfied with the decision of the licensing authority an opportunity to obtain speedy judicial review of the decision by resorting to a not unduly cumbersome court procedure.

The Supreme Court has recognized television and radio broadcasting are "affected by First Amendment interests." It has distinguished these media from other forms of communication, stating that "differences in characteristics * * * justify differences in the First Amendment standards applied to them." The Court has asserted that in this area "[i]t is the right of the viewers and listeners, not the right of the broadcasters, which is paramount * * *. It is the right of the public to receive suitable access to social, political, esthetic, moral, and other items and experiences which is crucial here." [8]

STANLEY v. GEORGIA

Supreme Court of the United States, 1969.
89 S.Ct. 1243, 394 U.S. 557, 22 L.Ed.2d 542.

Police officers obtained a warrant to search Stanley's home for evidence of bookmaking activities. In the course of their search they found little evidence of such activities but did find three reels of eight millimeter film. After viewing the film, they charged Stanley with "knowingly hav[ing] possession of * * * obscene matter" in violation of state law. Stanley was tried and convicted. The state supreme court affirmed. He appealed.

MR. JUSTICE MARSHALL delivered the opinion of the Court.

* * *

The State and appellant both agree that the question here before us is whether "a statute imposing criminal sanctions upon the mere [knowing] possession of obscene matter" is constitutional. In this context, Georgia concedes that the present case appears to be one of "first impression * * * on this exact point," but contends that since "obscenity is not within the area of constitutionally protected speech or press," Roth v. United States, * * * (1957), the States are free, subject to the limits of other provisions of the Constitution, * * *, to deal with it any way deemed necessary, just as they may deal with possession of other things thought to be detrimental to the welfare of their citizens. If the State can protect the body of a citizen, may it not, argues Georgia, protect his mind?

It is true that Roth does declare, seemingly without qualification, that obscenity is not protected by the First Amendment. That statement has been repeated in various forms in subsequent cases. * * * However, neither Roth nor any subsequent decision of this Court dealt with the precise problem involved in the present case. * * * None of the statements cited by the Court in Roth for the proposition that "this Court has always assumed that obscenity is not protected by the freedoms of speech and press" were made in the context of a statute punishing mere private possession of obscene material; * * * Moreover, none of this Court's decisions subsequent to Roth involved prosecution for private possession of obscene materials. * * *

In this context, we do not believe that this case can be decided simply by citing Roth. Roth and its progeny certainly do mean that the First and Fourteenth Amendments recognize a valid governmental interest in dealing with the problem of obscenity. But the assertion of that interest cannot, in every context, be insulated from all constitu-

---

8. Red Lion Broadcasting Co., Inc. v. F.
C. C., 89 S.Ct. 1794, 395 U.S. 367, 23
L.Ed.2d 371 (1969).

tional protections. Neither *Roth* nor any other decision of this Court reaches that far. * * * That holding cannot foreclose an examination of the constitutional implications of a statute forbidding mere private possession of such material.

It is now well established that the Constitution protects the right to receive information and ideas. "This freedom [of speech and press] * * * necessarily protects the right to receive * * *." * * * This right to receive information and ideas, regardless of their social worth, * * * is fundamental to our free society. Moreover, in the context of this case—a prosecution for mere possession of printed or filmed matter in the privacy of a person's own home—that right takes on an added dimension. For also fundamental is the right to be free, except in very limited circumstances, from unwanted governmental intrusions into one's privacy.

* * * Whatever may be the justifications for other statutes regulating obscenity, we do not think they reach into the privacy of one's own home. If the First Amendment means anything, it means that a State has no business telling a man, sitting alone in his own house, what books he may read or what films he may watch. Our whole constitutional heritage rebels at the thought of giving government the power to control men's minds.

And yet, in the face of these traditional notions of individual liberty, Georgia asserts the right to protect the individual's mind from the effects of obscenity. We are not certain that this argument amounts to anything more than the assertion that the State has the right to control the moral content of a person's thoughts. To some, this may be a noble purpose, but it is wholly inconsistent with the philosophy of the First Amendment. * * * Nor is it relevant that obscene materials in general, or the particular films before the Court, are arguably devoid of any ideological content. The line betwen the transmission of ideas and mere entertainment is much too elusive for this Court to draw, if indeed such a line can be drawn at all. * * * Whatever the power of the state to control public dissemination of ideas inimical to the public morality, it cannot constitutionally premise legislation on the desirability of controlling a person's private thoughts.

* * *

We hold that the First and Fourteenth Amendments prohibit making mere private possession of obscene material a crime. *Roth* and the cases following that decision are not impaired by today's holding. As we have said, the States retain broad power to regulate obscenity; that power simply does not extend to mere possession by the individual in the privacy of his own home. * * *

Judgment reversed and case remanded.

ROWAN v. UNITED STATES POST OFFICE

Supreme Court of the United States, 1970.
90 S.Ct. 1484, 397 U.S. 728, 25 L.Ed.2d 736.

The plaintiffs were publishers, distributors, owners, and operators of mail order houses, mailing list brokers, and owners and operators of mail service organizations. Their business activities were affected by § 4009 of Title 39 of the United States Code, entitled "Prohibition on Pandering Advertisements in the Mails." Under this section a householder could insulate himself from receiving advertisements that offered for sale material which he believed to be erotically arousing or sexually provocative by requesting the Postmaster to order the mailer to remove the householder's name from its mailing lists and not to communicate with him any further. If after a hearing the Postmaster concluded that his order to a mailer had been violated he could request a Federal District Court to direct compliance with his orders. Plaintiffs challenged the constitutionality of § 4009 on a variety of grounds. From a judgment in favor of the defendant, they appealed.

MR. CHIEF JUSTICE BURGER delivered the opinion of the Court.
    *   *   *

Section 4009 was a response to public and congressional concern with use of mail facilities to distribute unsolicited advertisements that recipients found to be offensive because of their lewd and salacious character. Such mail was found to be pressed upon minors as well as adults who did not seek and did not want it.   *   *   *

The essence of appellants' argument is that the statute violates their constitutional right to communicate. One sentence in appellants' brief perhaps characterizes their entire position:

"The freedom to communicate orally and by the written word and, indeed, in every manner whatsoever is imperative to a free and sane society." Brief for Appellants at 15.

Without doubt the public postal system is an indispensable adjunct of every civilized society and communication is imperative to a healthy social order. But the right of every person "to be let alone" must be placed in the scales with the right of others to communicate.

In today's complex society we are inescapably captive audiences for many purposes, but a sufficient measure of individual autonomy must survive to permit every householder to exercise control over unwanted mail. To make the householder the exclusive and final judge of what will cross his threshold undoubtedly has the effect of impeding the flow of ideas, information and arguments which, ideally, he should receive and consider. Today's merchandising methods, the plethora of mass mailings subsidized by low postal rates, and the growth of the sale of large mailing lists as an industry in itself have changed the mailman from a carrier of primarily private communications, as he was in a more leisurely day, and has made him an adjunct of the mass mailer who sends unsolicited and often unwanted mail into every home. It places no strain on the doctrine of judicial notice to observe that whether measured by pieces or pounds, Everyman's mail today is made up overwhelmingly of material he did not seek from persons he does not know. And all too often it is matter he finds offensive.

In Martin v. City of Struthers, * * * (1943), Mr. Justice Black, for the Court, while supporting the "[f]reedom to distribute information to every citizen," * * * acknowledged a limitation in terms of leaving "with the homeowner himself" the power to decide "whether distributors of literature may lawfully call at a home." * * * Weighing the highly important right to communicate, but without trying to determine where it fits into constitutional imperatives, against the very basic right to be free from sights, sounds and tangible matter we do not want, it seems to us that a mailer's right to communicate must stop at the mailbox of an unreceptive addressee.

The Court has traditionally respected the right of a householder to bar, by order or notice, solicitors, hawkers, and peddlers from his property. * * * In this case the mailer's right to communicate is circumscribed only by an affirmative act of the addressee giving notice that he wishes no further mailings from that mailer.

To hold less would tend to license a form of trespass and would make hardly more sense than to say that a radio or television viewer may not twist the dial to cut off an offensive or boring communication and thus bar its entering his home. Nothing in the Constitution compels us to listen to or view any unwanted communication, whatever its merits; we see no basis for according the printed word or pictures a different or more preferred status because they are sent by mail. The ancient concept that "a man's home is his castle" into which "not even the king may enter" has lost none of its vitality, and none of the recognized exceptions includes any right to communicate offensively with another. * * *

We therefore categorically reject the argument that a vendor has a right under the Constitution or otherwise to send unwanted material into the home of another. If this prohibition operates to impede the flow of even valid ideas, the answer is that no one has a right to press even "good" ideas on an unwilling recipient. That we are often "captives" outside the sanctuary of the home and subject to objectionable speech and other sound does not mean we must be captives everywhere. * * * The asserted right of a mailer, we repeat, stops at the outer boundary of every person's domain.

* * *

The appellants also contend that the requirement that the sender remove the addressee's name from all mailing lists in his possession violates the Fifth Amendment because it constitutes a taking without due process of law. The appellants are not prohibited from using, selling, or exchanging their mailing lists; they are simply required to delete the names of the complaining addressees from the lists and cease all mailings to those persons. Appellants next contend that compliance with the statute is confiscatory because the costs attending removal of the names are prohibitive. We agree with the conclusion of the District Court that the "burden does not amount to a violation of due process guaranteed by the Fifth Amendment. Particularly when in the context before the Court it is being applied to commercial enterprises." * * *

Judgment affirmed.

PROBLEMS

1. The defendant, the owner of a motion picture theater, was enjoined from displaying a film which the court found to be obscene. In his defense he argued that the film had a social message and therefore fell within the protection of the First Amendment. The court found the social message to be of secondary importance. In its opinion the message was simply "window dressing," purposely injected into the film in order to permit motion picture theaters to reap a large profit by displaying pornographic material. The court asserted that its decisions must be based on substance and not mere form. The defendant appealed. What judgment?

2. The defendant was charged with violating a statute which prohibited the sale of hard-core pornography to persons under eighteen years of age. He sold a fourteen year old boy a book which had a statement on its cover that read: "If the reader wants hard-core pornography, this is it. This book has been criticized in Denmark—remember, there everything can be shown and told. Real, raw, nothing left to your imagination." The name of the book was *Sex for Sex Sake*. The evidence established that the text of the book, at several points, stressed the importance of avoiding pre-marital or extra-marital sexual relations if one wished to have a happy family life. There were several color photographs of naked men and women, but no single photograph included both men and women. The defendant claimed that the book did not qualify as hard-core pornography and therefore the charges against him should be dismissed. What judgment?

3. A state statute's preamble declared that the legislature was concerned with the morals of young people, it was aware that young people visit bookstores, and it feared that while in a bookstore a young person might be exposed to lewd and obscene books. The statute prohibited booksellers from displaying a book which might be "harmful to the morals" of persons under eighteen. The statute defined a book as "harmful to the morals" of persons under eighteen if it sexually stimulated young people, aroused their curiosity about sex, or contained photographs of nude men or women. The statute provided that its provisions did not apply to bookstores which refused admittance to persons below the age of eighteen years. The defendant, a bookseller, challenged the statute on the grounds that it violated his rights to freedom of speech and press. What judgment?

4.   The defendant was convicted of selling hard-core pornography in violation of state law. On appeal his attorney conceded that the defendant had sold what, according to the test used by a majority of the Supreme Court, could be classified as obscene. He asked the court to reverse the conviction on the basis of *Stanley v. Georgia*. He argued that in *Stanley* the Court recognized the right of persons to privately possess hard-core pornography. The right to possess must, he insisted, include a right to receive. The defendant had personally delivered the material in question to the purchaser at the purchaser's home. The evidence established that the purchaser had himself viewed the material privately, for his own pleasure, in his own library. What judgment?

5.   The defendants, six young women, to protest what they regarded as sexual exploitation by *Playboy* magazine appeared stripped naked at a public meeting held at the college they were attending. They were convicted of violating a state public indecency statute which made it a crime for persons to appear in public unclothed. The six appealed, claimed that their conduct was protected under the First and Fourteenth Amendments since it was a form of communication of disapproval with the way in which *Playboy* treated women. What judgment?

Chapter 16

DISCRIMINATION

Since the end of World War II acceptance and implementation of egalitarian doctrine has marked judicial thought and action. Courts have formulated new principles to cover forms of discrimination which were once viewed as falling outside the periphery of the law's concern. Judicial insistence on equal treatment for all citizens, regardless of their race or color, has resulted in the striking down of discriminatory practices which were once only frowned upon, or considered immoral but lawful, or were condemned as inhumane but not illegal. During the same period of time legislators, executives, and administrators holding federal, state, or local office have likewise officially spoken out against discrimination on the basis of race, color, religion, sex, or age. As is the case with all rights which have their origin in legislation, executive orders, or administrative regulations, the courts are charged with the ultimate responsibility of seeing to it that such policies are carried out.

The Fourteenth Amendment expressly prohibits a state from denying persons equal protection of the laws. Among the types of state action this Amendment was found to prohibit in cases decided prior to 1950 were: (1) making use of zoning ordinances drawn to keep black and white persons from buying a home in a neighborhood in which more members of the other race already owned homes, (2) court enforcement of private agreements between white persons which by their terms barred the parties from later selling their homes to non-whites, and (3) indicting or trying a black person accused of having committed a crime by using a procedure by which all black persons were systematically kept off the grand or petit jury.

At one time the concept of separate but equal met the constitutional standard of equal protection of the laws. Under this test, for example, a dual system of state public schools, one for black students and one for white, was constitutional so long as the privileges available under the two systems were equal. In Brown v. Board of Education,[1] decided in 1954, the Supreme Court unanimously put aside the separate but equal test as a valid test of the constitutionality of state action. In the case before the Court the state operated a dual public school system. One's race determined which school he attended. The Court refused to find that simple equality of such tangible factors as a school's physical structure and the number of teachers in a school were true measures of equality of treatment. The Justices condemned separate but equal as "inherently unequal." The Court ruled that a state which maintained a dual public school system, with one set of

---

1. 74 S.Ct. 686, 347 U.S. 483, 98 L.Ed. 873 (1954).

schools for whites and one for blacks, was required to proceed in good faith and with "all deliberate speed" to put an end to such segregation and to establish but one school system. In 1969 the "all deliberate speed" requirement was replaced with the directive that those states which did not then satisfy the demands of the Fourteenth Amendment which required that there be no intentional separation of whites and blacks within their public school system proceed "at once * * * to operate now and hereafter only unitary schools."[2] No longer may the assignment of persons to any one school within a public school system be on the basis of race if the purpose of such an assignment is to keep white and black persons separate from one another.

The Constitution prohibits the federal government from discriminating against persons because of their race. This restraint is predicated on the Fifth Amendment's directive that persons shall not "be deprived of life, liberty, or property, without due process of law." The Supreme Court has ruled that due process includes protection from such discriminatory practices as are "so unjustifiable as to be violative of due process." Discrimination on the basis of race has been found to be a denial of due process. It was on the basis of the due process clause that the Supreme Court struck down a federally operated dual school system in the District of Columbia in which one's race determined which school he attended.[3]

Congress, acting under the power granted to it by the Thirteenth Amendment, has provided that all United States citizens shall enjoy the same right to inherit, purchase, lease, sell, hold, and convey real and personal property as enjoyed by white citizens. This directive, for example, bars all forms of private and public racial discrimination in the sale or rental of property. Exercising its power to regulate interstate commerce Congress has provided that "[a]ll persons must be entitled to the full and equal enjoyment of the goods, services, facilities, privileges, advantages, and accommodations of any place of public accommodation * * * without discrimination or segregation on the ground of race, color, religion, or national origin." Among the enterprises covered by this mandate are inns, hotels, and motels. Like restrictions have been imposed on restaurants, cafeterias, motion picture houses, and stadiums. Congress has also used its power over interstate commerce to prohibit certain employers and unions from discriminating against persons on account of their race, color, religion, or sex. Restrictions banning discrimination placed on those who own property, or operate a business, or engage in union activities have been found to be a valid exercise of the power of the government to oversee the use of property and activities affected with a public interest.

The Congressional mandate that employers not discriminate against persons on the basis of their sex seeks to put an end to one of mankind's oldest prejudices. By barring sex as a criterion of ac-

2. Alexander v. Holmes County Board of Education, 90 S.Ct. 29, 396 U.S. 19, 24 L.Ed.2d 19 (1969).

3. Bolling v. Sharpe, 74 S.Ct. 693, 347 U.S. 497, 98 L.Ed. 884 (1954).

ceptability or worth Congress has called for recognition of each person as an individual, not as either qualified or unqualified because that person is a man or a woman. It demands that employers not look to an applicant's or employee's sex to decide whether or not he or she will be hired, promoted, or discharged. The Supreme Court, carrying out this legislative policy, has ruled that an employer may not refuse to hire women solely because they have small children unless that employer also denies jobs to fathers of small children. An employer may not have "one hiring policy for women and another for men."

The equal protection of the law's clause of the Fourteenth Amendment does not permit government to discriminate against persons on account of their sex. A state may not enforce a policy which treats the mother of an illegitimate child as the child's parent but denies the father like treatment simply because of his sex. A factor other than sex must serve as the basis for the state's classification scheme of who may and who may not be regarded as a parent of an illegitimate child.

Federal law prohibits employers who are engaged in business which affects commerce and employ more than twenty-five persons from discriminating against persons between the ages of forty and sixty-five years on account of their age. This legislation, like the Civil Rights Act of 1964 which prohibits such employers from discriminating against persons on account of their race, color, religion, sex, or national origin in regard to hiring, promotion, and tenure, permits an employer to discriminate on the basis of age when done to satisfy a "bona fide occupational qualification." In each case in which an employer is charged with having engaged in an unlawful discriminatory practice and he defends his action on the ground that it was due to a "bona fide occupational qualification," it is the task of the trier of fact to decide whether what took place was done to satisfy an essential job requisite or is attributable to a prohibited form of discrimination. This approach would be used to decide if a test an employer requires a job applicant to pass was in fact a test of the applicant's ability or simply a means of disqualifying him because of his race. A test used to see if in fact an applicant can perform the tasks expected of him is lawful. But a test used to disqualify an applicant due to his race is unlawful. Similarly a test keyed to age rather than ability is illegal.

Public officials, legislative bodies, and courts are conscious of the fact that not every act of discrimination based on race contributes to keeping whites and blacks apart or is injurious to non-whites. At times, by classifying persons according to their race, steps can be taken to put an end to existing segregation and anti-black policies. Courts have approved each of the following procedures which make use of racial criteria because of the results the procedures were designed to achieve: (1) providing for the placing of black persons on grand juries because they are black when for a long period of time blacks had been barred from grand jury service, (2) assigning persons to schools on the basis of their race in an area in which purposeful segregation had once been practiced and *de facto* segregation continues to keep blacks and whites apart, and (3) making apartments in public housing available to blacks on a percentage basis when previously blacks were denied accommodations in such housing. The use of quotas to force the inclusion of non-whites in activities long dominated by whites has found a broad variety of uses. For example, courts have sustained the governmental practice of requiring employers to employ a minimum number of non-whites when in the past non-whites were denied employment. The use of a quota to perpetuate segregation or to promote the separation of the races continues to be classified as a form of invidious discrimination which is unconstitutional if carried on by government and unlawful when carried on by individuals in violation of federal, state, or local legislation.

One who has been the victim of unlawful discrimination may be awarded money damages. At times he may also be granted specific relief. This means, for example, that if one has been denied employment because of unlawful discrimination a court may grant him a judgment for money damages to compensate him for lost wages and also grant him an order directing the employer who had acted unlawfully to employ him. Money damages may also be awarded for the damage done to the psyche of one who has been illegally discriminated against. If one has been denied housing because of his race he may obtain a judgment granting him (1) reimbursement for the expenses caused him as a consequence of the unlawful discrimination, (2) compensation for the mental anguish and embarrassment he suffered due to the discrimination, (3) punitive damages, and (4) an order directing the landlord, when he has housing available, to rent it to him at the usual price charged for such a premises.

WALKER v. POINTER

United States District Court N.D. Texas, Dallas Division (1969).
304 F.Supp. 56.

In October of 1968, James and Cheryl Walker, the plaintiffs, white persons, rented an apartment from Pointer, one of the defendants. The Walkers and Pointer signed a one year lease. On several occasions the Walkers had black friends of theirs visit them. At about noon on December 14, 1968 Branscome, Pointer's manager, served a written notice on the plaintiffs, informing them that suit would be filed to evict them if they did not vacate the premises by 4:00 p.m. of that day. Two days later, while the plaintiffs were not at home, Branscome, together with three more of Pointer's employees, entered the plaintiffs' apartment and removed and hauled away their possessions. The Walkers sued Pointer and Branscome for compensatory and exemplary damages. They claimed that the defendants had evicted them because black persons had visited them and that such action violated 42 U.S.C. § 1982 which prohibits discrimination against persons in the rental of property because of race.

HUGHES, DISTRICT JUDGE. This case involves the scope of 42 U.S.C. section 1982 which provides that:

"All citizens of the United States shall have the same right, in every State and Territory, as is enjoyed by white citizens thereof to inherit, purchase, lease, sell, hold, and convey real and personal property."

* * *

There are few cases construing section 1982, but one case, Jones v. Alfred H. Mayer Co., 392 U.S. 409, * * * (1968), is of major importance in discussing the statute. In that case plaintiffs alleged that defendants had refused to sell them a home for the sole reason one of the plaintiffs was a Negro. The Supreme Court held that section 1982 applies to all discriminations against Negroes whether from private or public sources in the sale or rental of property. There is no doubt that if the plaintiffs in this case had been Negroes, the statute would apply. The fact that they are white distinguishes this case and makes it in part one of first impression.

Section 1982 in its original form was part of section 1 of the Civil Rights Act of 1866. This history of this Act, as outlined in Jones, reveals that it was passed to implement the Thirteenth Amendment which provides as follows:

"Neither slavery nor involuntary servitude, except as a punishment for crime whereof the party shall have been duly convicted, shall exist within the United States, or any place subject to their jurisdiction."

The discussion of the Court in Jones indicates that the institution of slavery prompting the Thirteenth Amendment was ordinarily associated with the black man. Yet whites too have historically been susceptible to enslavement in many countries throughout the centuries. In this country white slavery was known to exist during the antebellum period in the South. Current statutes punishing practices relating to slavery continually refer to the victimization of "any person." 18 U.S.C. §§ 1581–1588. The bar against involuntary servitude has been invoked by the courts in numerous contexts where race is immaterial.

The first six words of section 1982 appear to lead inescapably to the conclusion that the statute contemplates a reach as broad as the amendment upon which it is based. "All citizens of the United States" are to be protected. The inclusiveness of these words is reinforced by the Jones opinion which states that the rights granted in 1982 are granted "to all citizens without regard to race or color."

* * *

There is much in the language of Jones which would support protection of real property and personalty interests of any persons subjected to racial discrimination, whether on the basis of the color of their skin or the color of the skin of those with whom they choose to associate. The following statements seem particularly significant on this point. "We hold that § 1982 bars *all* racial discrimination, private as well as public, in the sale or rental of property, and that the statute, thus construed, is a valid exercise of the power of Congress to enforce the Thirteenth Amendment." * * * "§ 1982 grants to all citizens, without regard to race or color, 'the same right' to purchase and lease property 'as is enjoyed by white citizens.' " * * * "[I]f § 1982 'means what it says' * * * then it must encompass every racially motivated refusal to sell or rent and cannot be confined to officially sanctioned segregation in housing." (421–422, 88 S.Ct. 2194). "[W]hen Congress provided in § 1 of the Civil Rights Act that the right to purchase and lease property was to be enjoyed equally throughout the United States by Negro and white citizens alike, it plainly meant to secure that right against interference from any source whatever, whether governmental or private". * * *

Two Fourteenth Amendment cases indicate by analogy that protecting plaintiffs from the effects of racial discrimination against blacks would be rationally and legally supportable. In Lombard v. Louisiana, 373 U.S. 267, * * * (1963), four petitioners, including one white student, obtained reversals of their trespass convictions because they were adjudged victims of racial discrimination sufficiently involving state action. Though the court did not speak directly to the relative position of white petitioner, the reversal of *his* conviction can only be explained by a recognition of the court that he was a victim of discrimination against blacks and that he shared a position before the court with the blacks as one entitled to the same remedy.

Even stronger by analogy is the Third Circuit opinion, Valle v. Stengel, * * *. This case dealt with 42 U.S.C. § 1981. The statute states, "in terms that closely parallel those of § 1982", that all persons in the United States "shall have the same right * * * to make and enforce contracts, to sue, be parties, give evidence, and to the full and equal benefit of all laws and proceedings for the security of persons and property as enjoyed by white citizens * * *." The following language from Valle v. Stengel indicates that with a statute similar to the one in the instant case the character of the discrimination involved entitled whites in the company of black persons to relief.

* * * the plaintiffs were denied equal protection of the laws within the purview of the Fourteenth Amendment because they were Negroes *or acting in association with Negroes* when they attempted to gain admission to the pool at Palisade Park. They, or some of them, were ejected from the park, were assaulted and were imprisoned falsely, as alleged in the complaint, because they were Negros, *or were in association with Negroes*, and were denied the right to make or enforce contracts, all within the purview of and prohibited by the provisions of [1981].

It would not have been difficult for the Supreme Court in *Lombard* or the Court of Appeals in *Valle* to have denied relief to the white plaintiffs and their refusal to do so appears to suggest a right which would also exist (though under a different amendment) for plaintiffs here.

To deny jurisdiction under section 1982 to plaintiffs would be to hold in effect that only those suffering from discrimination against black people who happen to be black come within the protection of the statute. This would surely be to read in 1982 a racist purpose. * * *

It is the conclusion of this Court that the plaintiffs are within the jurisdictional scope of section 1982 in their own right—even though they are not Negro persons and irrespective of whatever harm might have befallen Negro persons as a result of the alleged interruption of the Walker leasehold by defendants.

* * *

The evidence thus establishes that the reason for the eviction and the termination of the lease was a policy of racial discrimination implemented by Branscome. The racially motivated termination of the lease violated section 1982 which expressly protects the right to "lease" real property. The evidence shows that as a result of this violation the Walkers suffered damages. Their clothing and other possessions were retained for almost three months and some were never returned. Others were returned in damaged condition. Branscome was employed by Pointer to manage the apartments. Pointer testified that Branscome had authority to ask tenants to move. Hence he as well as Branscome is liable for actual damages resulting from the eviction.

With regard to the claim for exemplary damages there is abundant evidence that Branscome acted with malice. There is credible testimony that on the day of eviction, Monday, December 16th, Branscome had James' car, which was legally parked next to the apartment building, backed into a lane and pushed 300 yards to a thoroughfare where it was left on the highway six feet from its edge. While James went after the car, Branscome with 3 employees entered the apartment with boxes, dumped all their clothes and food from the refrigerator into boxes and sheets from the bed and carried them away in a truck without advising either James or Cheryl, who had arrived while the eviction was taking place, where their belongings were to be taken. When James attempted to use the telephone, Branscome pulled the telephone out of the wall and threw it at James. When plaintiffs asked to be allowed to spend the night, Branscome said they could stay without heat and pulled the thermostat from the wall. Branscome had taken no action in the Justice Court to evict plaintiffs as he had said he would do in his notice of December 14th. The malice with which Branscome acted entitles plaintiffs to exemplary damages.

With reference to the claim for exemplary damages against Pointer, the Texas and federal rule is:

"a principal is not liable in exemplary damages on account of the acts of his agent unless such acts were authorized by the principal or subsequently ratified or approved with knowledge of the facts."

While Branscome had been authorized to evict tenants, there is no evidence that he was authorized to evict in the manner used in the case of plaintiffs, nor is there evidence that after the eviction Pointer knew of the facts surrounding the eviction and ratified or approved them. Recovery of exemplary damages is therefore denied against Pointer.

Judgment has been entered in accordance with this opinion.

HUNTER v. ERICKSON

Supreme Court of the United States, 1969.
89 S.Ct. 557, 393 U.S. 385, 21 L.Ed.2d 616.

Section 137, an amendment to Akron's City Charter, barred the City Council from implementing any ordinance dealing with racial, religious, or ancestral discrimination in housing without the prior approval of a majority of the city's voters. The council enacted a fair housing ordinance which barred discrimination in housing on the basis of race, color, religion, ancestry, or national origin. The ordinance provided for the establishment of a commission to enforce the act. When the plaintiff sought to have the commission assist her she was advised that as yet the ordinance was unenforceable since the City's voters had not approved it. She brought a mandamus action against the Mayor of Akron, asking that he be directed to convene the commission and that the commission be required to enforce the ordinance. The trial court held that section 137 made the ordinance inoperative. The state supreme court affirmed. The plaintiff appealed.

MR. JUSTICE WHITE delivered the opinion of the Court.

*   *   *

By adding § 137 to its Charter the City of Akron, which unquestionably wields state power, not only suspended the operation of the existing ordinance forbidding housing discrimination, but also required the approval of the electors before any future ordinance could take effect. Section 137 thus drew a distinction between those groups who sought the law's protection against racial, religious, or ancestral discriminations in the sale and rental of real estate and those who sought to regulate real property transactions in the pursuit of other ends.   *   *   *   The Akron charter obviously made it substantially more difficult to secure enactment of ordinances subject to § 137.

Only laws to end housing discrimination based on "race, color, religion, national origin or ancestry" must run § 137's gantlet. It is true that the section draws no distinctions among racial and religious groups. Negroes and whites, Jews and Catholics are all subject to the same requirements if there is housing discrimination against them which they wish to end. But § 137 nevertheless disadvantages those who would benefit from laws barring racial, religious, or ancestral discriminations as against those who would bar other discriminations or who would otherwise regulate the real estate market in their favor.

The automatic referendum system does not reach housing discrimination on sexual or political grounds, or against those with children or dogs, nor does it affect tenants seeking more heat or better maintenance from landlords, nor those seeking rent control, urban renewal, public housing, or new building codes.

Moreover, although the law on its face treats Negro and white, Jew and gentile in an identical manner, the reality is that the law's impact falls on the minority. The majority needs no protection against discrimination and if it did, a referendum might be bothersome but no more than that. Like the law requiring specification of candidates' race on the ballot, * * * § 137 places special burdens on racial minorities within the governmental process. This is no more permissible than denying them the vote, on an equal basis with others. * * * The preamble to the open housing ordinance which was suspended by § 137 recited that the population of Akron consists of "people of different race, color, religion, ancestry or national origin, many of whom live in circumscribed and segregated areas, under substandard unhealthful, unsafe, unsanitary and overcrowded conditions, because of discrimination in the sale, lease, rental and financing of housing." Such was the situation in Akron. It is against this background that the referendum required by § 137 must be assessed.

Because the core of the Fourteenth Amendment is the prevention of meaningful and unjustified official distinctions based on race, * * * racial classifications are "constitutionally suspect," * * * and subject to the "most rigid scrutiny," * * *. * * * They "bear a far heavier burden of justification" than other classifications, * * *.

We are unimpressed with any of Akron's justifications for its discrimination. Characterizing it simply as a public decision to move slowly in the delicate area of race relations emphasizes the impact and burden of § 137, but does not justify it. * * * Even though Akron might have proceeded by majority vote at town meeting on all its municipal legislation, it has instead chosen a more complex system. Having done so, the State may no more disadvantage any particular group by making it more difficult to enact legislation in its behalf than it may dilute any person's vote or give any group a smaller representation than another of comparable size. * * *

We hold that § 137 discriminates against minorities, and constitutes a real, substantial, and invidious denial of the equal protection of the laws.

Reversed.

PROBLEMS

1. A municipal police department assigned black police officers to areas inhabited predominantly by black persons. The plaintiff brought a suit to enjoin this practice, claiming that it was unconsti-

tutional. The police department defended its assignment policy on the ground that it contributed to departmental efficiency. What judgment?

2.   To achieve racial balance in what had been an intentionally segregated public school system, the school board used a racial test to decide which school students would attend. The plaintiffs claimed that this procedure was unconstitutional. The board defended the practice on the ground that it was intended to put an end to *de facto* segregation which was the result of past segregation policies. What judgment?

3.   The petitioner, a black, was indicted by a grand jury to which blacks had been intentionally assigned. He claimed that purposeful inclusion of blacks in a locality in which blacks constituted 10% of the population denied him equal protection of the laws. In support of a quota to insure that blacks served on grand juries it was argued that since American society is dedicated to bringing an end to the remnants of segregation the intentional inclusion of blacks satisfies the Constitution. What judgment?

4.   A state statute provided that women might not serve as jurors. Is such a statute constitutional? Would a statute be constitutional if it gave women an option to refuse jury service without having to state any reason for refusal, while it did not confer a like option on men?

5.   The petitioner, unwed, while a member of the armed forces, became pregnant and gave birth to a child which she offered for adoption. In accordance with Army Regulations, when she became pregnant she was informed that since she had become pregnant she would be honorably discharged. The Regulation made no distinction between married and unmarried women. The petitioner brought a suit to bar her discharge on the ground that a regulation which permitted men who fathered children to remain in the service, but barred a woman who became pregnant from future army service, was a denial of due process. What judgment?

6.   The plaintiff sought employment as a longshoreman. Under state law one seeking such employment had to be approved by a designated state commission. The commission denied him employment because of his criminal record. He had been repeatedly arrested and convicted for various forms of larceny, including the receiving of goods stolen from docks. The plaintiff insisted that since all of the arrests and convictions occurred more than fifteen years before he applied for the job the commission could not take them into consideration when passing on his application. Professional social workers, the family physician, and neighbors testified that he had been rehabilitated. He had an ailing wife and a child. He had been supporting them and himself for 10 years on welfare payments. The plaintiff appeals from the commission's action. What judgment?

7.   The state constitution provided that before low-income housing could be built in a community the local citizens would have to

approve it. Mexican-Americans brought a suit asking the court to declare the constitutional provision unconstitutional under the Fourteenth Amendment. Local voters had repeatedly disapproved requests for permission to build such housing. Is the provision constitutional?

8. The plaintiff, a male, 18 years of age, who had been an outstanding quarterback in high school, applied for admission to a state's women's college. He was denied admission because of his sex. He brought an action asking the court to order that he be admitted on the ground that the state's action denied him equal protection of the laws. What judgment?

Chapter 17

ONE MAN ONE VOTE

The Constitution provides for the establishment and preservation of a federal system of government. It distributes the powers of government between the national and state governments. The powers entrusted to the federal government are arranged in three distinct categories: executive, legislative, and judicial. This tripartite classification manifests acceptance of the separation of powers doctrine. This doctrine requires each sector of government to act only within its designated sphere of competence and to refrain from encroaching upon an area of competence assigned to one of the other branches of government. This three category approach at times allows one branch of government to act as a policeman. When using its policing power one sector may take steps to prevent an errant sector from going astray. Illustrative of this policing power are the power of the president to veto legislation and the power of the Congress to override a presidential veto. The doctrine which calls for the possession and use of such power is known as checks and balances. The judicial branch of government has the power of judicial review. This means that the judiciary has the power to adjudge executive or legislative action unconstitutional and therefore void. The judiciary may use this power when it finds that action taken by either of these two branches of government violates one or more constitutional mandates. The federal judiciary may set aside action taken by any of the three branches of state government which it finds to be unconstitutional by making use of its power of judicial review.

The Constitution proclaims that its directives, laws made in accordance with its pronouncements, and treaties entered into by the federal government are "the supreme law of the land." Article IV, § 4 provides "[t]he United States shall guarantee to every State in this Union a Republican Form of Government." Article I, § 2 directs that the "House of Representatives shall be composed of Members chosen * * * by the People of the several States." Section 1 of the Fourteenth Amendment prohibits a state from denying "to any person within its jurisdiction the equal protection of the laws." The Twenty-fourth Amendment declares that a citizen of the United States may not be denied the right to "vote in any primary or other election for President or Vice President, for electors for President or Vice President, or for Senator or Representative in Congress * * * by reason of failure to pay any poll tax or any other tax."

As late as 1961 courts refused to rule on challenges litigants made to the constitutionality of state legislative schemes which apportioned elective public officials among the electorate. Those who challenged

146

an apportionment plan on the ground that it resulted in their vote having less weight than the vote of more favored voters were told that they could not look to the courts for relief. The Constitution's declaration that states were guaranteed a republican form of government was not interpreted as an edict which empowered the courts to rule on the constitutionality of apportionment plans enacted by a state legislature. The question of whether or not a challenged plan assigned the proper weight to the vote of each voter was said to be nonjusticiable, that is, beyond the power of the judiciary to decide. Courts insisted that the propriety of such legislative action was a political question, to be dealt with, if at all, by the executive, or the electorate, or the legislature itself. The separation of powers doctrine was pointed to as precluding judicial involvement in what the Supreme Court labeled the "political thicket."

In Baker v. Carr,[1] decided in 1962, the Supreme Court announced an abrupt shift in judicial thought. It ruled that the right to vote was a constitutionally protected political right and that courts had the power to decide if state apportionment legislation satisfied the equal protection of the laws clause of the Fourteenth Amendment. *Baker* set the stage for future extensive judicial involvement in apportionment legislation and led to judicial enforcement of the constitutional principle that apportionment legislation having to do with the election of persons to a state legislature must establish election districts of equal population. *Baker*, and the apportionment decisions which have followed, are the product of judicial insistence that every voter should have one vote and that each vote be of equal worth. Under this "one man one vote" doctrine the weight of every person's vote must be the same regardless of the election district in which he casts his ballot. A minority of the population should not, through the use of clever and devious apportionment formulas, deny a majority of the population the power to select those who shall serve in the legislative branch of state government.

Soon after the Court handed down *Baker* it ruled that the one man one vote principle equally applied to Congressional apportionment formulas. This time its decision was not based on the Fourteenth Amendment but on the Constitution's command "that the House of Representatives shall be composed of Members chosen * * * by the People of the several States." This provision, said the Court, requires "that as nearly as is practicable one man's vote in a congressional election is to be worth as much as another's." [2]

Since 1962 the Supreme Court has frequently spoken out on what is and what is not demanded by the one man one vote rule. It applies to elections in which persons are selected to serve in a legislative body or a body which exercises "general governmental powers over the en-

1. 82 S.Ct. 691, 369 U.S. 186, 7 L.Ed.2d 663 (1962).

2. Wesberry v. Sanders, 84 S.Ct. 526, 376 U.S. 1, 11 L.Ed.2d 481 (1964).

tire geographic area." [3]   In such elections there must be "no substantial variation from equal population in [any of the election] * * * districts." [4]   When speaking of permissible population variation the Court has pointed out that the only constitutionally permissible variance is one that is "unavoidable despite good faith effort to achieve absolute equality, or for which justification is shown." [5]   An apportionment plan may not allow inequality of population between districts if such inequality is intended to recognize differences in community interests, such as the assumed unique interests of individual counties, or towns, or any other geographical grouping.   Size of population rather than any new or existing geographic grouping of persons must be used to determine each election district's boundaries.   The one man one vote principle prohibits any unexplained population variance however small it may be.

The Supreme Court has expressly disclaimed any intention to prevent state or local governments from experimenting with new techniques designed to help solve state or local problems.   So far the Court has refused to say which types of public offices must be elective and which may be filled by appointment.   In each of the following cases the Court refused to strike down the challenged procedure, failing to find that it violated the one man one vote principle: (1) Each of several locally elected school boards representing communities with different size populations sent a single delegate to a convention to vote in an election held to select members of the county school board.   The Court described the county board's duties as "nonlegislative in character."   (2) Members of a city council were selected on an at-large basis.   A number of the candidates for the council were required to reside in boroughs which had different size populations.   (3) The New York City Board of Estimate had among its members five borough presidents.   They were selected by residents of boroughs having different size populations.   The five presidents did not make up a majority of the Board.   A majority of the Board members were elected in city-wide elections.   The Board could not pass any laws but could make budget recommendations to the City Council.   The City Council possessed legislative powers.   Its members were selected in accordance with the demands of the one man one vote principle.

State laws specifying who may vote and who may not are subject to the Nineteenth Amendment's bar on denying one the right to vote "on account of sex," the already mentioned Twenty-fourth Amendment, and the Fourteenth Amendment's equal protection of the laws clause.   The last of the three prohibits a state from withholding the franchise from any person unless it appears that there is a rational basis for such action.   When confronted with a challenge to a state law which does not allow a class of persons to vote, the court must balance the state interest supposedly served by such an arrangement

3. Avery v. Midland County, 88 S.Ct. 1114, 390 U.S. 474, 20 L.Ed.2d 45 (1968).

4. Ibid.

5. Kirkpatrick v. Preisler, 89 S.Ct. 1225, 394 U.S. 526, 22 L.Ed.2d 519 (1969).

and the constitutional requirement that all persons enjoy equal treatment under state law. If it appears that the state has acted in an arbitrary fashion, or has been guilty of an invidious discrimination, or the state interest sought to be protected by denying a group of persons the right to vote is either not in fact served, is not permissible under the Constitution, or is less compelling than the desirability of every state granting all of its citizens an equal opportunity to vote, the state statute is unconstitutional.

The following are examples of state election procedures which the Supreme Court has declared unconstitutional: (1) a state statute provided that to vote one must either pay a poll tax or "file a witnessed or notarized certificate of residence," (2) a state law prohibited a member of the armed forces who had once resided in another state to vote in any state election so long as he was a member of the armed forces regardless of how long he lived in the state and even if it was his intention to become a permanent state resident, and (3) state law permitted only taxpayers who had a certain type of property interest to vote in an election held to approve or disapprove the issuance of revenue bonds by a municipally owned and operated utility. In the first example the Court ruled that the statute violated the Twenty-fourth Amendment. In the second the state interest intended to be protected was found to be insufficient to withhold the franchise. In the last example the Court rejected the argument that only those with particular property interests had the necessary "special interest" to vote.

In the Voting Rights Act of 1970 Congress (1) lowered the minimum age of voters in federal elections to eighteen, (2) lowered the minimum age of voters in state elections to eighteen, (3) barred the use of any form of literacy test as a criterion of eligibility to vote in any national, state, or local election until 1975, (4) forbid states from imposing minimum residency requirements in Presidential and Vice-Presidential elections, and (5) established uniform absentee ballot regulations to be used by each of the fifty states in Presidential and Vice-Presidential elections.

A majority of the Supreme Court concluded: (1) Congress has the power to prescribe minimum age eligibility in elections held for the selection of presidential and vice-presidential electors and United States Senators and Representatives. The Court pointed to (a) Article I, § 4 of the Constitution which permits Congress to alter state regulations governing the selection of members of Congress and (b) Article I, § 8, clause 18 which empowers Congress to do what is necessary and proper to carry out constitutional powers expressly delegated to it. It was the opinion of the Court that "it is the prerogative of Congress to oversee the conduct of presidential and vice-presidential elections and to set the qualifications for voters for electors for those offices." (2) Congress does not have the power to set minimum age requirements for voters in state elections. The Tenth Amendment reserves to the states the power to maintain their own governments and to regulate state and local elections, except as provided for by the Fourteenth, Fifteenth, Nineteenth, and Twenty-fourth Amendments. (3) The literacy test ban is a valid exercise of the power granted to Congress under the Fifteenth Amendment. This Amendment bars states from denying persons the right to vote on account of race or color and empowers Congress to pass legislation to prevent such discrimination. The Court declared that there was substantial evidence to support the Congressional finding that states used literacy tests to keep non-whites from voting. The Congressional ban was in accord with the directive found in the Thirteenth Amendment outlawing slavery, the equal protection of the laws clause of the Fourteenth Amendment, and the enforcement power given to Congress by each of these Amendments. The misuse of literacy tests was viewed as a national problem, quite properly a matter for Congressional action. (4) The prohibition of minimum residency requirements was a proper use of Congressional power to regulate federal elections and to insure equal protection of the laws. (5) The uniform absentee ballot legislation was sustained on the same grounds as the legislation barring minimum residency requirements.

The right to vote can be debased if persons are not allowed to associate with one another and offer candidates for election to public office. The Supreme Court recognizes that the acts of banding together for political purposes and the offering of persons for election to public office are constitutionally protected political rights. A statute which outlaws either of such activities is unconstitutional unless it can pass the "clear and present danger" test. A statute drawn to keep only established major political parties in power is unconstitutional. Political parties have no right to insulate themselves from challenge. No law may bar the free exchange of political philosophy in the market place of ideas.

WILLIAMS v. RHODES

Supreme Court of the United States, 1968.
89 S.Ct. 5, 393 U.S. 23, 21 L.Ed.2d 24.

Under Ohio law a new political party could not appear on the state ballot and designate electors pledged to particular candidates for the Presidency and Vice Presidency unless it obtained petitions signed by qualified electors totaling 15% of the number of ballots cast in the last preceding gubernatorial election. An already established party could retain its position on the ballot without filing petitions if it obtained 10% of the votes cast in the last gubernatorial election.

The Ohio American Independent Party was formed in January 1968 and in the course of six months obtained petitions with more than the required number of signatures. However, it was barred from filing them since under Ohio law the petitions had to be filed by February 7, 1968. The Socialist Labor Party, composed of 108 persons, did not obtain petitions with the required number of signatures. It was also denied a place on the ballot. The Independent Party commenced a suit in the District Court, claiming the state procedure was unconstitutional. The Socialist Party brought a similar suit. In each case the Court ruled that the Ohio law violated the equal protection of the laws clause of the Fourteenth Amendment. It ordered that a space be provided for each party on the ballot so that there could be write in votes. The Court refused to rule that the parties could have their names printed on the ballot on the ground that they commenced their suits too late to permit the Ohio legislature to change the law before the forthcoming election. Each party and the State of Ohio appealed. Justice Stewart of the Supreme Court ordered that the judgment of the District Court handed down in the Independent Party case be enjoined until the entire Court could hear the appeal. Because of the stay Ohio included the name of the Independent Party and its electors on its printed ballot. Justice Stewart denied a subsequent request for like relief made by the Socialist Party.

MR. JUSTICE BLACK delivered the opinion of the Court.

* * *

* * * It is true that this Court has firmly established the principle that the Equal Protection Clause does not make every minor difference in the application of laws to different groups a violation of our Constitution. But we have also held many times that "invidious" distinctions cannot be enacted without a violation of the Equal Protection Clause. In determining whether or not a state law violates the Equal Protection Clause, we must consider the facts and circumstances behind the law, the interests which the State claims to be protecting, and the interests of those who are disadvantaged by the classification. In the present situation the state laws place burdens on two different, although overlapping, kinds of rights—the right of individuals to associate for the advancement of political beliefs, and the right of qualified voters, regardless of their political persuasion, to cast their votes effectively. Both of these rights, of course, rank among our most precious freedoms. We have repeatedly held that freedom of association is protected by the First Amendment. And of course this freedom protected against federal encroachment by the First Amendment is entitled under the Fourteenth Amendment to the same protection from infringement by the States. Similarly we have said with reference to the right to vote: "No right is more precious in a free country than that of having a voice in the election of those who make the laws under which, as good citizens, we must live. Other rights, even the most basic, are illusory if the right to vote is undermined."

No extended discussion is required to establish that the Ohio laws before us give the two old, established parties a decided advantage over any new parties struggling for existence and thus place substantially unequal burdens on both the right to vote and the right to associate. The right to form a party for the advancement of political goals means little if a party can be kept off the election ballot and thus denied an equal opportunity to win votes. So also, the right to vote is heavily burdened if that vote may be cast only for one of two parties at a time when other parties are clamoring for a place on the ballot. In determining whether the State has power to place such unequal burdens on minority groups where rights of this kind are at stake, the decisions of this Court have consistently held that "only a compelling state interest in the regulation of a subject within the State's constitutional power to regulate can justify limiting First Amendment freedoms." * * *

The State has here failed to show any "compelling interest" which justifies imposing such heavy burdens on the right to vote and to associate.

The State asserts that the following interests are served by the restrictions it imposes. It claims that the State may validly promote a two-party system in order to encourage compromise and political stability. The fact is, however, that the Ohio system does not merely favor a "two-party system"; it favors two particular parties—the Republicans and the Democrats—and in effect tends to give them a complete monopoly. There is, of course, no reason why two parties should retain a permanent monopoly on the right to have people vote for or against them. Competition in ideas and governmental policies is at the core of our electoral process and of the First Amendment freedoms. New parties struggling for their place must have the time and opportunity to organize in order to meet reasonable requirements for ballot position, just as the old parties have had in the past.

Ohio makes a variety of other arguments to support its very re- strictive election laws. It points out, for example, that if three or more parties are on the ballot, it is possible that no one party would obtain 50% of the vote, and the runner-up might have been preferred to the plurality winner by a majority of the voters. Concededly, the State does have an interest in attempting to see that the election win- ner be the choice of a majority of its voters. But to grant the State power to keep all political parties off the ballot until they have enough members to win would stifle the growth of all new parties working to increase their strength from year to year. Considering these Ohio laws in their totality, this interest cannot justify the very severe re- strictions on voting and associational rights which Ohio has imposed.

  * * *

  * * * Of course, the number of voters in favor of a party, along with other circumstances, is relevant in considering whether state laws violate the Equal Protection Clause. And, as we have said, the State is left with broad powers to regulate voting, which may include laws relating to the qualification and functions of electors. But here the totality of the Ohio restrictive laws taken as a whole imposes a burden on voting and associational rights which we hold is an invidious discrimination, in violation of the Equal Protection Clause.

* * * Certainly at this late date it would be extremely difficult, if not impossible, for Ohio to provide still another set of ballots. Moreover, the confusion that would attend such a last-minute change poses a risk of interference with the rights of other Ohio citizens, for example, absentee voters. Under the circumstances we require Ohio to permit the Independent Party to remain on the ballot, along with its candidates for President and Vice President, subject, of course, to compliance with valid regulatory laws of Ohio, including the law relating to the qualification and functions of electors. We do not require Ohio to place the Socialist Party on the ballot for this election. The District Court's judgment is affirmed with reference to * * * the Socialist Labor Party case, but is modified in * * * the Independent Party case, with reference to granting that Party the right to have its name printed on the ballot. It is so ordered.

FORTSON v. MORRIS

Supreme Court of the United States, 1967.
87 S.Ct. 446, 385 U.S. 231, 17 L.Ed.2d 330.

Article V of Georgia's Constitution provides that if no candidate for governor receives a majority of the votes cast in a gubernatorial election then a majority of the members of the General Assembly select the Governor "from the two persons having the highest number of votes." The District Court found that this procedure violated the equal protection of the laws clause of the Fourteenth Amendment. The Secretary of State of Georgia appealed.

MR. JUSTICE BLACK delivered the opinion of the Court.

* * *

The language of Article V of the State Constitution struck down by the District Court has been a part of Georgia's State Constitution since 1824 and was readopted by the people in 1945. * * * There is no provision of the United States Constitution or any of its amendments which either expressly or impliedly dictates the method a State must use to select its Governor. A method which would be valid if initially employed is equally valid when employed as an alternative. It would be surprising to conclude that, after a State has already held two primaries and one general election to try to elect by a majority, the United States Constitution compels it to continue to hold elections in a futile effort to obtain a majority for some particular candidate. Statewide elections cost time and money and it is not strange that Georgia's people decided to avoid repeated elections. The method they chose for this purpose was not unique, but was well known and frequently utilized before and since the Revolutionary War. Georgia Governors were selected by the State Legislature, not the people, until 1824. At that time a new constitution provided for popular election, but with the provision that upon the failure of any one candidate to receive a majority, the General Assembly should elect.

Two States, Mississippi and Vermont, that provide for majority voting also provide for state legislative election of their governors in case of no majority in the general election. Thirty-eight States of the Union which today provide for election of their governors by a plurality also provide that in case of a tie vote the State Legislatures shall elect. * * * It thus turns out that Georgia, clearly acting within its rights as a State, has decided that, any one candidate failing to obtain a majority in a general election, its General Assembly will elect its Governor. Its clear choice has remained in its constitution for 142 years. * * *

Article V of Georgia's Constitution provides a method for selecting the Governor which is as old as the Nation itself. Georgia does not violate the Equal Protection Clause by following this article as it was written.

Reversed.

PROBLEMS

1. The mayor, a Democrat, required all Democrats who held non-civil service city employment to work in the precincts in which they lived to elect Democratic candidates. They were told that if they failed to do so they would be discharged from their municipal jobs. Is this practice constitutional?

2. By state law persons residing in a federal enclave in Maryland were not permitted to vote in state elections. Does this contravene the Fourteenth Amendment?

3. New York law provided that a naturalized citizen could not vote in a state election unless prior to the election he had been a naturalized citizen for at least 90 days. Is such a restraint constitutional?

4. In precinct elections registered members of the Democratic Party could select delegates who in turn chose Party county delegates. The precinct elections were conducted on a one man one vote basis. Delegates to the county convention, selected by those elected in precinct elections, were not chosen on the basis of the one man one vote principle. Is such a procedure constitutional?

5. State law required that a candidate's race be indicated on ballots used in primary and general elections. Is such a statute constitutional?

6. May a state legislature bar from its membership a person who was elected to the legislature on the ground that he had publicly endorsed a civil rights group's support of black persons who refused to comply with the Selective Service Act?

7. A state legislature apportioned election districts on the basis of equal numbers of registered voters rather than on the basis of an equal number of residents. Does this procedure satisfy the one man one vote requirement?

8.   A state legislature designed election districts so that so far as the number of persons living in each district was concerned the one man one vote principle was satisfied.   However, the party which dominated the legislature structured the districts in such a fashion as to favor its future candidates.   Is such a procedure constitutional?

9.   A state statute provided that if any organization which indorsed a candidate in a primary election made use of the name of any political party in its title it had to state in its advertisements that it was an unofficial political group.   The California Democratic Council, an unofficial group, contended that such a statute violated the due process clause and was an unconstitutional abridgement of freedom of speech.   What judgment?

10.   State law required that any person who sought to have his named placed on the ballot in a primary election pay a $300 fee.   Another section of the law exempted from this requirement persons whose names were written on the ballot by individual electors.   Does this statute violate the due process or equal protection of the laws clauses?

11.   Municipal law required that only persons who paid property taxes could vote for members of the school board.   Is this law constitutional?

12.   A town charter provided that only persons who had children enrolled in the town's public school system could vote on questions having to do with the operation of the town's schools and matters having to do with the school budget.   Is this charter provision constitutional?

●

Part Five

CONSUMERS AND DEBTORS

Chapter 18

CONSUMERS' RIGHTS

Dissatisfaction with dishonest, immoral, and dangerous business practices has brought forth demands that consumers be granted a "bill of rights" which would guarantee them redress in the courts and before administrative agencies. Advocates of consumers' rights insist that consumers have a right to (1) safety, (2) information, (3) choice, (4) be heard, and (5) recovery. Steps have already been taken to protect the consumer in each of these five categories.

Federal, state, and local legislation prohibit the sale of various sorts of products which can injure consumers. Commonly barred from sale are highly inflammable materials, toys hazardous to infants, and dangerous foods and drugs. Administrative agencies are entrusted with the task of investigating and regulating the sale of such goods.

Courts invoke a number of principles to assist consumers who have been injured by unsafe products. (1) Consumers may sue their immediate seller and those who played some part in the manufacture or distribution of the unsafe goods if their failure to exercise reasonable care caused injury. (2) A consumer may sue one who expressly promised that the goods possessed particular qualities when they did not and the absence of such qualities caused injury. (3) The Uniform Commercial Code, in force in forty-nine states and the District of Columbia, provides that when a merchant sells goods he impliedly promises his customer that they are fit for the purpose for which they are sold or for the purpose for which he knows they are planned to be used and that the goods would pass in the trade as goods sold for such use. For example, when a merchant sells shaving cream or perfume he is treated as having promised that the product has the same characteristics generally found in shaving cream or perfume. Neither should contain elements which would burn one's skin. If either did, the merchant would be obliged to compensate the consumer for his or her injuries. Many courts now allow an injured consumer to recover damages from a manufacturer or middle man whose product caused injury because it was not fit for the purpose for which it was sold or did not possess the characteristics generally possessed by such products. When allowing recovery courts rely either on the ground that the manufacturer or middle man impliedly promised that the

157

goods were fit or possessed such generally found characteristics or on the ground that it is a legal wrong to make or handle such defective goods. (4) Some courts impose liability on a manufacturer when the evidence establishes that the product which injured the consumer was so defectively designed or constructed that it was unreasonably dangerous, even in the absence of a showing that the manufacturer had failed to exercise reasonable care.

Legislation and some court formulated principles require manufacturers and merchants to inform consumers of particular kinds of information. For example, affixed to every new automobile offered for sale must be a statement of the manufacturer's suggested selling price. The Truth in Lending Act requires lenders to inform borrowers of the true cost of their loan. Statutes require particular products to be fairly packaged in terms of the relationship between the size of the package and its contents and that packages have labels which accurately states their contents. At one time courts rigorously enforced the precept "caveat emptor," buyer beware. Today courts are prone to carefully probe the relationship between the merchant and the consumer to see if the merchant had a duty to disclose a defect known to the merchant but not readily apparent to the consumer. In those instances in which a court finds that a merchant had such a duty but failed to satisfy his legal obligation the consumer may, if he wishes, cancel the transaction, or if he is injured due to the defect sue for damages.

Our antitrust laws outlaw (1) agreements and combinations which restrain trade, (2) most kinds of price-fixing arrangements, (3) monopolies, (4) the combination of business enterprises when their combining would probably have an adverse effect on competition or probably lead to monopoly, (5) some forms of price cutting arrangements which have an adverse effect on competition, and (6) unfair trade practices which restrict or eliminate competition. Proper enforcement of the antitrust laws can help guarantee to consumers the opportunity to choose the products they wish from among the offerings of a large number of sellers, each of whom is vying for their patronage.

Consumers make themselves heard by the choices they make in the market place and by direct communication with government and business. Within the last decade government and business have each displayed a greater willingness to listen and pay heed to consumer needs and desires. On the federal level of government, as well as in many states and municipalities, governmental officers have been charged with the task of looking after consumer affairs. Courts and administrative agencies have been giving consumers the opportunity to speak in forums in which they have never before had the opportunity to do so. By judges and administrators making use of a more liberal interpretation than in the past of what is meant by the terms "aggrieved party" and "standing to sue," two concepts considered in Chapter 1, the doors of the nation's courthouses and administrative offices are now open to consumers in cases in which just a short time ago they were closed. A growing number of business enterprises are actively trying to find out what consumers think and want and are reacting positively to what they learn. But ardent proponents of consumers' rights remain unsatisfied. They insist that a great deal more must be done to make the consumers' right to be heard more effective than it is at present. They look forward to the day when consumers will have a much louder voice in the policy-making councils of government and business, when courts and administrative agencies will further expand the right of consumers to be heard in the courtroom and the agency office, and when the right to be heard will be accompanied by more meaningful responses by the executive and legislative branches of government, courts, agencies, and business organizations.

Intertwined with consumers' rights to safety, information, choice, and to be heard is the right to recovery. The greater the scope of the protection each of these four rights confers on consumers, the broader is a consumer's right to recovery.

When a consumer has been denied a right conferred upon him by the law he is generally entitled to compensatory damages. Such damages are intended to make the injured party "whole again" by adjudging that the wrongdoer pay him a sum of money believed to be equivalent to the harm he has suffered. For example, if a manufacturer has violated his duty to make and market safe products, a consumer injured by the product is entitled to a judgment which would compensate him for his bodily injuries, as well as such things as medical and hospital expenses, and his loss of earnings.

A consumer may wish other than compensatory damages. For example, if a merchant has been guilty of fraud the consumer may prefer to return the merchandise he has bought and have his money refunded to him. The consumer may obtain a judgment which grants him such relief. The judgment will provide for the cancellation of the sale agreement and adjudge the merchant indebted to the consumer for an amount equal to the purchase price paid, together with court costs and interest. In cases in which the consumer's damages exceed the refund of what he has paid the court may in addition grant him compensatory damages in an amount sufficient to make him "whole again."

In cases involving fraud or defamation a court may grant the injured party punitive as well as compensatory damages. Such damages are intended to punish the wrongdoer and to deter others from engaging in like conduct. Accordingly, punitive damages are determined on the basis of the defendant's wealth. Persons of little wealth can be punished or deterred by judgments for small sums of money while those of great wealth would not be punished or deterred by punitive damages unless plaintiffs are awarded judgments for substantial sums of money.

When a consumer's loss is small the cost of his seeking redress by recourse to ordinary court procedures is prohibitive. To overcome this states have established small claims courts. In such courts the cost of processing a case is no more than several dollars, procedures are simple, and a lawyer's services are unnecessary. While state practice varies, usually $500 is the maximum judgment such courts can award.

Class suits likewise serve to reduce the cost of consumer litigation. Court practice differs, but the basic philosophy of the class suit is the same everywhere. It permits one or several consumers who have been similiarly injured because of the failure of a business enterprise to meet its legal obligation to sue that enterprise on their own behalf as well as on behalf of all other consumers who have been likewise injured. If the plaintiff or plaintiffs are successful the court enters a judgment in their favor as well as in favor of all others on whose behalf they acted. This form of litigation has been used to recover damages for consumers who have been injured in violation of our antitrust laws. In such a class suit the court awards a judgment against the defendants in an amount sufficient to satisfy the claims of all persons who have been injured. To obtain what is due to him a consumer need not commence his own lawsuit. After the judgment is entered he need only present evidence that he purchased the merchandise from the defendants at the illegally fixed price. He may then receive payment under the terms of the court's judgment. Besides making it less costly for consumers to enforce their right to recovery class suits may also deter businessmen from engaging in unlawful practices. A businessman may not be fearful of individuals who have suffered a small loss bringing a suit to recover damages. Few seek to recover judgments for small sums of money. But in a single class suit a court can enter a judgment for thousands of consumers, each of whom has a small claim. The judgment can amount to hundreds of thousands, if not millions, of dollars. Obviously judgments of this size can induce businessmen who might not otherwise do so to comply with the law's demands.

———

CONNOR v. GREAT WESTERN SAVINGS AND LOAN ASSOCIATION

Supreme Court of California, 1968.
73 Cal.Rptr. 369, 447 P.2d 609, 69 Cal.2d 850.

Conejo and the defendant agreed that the defendant would supply Conejo with funds to purchase a tract of land on which Conejo would build a large number of one family homes. In return the defendant obtained rights (1) to make construction loans on each of the homes built and (2) to demand each purchaser of a home to first seek a mortgage from the defendant before applying elsewhere. The land and homes served as security for the defendant's loan to Conejo.

In its relationship with Conejo the defendant departed from its normal procedures. It expected to earn a larger profit on its loan to Conejo than it ordinarily made. The defendant knew that Conejo's officers, Goldberg and Brown, had little experience in the field and knew that 64/65 of Conejo's reported capital represented anticipated profits on the sale of homes yet to be built. The defendant adopted a scheme to circumvent a state statute which prohibited it from making the type of loan it made to Conejo by "disguising" the loan "as the kind of investment in real property" permitted by law. The defendant had extensive control over the way in which Conejo constructed the homes but it never examined the building plans nor did it inspect the foundations of any of the homes Conejo built.

Each plaintiff purchased a home from Conejo. Shortly thereafter their homes "suffered serious damage from cracking caused by ill-designed foundations that could not withstand the expansion and contraction of [the] adobe soil" on which they were built. The plaintiffs brought an action against the defendant asking in part for money damages. The trial court entered a judgment for the defendant. The plaintiffs appealed.

TRAYNOR, CHIEF JUSTICE.

* * *

The fact that Great Western was not in privity of contract with any of the plaintiffs except as a lender does not absolve it of liability for its own negligence in creating an unreasonable risk of harm to them. "Privity of contract is not necessary to establish the existence of a duty to exercise ordinary care not to injure another, but such duty may arise out of a voluntarily assumed relationship if public policy dictates the existence of such a duty." * * * The basic tests for determining the existence of such a duty are * * * as follows: "The determination whether in a specific case the defendant will be held liable to a third person not in privity is a matter of policy and involves the balancing of various factors, among which are [1] the extent to which the transaction was intended to affect the plaintiff, [2] the foreseeability of harm to him, [3] the degree of certainty that the plaintiff suffered injury, [4] the closeness of the connection between the defendant's conduct and the injury suffered, [5] the moral blame attached to the defendant's conduct, and [6] the policy of preventing future harm."

* * *

[1] Great Western's transactions were intended to affect the plaintiffs significantly.

The success of Great Western's transactions with South Gate and Conejo depended entirely upon the ability of the parties to induce plaintiffs to buy homes in the Weathersfield tract and to finance the purchases with funds supplied by Great Western. * * *

[2] Great Western could reasonably have foreseen the risk of harm to plaintiffs.

Great Western knew or should have known that neither Goldberg nor Brown had ever developed a tract of similar magnitude. Great Western knew or should have known that Conejo was operating on a dangerously thin capitalization, creating a readily foreseeable risk that it would be driven to cutting corners in construction. That risk was enlarged still further by the additional pressures on Conejo ensuing from its onerous burdens as a borrower from Great Western.

[3] It is certain that plaintiffs suffered injury.

Counsel stipulated that each of the plaintiff homeowners, if called, would testify that their respective homes sustained damage in varying degrees "of the character of which we have been concerned in this action." Sufficient evidence was presented to show by way of example the existence of damage to the homes and therefore injury to plaintiffs.
* * *

[4] The injury suffered by plaintiffs was closely connected with Great Western's conduct.

Great Western not only financed the development of the Weathersfield tract but controlled the course it would take. Had it exercised reasonable care in the exercise of its control, it would have discovered that the pre-packaged plans purchased by Conejo required correction and would have withheld financing until the plans were corrected.

[5] Substantial moral blame attaches to Great Western's conduct.

The value of the security for Great Western's construction loans as well as the projected security for its long-term loans to plaintiffs depended on the soundness of construction, Great Western failed of its obligation to its own shareholders when it failed to exercise reasonable care to preclude major structural defects in the homes whose construction it financed and controlled. It also failed of its obligation to the buyers, the more so because it was well aware that the usual buyer of a home, is ill-equipped with experience or financial means to discern such structural defects. * * * Moreover a home is not only a major investment for the usual buyer but also the only shelter he has. Hence it becomes doubly important to protect him against structural defects that could prove beyond his capacity to remedy.

[6] The admonitory policy of the law of torts calls for the imposition of liability on Great Western for its conduct in this case. Rules that tend to discourage misconduct are particularly appropriate when applied to an established industry.

By all the foregoing tests, Great Western had a duty to exercise reasonable care to prevent the construction and sale of seriously defective homes to plaintiffs. The countervailing considerations invoked by Great Western and amici curiae are that the imposition of the duty in question upon a lender will increase housing costs, drive marginal builders out of business, and decrease total housing at a time of great need. These are conjectural claims. In any event, there is no enduring social utility in fostering the construction of seriously defective homes. If reliable construction is the norm, the recognition of a duty on the part of tract financiers to home buyers should not materially increase the cost of housing or drive small builders out of business. If existing sanctions are inadequate, imposition of a duty at the point of effective financial control of tract building will insure responsible building practices. Moreover, in either event the losses of family savings invested in seriously defective homes would be devastating economic blows if no redress were available.

Defendants contend, however, that the question of their liability is one of policy, and hence should be resolved only by the Legislature after a marshalling of relevant economic and social data. There is no assurance, however, that the Legislature will undertake such a task, even though tract financing grows apace. In the absence of actual or prospective legislative policy, the court is free to resolve the case before it, and indeed must resolve it in terms of common law.

Great Western contends that lending institutions have relied on an assumption of nonliability and hence that a rule imposing liability should operate prospectively only. In the past, judicial decisions have been limited to prospective operation when they overruled earlier decisions upon which parties had reasonably relied and when considerations of fairness and public policy precluded retroactive effect. * * * Conceivably such a limitation might also be justified when there appeared to be a general consensus that there would be no extension of liability. Such is not the case here. At least since Mac-Pherson v. Buick Motor Co. (1916) * * *, there has been a steady expansion of liability for harm caused by the failure of defendants to exercise reasonable care to protect others from reasonably foreseeable risks. * * * By the time of the decision in Sabella v. Wisler (1963), * * * such liability had been imposed on a builder who negligently constructed a seriously defective home. * * * Those in the business of financing tract builders could therefore reasonably foresee the possibility that they might be under a duty to exercise their power over tract developments to protect home buyers from seriously defective construction. Moreover, since the value of their own security depends on the construction of sound homes, they have always been under a duty to their shareholders to exercise reasonable care to prevent the construction of defective homes. Given that traditional duty of care, a lending institution should have been farsighted enough to make such provisions for potential liability as would enable it to withstand the effects of a decision of normal retrospective effect.

Great Western contends finally that the negligence of Conejo in constructing the homes and the negligence of the county building inspectors in approving the construction were superseding causes that insulate it from liability. Conejo's negligence could not be a superseding cause, for the risk that it might occur was the primary hazard that gave rise to Great Western's duty. " 'If the realizable likelihood that a third person may act in a particular manner is the hazard or one of the hazards which makes the actor negligent, such an act whether innocent, negligent, intentionally tortious or criminal does not prevent the actor from being liable for harm caused thereby.' " * * * The negligence of the building inspectors, confined as it was to inspection, could not serve to diminish, let alone spirit away, the negligence of the lender. Great Western's duty to plaintiffs was to exercise reasonable care to protect them from seriously defective construction whether caused by defective plans, defective inspection, or both, and its argument that there was a superseding cause of the harm "is answered by the settled rule that two separate acts of negligence may be the concurring proximate causes of an injury. * * * *"

* * * The judgment is reversed.

BARRERA v. STATE FARM MUTUAL AUTOMOBILE INSURANCE COMPANY

Supreme Court of California (1969).
79 Cal.Rptr. 106, 456 P.2d 674, 71 Cal.2d 659.

On April 29, 1958 Mr. Avles applied to the defendant for automobile liability insurance. On the same day the defendant issued him a policy insuring him and his wife against claims made for personal injuries he or she caused other persons by their negligent operation of an automobile. In September 1958 the defendant paid a claim made against Mr. Avles. In November 1959 Mrs. Avles, while driving an automobile, injured the plaintiff. In December 1959 the plaintiff's attorneys notified the defendant of the accident. In April 1960 the defendant advised Mr. Avles that it cancelled the policy. It returned to him the premiums he had paid. The plaintiff sued the Avleses in July 1960. The defendant advised the Avleses that it would not defend the action. On November 3, 1960 a judgment was entered in favor of the plaintiff against the Avleses. It was not paid. Under state law if a judgment against an insured person remains unpaid the plaintiff is entitled to proceed directly against the insurance company to recover the amount of the unpaid judgment up to the face amount of the policy.

The plaintiff sued the defendant. The defendant denied liability and filed a cross-suit asking the court to declare the policy issued on April 29, 1958 to be void *ab initio* since it was issued in reliance on a material misrepresentation Mr. Avles had made in his application. The plaintiff contended that the defendant was estopped to rescind the policy at such a late date. In part the plaintiff relied upon the state's financial responsibility law which provided that once a driver caused injury to another person or another's property due to his negligent operation of an automobile he might not thereafter lawfully operate an automobile unless he established that he was financially responsible. Under the statute one could establish that he was financially responsible by obtaining an automobile liability insurance policy. From a judgment for the defendant the plaintiff appealed.

Tobriner, Justice.

* * *

Because of the "quasi-public" nature of the insurance business and the relationship between the insurer and the insured * * *, the rights and obligations of the insurer cannot be determined solely on the basis of rules pertaining to private contracts negotiated by individual parties of relatively equal bargaining strength. In the case of the standarized contract prepared by the economically powerful entity and the comparatively weak consumer we look to the reasonable expectation of the public and the type of service which the entity holds itself out as ready to offer.

The reasonable expectation of both the public and the insured is that the insurer will duly perform its basic commitment: to provide insurance. * * *

A rule which would permit an automobile liability insurer indefinitely to postpone determination of the validity of a liability policy and to retain its right to rescind the policy in the absence of the filing of a suit against it by a judgment creditor of the insured, defeats not only the public service obligations of the insurer but also the basic policy of the Financial Responsibility Law. That law aims "to make owners of motor vehicles financially responsible to those injured by them in the operation of such vehicles." * * *

The public policy expressed in the Financial Responsibility and related laws requires that we construe statutes applicable to automobile liability insurance policies, as well as contractual provisions in those policies, in light of its purpose to protect those who may be injured by the use of automobiles. * * * We therefore cannot accept a construction of the statute governing rescission of insurance policies, insofar as it applies to automobile liability insurers, which would serve only the financial interest of the insurer and directly thwart that public policy.

State Farm's alleged practice of postponing its investigation of insurability until after the assertion of a "significant" claim produces the dangerous condition that owners of cars will be driving on the streets and highways in the erroneous belief that they are insured and that the public generally will utilize these streets and highways with the frustrated expectation that insurance companies would conduct their business in such a way as to fulfill, not thwart, the basic purposes of the Financial Responsibility Law. This latter expectation can only be fulfilled, however, by recognition of the duty of the automobile liability insurer to undertake within a reasonable time from issuance of the policy a reasonable investigation of insurability and by penalizing the breach of that duty by loss of the right of rescission.

* * *

Our conclusion that an automobile liability insurer incurs the duty to conduct a reasonable investigation of insurability within a reasonable period of time after issuance of the policy, paralleling the line of decisions that hold that an insurer has a duty to act promptly on applications, "recognize[s] facts to be what they are. * * * "

The requirement that the carrier act promptly to determine insurability after issuance of an automobile liability insurance policy inures primarily to the benefit of those members of the public who suffer injury from negligent motorists and seek recovery against the responsible tortfeasors. The duty arises from the public policy that protects the innocent victim of the careless use of automobiles from an inability to sue a financially responsible defendant. This duty, which the insurer incurs with the issuance of an automobile liability policy, therefore runs directly to the class of potential victims of the insured. Consequently, when the insurer breaches that duty, it may not defeat recovery by the injured person, who has recovered a judgment against the insured, by relying on an untimely attempt to rescind.

*   *   *

State Farm contends that the "rule" that an injured person "stands in the shoes of" the insured bars the injured person's recovery against the insurer when the insured procured the policy through misrepresentation. It argues that the Alveses could not compel it to pay them if they had satisfied the judgment obtained by plaintiff, and that therefore plaintiff lacks any basis upon which to sue it on the policy.

State Farm's contention overlooks the fact that the automobile liability insurer's duty to conduct a reasonable investigation of insurability with due diligence inures directly to the benefit of persons such as the plaintiff who may be injured by the insured's use of his automobile. Upon the imposition of analogous duties in other contexts, we have held that the real beneficiary of such a duty cannot lose his remedy merely because the party whose relationship with the defendant gave rise to the duty would be barred from recovery.

Likewise, in the instant case, to allow the defendant to raise the defense of the insured's misrepresentation to an action by a person injured by the insured's automobile would frustrate the purpose of the imposition of a duty upon the insurer to undertake a reasonable investigation of insurability within a reasonable time from the acceptance of the application and issuance of the policy. The purpose of the imposition of such a duty is to reduce the number of motorists on our highways who are, in fact, financially irresponsible; the goal is to protect the motoring public generally against the inability to recover compensation for death or injuries caused by automobile accidents. Prompt notice to the insured of the revocation of his policy of insurance will most certainly impel him to seek other means of compliance with the potential requirements of the Financial Responsibility Law.
*   *   *

The judgment on plaintiff Barrera's complaint and defendant State Farm's cross-complaint is reversed. The cause is remanded for proceedings consistent with this opinion.

PROBLEMS

1. The plaintiff's husband and brother were occupants in an automobile which was hit from the rear by another automobile. The crash caused the gas tank in the automobile they occupied to rupture. They were burned to death in the fire which followed. The plaintiff brought an action under a wrongful death statute against the manufacturer of the automobile asking for money damages for the loss of her husband and brother. The evidence established that the automobile's design was defective in that the gas tank was subject to displacement and rupture by a variety of applied forces and the glass fiber bulkhead which separated the gas tank from the car's occupants was fragile and readily destructible. What judgment?

2. The plaintiff, a beauty salon patron, asked that her hair be dyed. The salon operator used a dye which caused the plaintiff physical injury. The plaintiff sues the manufacturer of the dye. What judgment?

3. The defendant was a drug manufacturer. It manufactured a drug for use by arthritis sufferers which was medically known to occasionally have an adverse effect upon one's vision. The plaintiff used this drug in accordance with the advice of his physician. The drug caused the plaintiff to suffer loss of vision. The plaintiff seeks money damages from the defendant. What judgment?

4. An automobile manufacturer prepared and distributed to each of its dealers a repair manual. This manual listed each of the various types of repairs that a dealer might make and then set forth the suggested charge for such repairs. Each dealer abided by the manual's rate schedule. The plaintiff had a dealer repair his automobile. He was charged the prescribed rate. He brought a class suit under the antitrust laws against the manufacturer and dealer, asking for triple damages and counsel fees on behalf of all persons who had made payments to the dealer in accordance with the repair manual's schedule of rates. The plaintiff contended that if the cost of repairs had been set independently by each dealer the repairs would have cost less. The defendants moved to dismiss the action. What judgment?

5. The plaintiff, prior to purchasing a home, inquired of the defendant insurance company if it issued policies to home owners in the geographic area in which the home was located. The plaintiff was advised that it did. The plaintiff purchased the home. Thereafter he applied for and received a home owner's policy which included fire and burglary provisions. It provided that "either party may cancel this agreement on 10 days notice." Two weeks later the defendant advised the plaintiff that it had decided to cancel the policy due to "unprecedented and unforeseeable losses" in the neighborhood. The plaintiff brought suit asking the court for an order directing the policy to be kept in force. What judgment?

Tucker, Adjudication Social Issues Pamph. MCB—12

Chapter 19

DEBTORS' RIGHTS

Imprisonment of debtors was once looked upon as an acceptable civil remedy. However, widespread hostility to this cruel form of relief, increased interest in the plight of debtors, and aloofness from the needs and desires of creditors brought an end to debtors' prisons. During the last two decades many voices have been heard severely criticizing and forcefully condemning a number of other once generally approved ways of treating debtors who fail to meet their financial obligations. As a result, by legislation or judicial decision, a number of remedies available to creditors as late as the early 1950's have been either narrowed or outlawed.

The seizure of a portion of a debtor's wages has long been popular with creditors and their attorneys as a means of obtaining payment from a recalcitrant debtor. Such seizure can be accomplished by use of a wage assignment or garnishment. Each requires the debtor's employer to deduct and forward to the creditor a sum of money from the debtor's wages at the end of each wage period until the indebtedness is paid. These two procedures differ in the way in which they come about. A wage assignment is an agreement between a creditor and a debtor in which the debtor consents to his employer deducting and transmitting part of his wages to the creditor in the event the debtor fails to pay his indebtedness. Garnishment is a court proceeding in which a court orders the employer to deduct a percentage of the employee's wages and to send that sum to the creditor or his attorney to reduce the indebtedness. The court's order is generally known as a garnishee order. The failure of an employer to comply with either a wage assignment or garnishee order renders him liable to the creditor for the amount of money he should have but failed to deduct from his employee's earnings.

State laws now impose various restrictions on the use of wage assignments and garnishee orders. Statutes may prescribe the format and minimum size print which may be used in wage assignments. The Uniform Consumer Credit Code, adopted by a few states, prohibits the use of wage assignments to collect a debt arising out of a consumer credit sale. Several states have outlawed garnishee orders. The Supreme Court has prohibited the use of garnishee orders in state proceedings until after the debtor has had the opportunity to challenge the creditor's claim that there is an outstanding indebtedness. The Uniform Consumer Credit Code bars use of garnishment proceedings before the entry of a judgment. The Consumer Credit Protection Act passed by Congress in 1968 limits the amount a state may require be deducted under a garnishment order to the lesser of (1) twenty-five percent of the disposable weekly earnings of the debtor or

(2) the amount by which the disposable earnings of the debtor exceed thirty times the federally established minimum hourly wage. Disposable earnings is defined as the amount remaining after the employer has deducted such sums from the employee's wages as required by law to be withheld, such as income tax and social security contributions. This restriction does not apply to (1) debts due to unpaid federal or state taxes and (2) court orders (a) calling for the support of any person or (b) issued pursuant to the bankruptcy laws.

Some employers, to avoid the cost and inconvenience of the record keeping involved in complying with garnishee orders, choose to discharge those employees against whom such orders are directed. The 1968 Consumer Credit Protection Act makes it a crime for an employer to discharge an employee whose wages are subject to but one garnishee order. The Act expressly allows states to place a more extensive prohibition on employers. Connecticut, for example, prohibits an employer from disciplining, suspending, or discharging an employee because of the placing of garnishee orders on his wages, unless more than seven orders are served on the employer in any one calendar year.

The amount of money a lender charges a borrower for the use of money is known as interest. Interest charges have been regulated since ancient times. At present statutes prescribe different maximum interest rates for different types of loans. Rates usually vary from six to eighteen percent. Ordinarily corporate borrowers may be charged whatever rate of interest the parties to the loan agree upon. When a lender charges a sum of interest greater than allowed by law he is said to be guilty of usury. Usury is generally treated as a crime as well as a civil wrong. Depending on the applicable law, a lender who has made a usurious loan may (1) be denied the right to recover either interest or the amount of the loan, or (2) be denied recovery of any interest or only the amount of the overcharge, or (3) be obliged to pay the borrower two times the amount of the overcharge. The Consumer Credit Protection Act of 1968 requires that those who extend consumer credit disclose to the borrower, clearly and conspicuously, in writing, the rate of interest he will have to pay for the loan. All lenders must use the formula prescribed by the Federal Reserve Board when stating the rate of interest they are demanding of the borrower. In addition, every individual cost element of the loan must be itemized and the total dollar cost stated in writing.

It has long been the practice for consumers who purchase merchandise on credit to agree that should the purchaser fail to pay his indebtedness the seller may arrange for the retaking and resale of the sold merchandise. Should the resale fail to yield a sum sufficient to satisfy the purchaser's outstanding indebtedness the seller by law is entitled to recover a deficiency judgment against the debtor. This judgment is equal to the balance due the seller after making allowance for the sum paid by the purchaser and the amount recovered as a result of the resale.

To prevent a seller from taking unfair advantage of a purchaser whose merchandise is retaken and resold state law generally details the steps a creditor must follow to lawfully retake and resell merchandise if he wishes to thereafter obtain a deficiency judgment.

Advocates of debtors' rights see deficiency judgments as oppressive and unfair and ask that they be outlawed. They object to them on several grounds. Such judgments oblige a debtor to pay in full for merchandise he can no longer enjoy. Some merchants sell goods to persons whom they know cannot afford to make the purchase but they make the sale anyway since if they are not paid they can regain the merchandise and keep whatever sums of money they received from the purchaser as well as by way of resale. If the purchaser is employed a merchant who obtains a deficiency judgment can force payment by resorting to garnishment proceedings. Those who oppose the use of deficiency judgments have garnered the support of a number of state legislatures. In those states in which the Uniform Consumer Credit Code has been adopted a merchant may not obtain a deficiency judgment against one who has bought consumer goods which cost $1,000 or less unless the debtor intentionally damaged the goods or refused to allow the merchant to repossess it. State legislation independent of the Code may bar the entry of a deficiency judgment in cases in which a creditor has repossessed consumer goods.

A lost credit card has been a source of serious financial loss for some credit card holders. Those who use credit cards invariably agree that until they notify the issuer in writing of the loss or theft of the card they are responsible for the unauthorized use of the card. Thieves, adept at obtaining and using stolen credit cards, have forced courts to decide under what circumstances card holders are responsible for the unauthorized use of their cards. A number of courts have, under certain circumstances, invoked equitable principles to shield a card holder from liability. For example, should it appear that the card holder has never made more than sporadic use of his card, and then only to purchase inexpensive items, continuous use of the card by the thief to make costly purchases has served as a basis for a court refusing to hold the card owner liable for the thief's purchases on the ground that the unusual use of the card should have alerted the card issuer to the fact that the card was being used without the owner's consent. Similarly, when it appeared that the card holder was of the opinion that his credit card was safely stored away but it had in fact been stolen, the card holder was excused from having to pay the card issuer for the indebtedness incurred by the unauthorized use of the card. In general, however, card holders have been held liable for the full amount of the indebtedness incurred by one who made use of the card without the owner's consent before the owner notified the issuer of the theft or loss of his card.

A 1970 Amendment to the Federal Truth in Lending Act has placed a limit on the card holder's responsibility for the unauthorized use of his credit card. Under the law, after January 23, 1971, the card holder of a newly issued credit card cannot be held liable for more than fifty dollars for the unauthorized use of his card and then only if the issuer "gives adequate notice to the card holder of the potential liability, the card issuer has provided the card holder with a self-addressed, prestamped notification to be mailed by the card holder in the event of the loss or theft of the credit card, and the unauthorized use occurs before the card holder has notified the card issuer that an unauthorized use of the credit card has occurred or may occur as the result of the loss, theft, or otherwise." In addition the card issuer must provide "a method whereby the user of such card can be identified as the person authorized to use it." Presumably a photograph of the card holder or a place on the card on which he must affix his signature would satisfy this identification requirement. Under the Amendment "a card holder notifies a card issuer by taking such steps as may be reasonably required in the ordinary course of business to provide the card issuer with the pertinent information whether or not any particular officer, employee, or agent of the card issuer does in fact receive such information." This portion of the Amendment suggests that when a card holder mails a notice to the issuer stating that his card has been stolen or lost he has done what the law requires of him to avoid liability for any unauthorized use of the card made after he has so notified the card issuer.

During the 1960's there was widespread dissatisfaction with the practice of business and financial enterprises mailing credit cards to persons without the recipients having requested that a card be issued to them. This often resulted in recipients incurring debts which accrued interest at the rate of eighteen percent per annum. Many such card holders lacked the financial wherewithal with which to pay the debts which arose as a result of their unwise use of credit cards which were intentionally placed in their hands by the issuer. At times unasked for credit cards ended up in the hands of thieves and the person named as the card holder was forced to defend himself against the issuer's claims that the card was used with his consent or was used after he received and then lost it. In the 1970 Amendment to the Truth in Lending Act Congress prohibited the issuance of credit cards "except in response to a request or application therefor" unless the new card is a renewal or a substitute for a previously accepted card.

In consumer creditor-debtor relationships it is usually the creditor who prepares the agreement. In most cases the only contribution the debtor makes to the agreement is his signature. As authors creditors invariably include provisions which maximize their rights and minimize their obligations. Some of the contract clauses commonly used to attain these objectives are: (1) Exculpatory clauses. These limit or eliminate the liability of the creditor for particular kinds of conduct or consequences. For example, a contract may provide that in the event goods are defective the creditor's total obligation, regardless of the loss caused the debtor, is to replace the defective goods. (2) Waiver provisions. These provide that the debtor surrenders particular rights, such as the right to a trial by jury, in the event he is sued by the creditor on account of a breach of the agreement. On the other hand, the creditor expressly retains all of his rights under the terms of the agreement. The agreement may provide that the failure of the creditor to insist upon his rights shall not be construed as a waiver of such rights. (3) Small size print. All or portions of the agreement may be in such small size print that a provision is almost illegible. Frequently exculpatory clauses and clauses which set forth that the debtor waives one or more of his rights appear in exceedingly small print. (4) Attorneys' fees. A debtor may agree that in the event the creditor sues him because he failed to meet his obligations he will pay the creditor's attorneys' fees.

At times courts refuse to enforce exculpatory or waiver provisions for such reasons as: (1) the provision violates public policy or places an unreasonable burden on the debtor or is unconscionable, (2) there was too great a disparity of bargaining power between the creditor and the debtor, with the debtor having nothing to say about the terms of the agreement, (3) the print used was so small that it was virtually invisible in the context in which it appeared, or (4) the creditor's conduct was so inconsistent with the agreement that it is the creditor's conduct rather than the agreement which must determine the rights and duties of the parties. The Uniform Commercial Code bars the enforcement of unconscionable arrangements in sale agreements. The Uniform Consumer Credit Code suggests that states either limit a debtor's obligation to pay attorneys' fees to fifteen percent of the indebtedness due after default or make all agreements to pay counsel fees unenforceable.

When a debtor signs a negotiable instrument in favor of a creditor the creditor may negotiate the instrument to a third party. If this party gives value for the instrument, takes it in good faith before it is overdue, without any notice of any reason why the debtor should not be required to pay the instrument, he may claim the benefits of a holder in due course. Under the law governing negotiable instruments a debtor is obliged to pay the amount due by the terms of a negotiable instrument to a holder in due course when he would be excused from paying the seller to whom he first delivered the instrument. A purchaser of merchandise who delivers a negotiable instrument to a seller, for example, would not be obliged to pay the seller if the seller failed to deliver the merchandise, had misrepresented its nature or quality, or delivered defective goods. Such defenses may not be used against a holder in due course. A holder in due course can demand payment in full even though the purchaser did not get the benefit of his bargain.

A number of courts have ruled that when there is a very close relationship between a seller of consumer goods and the holder in due course the purchaser may use the same defense against the holder in due course as he could if he was sued by the seller. Some states, by statute, have prohibited the use of negotiable instruments in sales made in the purchaser's home if the seller came to the purchaser's home without a prior invitation. The Uniform Consumer Credit Act provides that the only kind of negotiable instrument a seller of consumer goods can lawfully take from a purchaser is a check. **One of** the options a state may elect if it decides to adopt the Act is to reject the holder in due course concept in all consumer credit sales.

SNIADACH v. FAMILY FINANCE CORPORATION OF BAY VIEW

Supreme Court of the United States, 1969.
89 S.Ct. 1820, 395 U.S. 337, 23 L.Ed.2d 349.

Wisconsin law permitted garnishment proceedings to be instituted without a court first deciding whether or not there was a valid claim against the individual whose wages were to be seized. The defendant commenced a garnishment proceeding against the plaintiff. The plaintiff's employer was directed to withhold one-half of the plaintiff's wages. The plaintiff brought an action to set the garnishment proceedings aside. She claimed that the procedure denied her due process of law since she had been deprived of the use of one-half of her wages without a hearing. The trial court upheld the state's procedure. The state supreme court affirmed. Certiorari was granted.

MR. JUSTICE DOUGLAS delivered the opinion of the Court.

* * *

The question is not whether the Wisconsin law is a wise law or unwise law. Our concern is not what philosophy Wisconsin should or should not embrace. * * * We do not sit as a super-legislative body. In this case the sole question is whether there has been a taking of property without that procedural due process that is required by the Fourteenth Amendment. We have dealt over and over again with the question of what constitutes "the right to be heard" * * * within the meaning of procedural due process. * * * In the context of this case the question is whether the interim freezing of the wages without a chance to be heard violates procedural due process.

* * * The fact that a procedure would pass muster under a feudal regime does not mean it gives necessary protection to all property in its modern forms. We deal here with wages—a specialized type of property presenting distinct problems in our economic system. * * *

A prejudgment garnishment of the Wisconsin type is a taking which may impose tremendous hardship on wage earners with families to support. Until a recent Act of Congress, * * * which forbids discharge of employees on the ground that their wages have been garnished, garnishment often meant the loss of a job. Over and beyond that was the great drain on family income. As stated by Congressman Reuss:

"The idea of wage garnishment in advance of judgment, of trustee process, of wage attachment, or whatever it is called is a most inhuman doctrine. It compels the wage earner, trying to keep his family together, to be driven below the poverty level."

Recent investigations of the problem have disclosed the grave injustices made possible by prejudgment garnishment whereby the sole opportunity to be heard comes after the taking. * * *

The leverage of the creditor on the wage earner is enormous. The creditor tenders not only the original debt but the "collection fees" incurred by his attorneys in the garnishment proceedings:

"The debtor whose wages are tied up by a writ of garnishment, and who is usually in need of money, is in no position to resist demands for collection fees. If the debt is small, the debtor will be under considerable pressure to pay the debt and collection charges in order to get his wages back. If the debt is large, he will often sign a new contract of 'payment schedule' which incorporates these additional charges."

Apart from those collateral consequences, it appears that in Wisconsin the statutory exemption granted the wage earner is "generally insufficient to support the debtor for any one week."

The result is that a prejudgment garnishment of the Wisconsin type may as a practical matter drive a wage-earning family to the wall. Where the taking of one's property is so obvious, it needs no extended argument to conclude that absent notice and a prior hearing * * * this prejudgment garnishment procedure violates the fundamental principles of due process.

Reversed.

LISI v. ALITALIA–LINEE AEREE ITALIANE, S.p.A.

United States Court of Appeals, Second Circuit, 1966.
370 F.2d 508, affirmed 88 S.Ct. 1193, 390 U.S. 455, 20 L.Ed.2d 27,
rehearing denied 88 S.Ct. 1801, 391 U.S. 929, 20 L.Ed.2d 671.

Article 3 of the Warsaw Convention, a treaty to which the United States is a party, permits an airline engaged in "international transportation" to limit its liability to approximately $8300 for each passenger injured or killed on one of its flights. To take advantage of the $8300 limit an airline must call it to the attention of its passengers by including a statement to this effect on that portion of its tickets and baggage checks it delivers to them. The Convention permits an airline and an individual passenger to agree to a higher limit.

The next of kin of several passengers who were killed in a crash of an airplane operated by the defendant sued the defendant for money damages in excess of $8300. As a partial defense to the suit, the defendant set forth in its answer that it had complied with the Warsaw Convention and accordingly the plaintiffs could recover no more than $8300. The plaintiffs claimed that the defendant had failed to comply with the Treaty since the print on its tickets and baggage checks was too small to be noticed. The trial court rejected the partial defense pleaded by the defendant. The defendant appealed.

IRVING R. KAUFMAN, CIRCUIT JUDGE:

* * *

It is conceded that the flight in question meets the definition of "international transportation" contained in Article 1 of the Convention. Therefore, the provisions of the Convention quite properly govern the present action. * * *

It is apparent that Alitalia relies on a literal reading of the Convention for its assertions. We reject the interpretation it urges upon us. While it is true that the language of the Convention is relevant to our decision, it must not become, as Justice Frankfurter stated it, a "verbal prison." * * * The task of ascertaining the meaning of words is difficult, and one certain way of misinterpreting them is by a literal reading. As Learned Hand put it, "words are such temperamental beings that the surest way to lose their essence to to take them at their face." * * * Thus, the language of Article 3 cannot be considered in isolation; rather, it must be viewed in light of the other Articles and the overall purposes of the Convention. * * *

This is not the first occasion on which we have been called upon to interpret the language of the Convention's delimiting provisions. For example, in Mertens v. Flying Tiger Line, * * * we were asked to decide whether presenting a ticket to a passenger after he boarded the carrier's plane, constituted a "delivery" within the meaning of Article 3(2). We stated:

We read Article 3(2) to require that the *ticket be delivered to the passenger in such a manner as to afford him a reasonable opportunity to take measures to protect himself against the limitation of liability.* Such self-protective measures, could consist of, for example, deciding not to take the flight, entering in a special contract with the carrier, or taking out additional insurance for the flight. The Convention specifically provides that "the carrier and the passenger may agree to a higher limit of liability" (Article 22(1)) and there would be little reason to make this provision, to require that the ticket state that the liability of the carrier is limited (Article 3(1) (e)), and to require that such a ticket be delivered to the passenger unless the Convention also required that the ticket *be delivered in such circumstances as to afford the passenger a reasonable opportunity to take these self-protective measures.* * * * (emphasis added).

We held, accordingly, that the delivery was inadequate, and the Convention's fixed limits of liability were not available.

Later, a similar result was reached by the Ninth Circuit in Warren v. Flying Tiger Line, Inc., * * *. There the passenger was given a "boarding ticket" or "pass" at the foot of the ramp leading to the aircraft. The Court decided that the "delivery" must be made sufficiently in advance so that the passenger will have the opportunity to take self-protective measures, such as purchasing additional insurance if he so chooses. The "delivery" of a boarding ticket at the foot of the ramp as the plane was about to depart, did not suffice therefor. The carrier, accordingly, was barred by Article 3(2) from availing itself of the Convention's liability limitation provisions.

We believe that the reasoning of the *Mertens* and *Warren* decisions is apposite to the case now before us. The Convention's arbitrary limitations on liability—which have been severely and repeatedly criticized—are advantageous to the carrier. But the *quid pro quo* for this one-sided advantage is delivery to the passenger of a ticket and baggage check which give him notice that on the air trip he is about to take, the amount of recovery to him or his family in the event of a crash, is limited very substantially. Thus the passenger is given the opportunity to purchase additional flight insurance or to take such other steps for his self-protection as he sees fit.

This notice to passengers is especially important in this country where the overwhelming number of people who travel by air do so on domestic flights, for which the Convention's restrictions on liability are inapplicable. It is too much to expect these passengers to be sufficiently sophisticated to realize that although they are traveling the same number of miles on an international flight that they have frequently traveled domestically, the amount they may recover in the event of an accident is drastically reduced. In short, it is clear from the *ratio decidendi* of the *Mertens* and *Warren* cases, that the inquiry that must be made if the Convention's Articles are to be given meaning, is "[w]hether the ticket was delivered to the passenger in such a manner as to afford him a reasonable opportunity to take self-protective measures * * *." * * *

We proceed to determine, therefore, whether the particular tickets and baggage checks involved in the present case gave the appellees adequate notice. On the front of the ticket and baggage check, in exceedingly small print, was the following message: "Each passenger should carefully examine this ticket, particularly the Conditions on page 4." And, at this point, we note that one of our reasons in Mertens v. Flying Tiger Line, Inc., * * * for precluding the carrier from limiting its liability under the Convention was that the required statement on the ticket "was printed in such a manner as to virtually be unnoticeable and unreadable * * *."

Judge MacMahon appropriately characterized the "notice" to the passengers in his pithy conclusion as "camouflaged in Lilliputian print in a thicket of 'Conditions of Contract' * * *. Indeed the exculpatory statements on which defendant relies are virtually invisible. They are ineffectively positioned, diminutively sized, and unemphasized by bold face type, contrasting color, or anything else. The simple truth is that they are so artfully camouflaged that their presence is concealed." * * *

We agree that a jury could not reasonably have found that the tickets and baggage checks gave the passengers the required notice.

The District Court properly granted partial summary judgment striking out these affirmative defenses of appellant.

Affirmed.

PROBLEMS

1. The plaintiff obtained a judgment against the defendant. It was not paid. To prevent the plaintiff from seizing his assets the defendant transferred them to a close friend. On discovering what had taken place, the plaintiff brought a second lawsuit against the defendant, claiming that the defendant's conduct constituted a new wrong to him for which he was entitled to a judgment for the additional damages he suffered due to the transfer. Is the creditor entitled to a second judgment?

2. The defendants, husband and wife, entered into an agreement with the plaintiff which required them to make monthly payments for coupons delivered to them by the plaintiff. The coupons could be used to purchase merchandise from the plaintiff. The defendants never used the coupons to purchase any merchandise. Under the terms of the agreement the defendants were obliged to make monthly payments to pay for the coupons and to pay interest on the unpaid balance due for the cost of the coupons even if they never used them. Is the plaintiff entitled to a judgment against the defendants for (1) the cost of the coupons and (2) the interest?

3. A finance company purchased a negotiable instrument at 20% of its face value. The defendant had signed the instrument in favor of a disruptable home improvement firm. The firm failed to keep its contract with the defendant. Is the finance company entitled to a judgment against the defendant for the face amount of the instrument?

4. The sale agreement provided that in the event the defendant delivered merchandise which was not as warranted its liability was limited to replacing the defective merchandise. The defendant sold the plaintiff a quantity of rubber hose. It was installed in equipment owned by the plaintiff. The hose was not as warranted. While the equipment was in use the hose burst, causing substantial damage to the equipment. The plaintiff brought a lawsuit against the defendant asking for money damages in an amount necessary to pay for the cost of repairing the damaged equipment. The defendant insisted that its liability was limited to supplying the plaintiff with more rubber hose. Judgment for whom?

5. By state statute a welfare recipient was excused from paying rent to the landlord of a premises which did not comply with the building code requirement that residential property not be in a dangerous or hazardous condition or be in such a state that it was detrimental to life or health. The landlord contended that this statute denied him of his property without due process of law. What judgment?

6. The plaintiff, a credit card club, agreed with the defendant, a card holder, that it would pay all sellers of merchandise who had valid claims due to them as a result of the defendant's use of his credit card. The plaintiff would then charge the defendant for the amount it had dispersed to such sellers. After the defendant notified the club he had lost his credit card the club proceeded to pay sellers who delivered merchandise to a thief who had used the card and had forged the defendant's signature on purchase slips. The plaintiff was not legally obliged to pay the sellers. Is the plaintiff entitled to a judgment against the defendant for the sums of money it voluntarily paid the sellers?

7. Under state law a creditor, prior to a court hearing, could use garnishment proceedings to prevent the person the creditor claimed was indebted to him from using any money the supposed debtor had on deposit with a bank. The alleged debtor claimed that use of garnishment proceedings to deny him use of his money in his bank account prior to a hearing in which it was adjudged that he was indebted to the creditor denied him due process of law. Is he correct?

8. State law permitted a seller to enter the home of a purchaser who failed to make payments on merchandise he bought on credit and to repossess the merchandise. The plaintiff, a purchaser of merchandise on credit, challenged the law on the ground that it violated his right to privacy. What judgment?

Part Six

THE POOR

Chapter 20

THE INDIGENT AND COURT PROCEEDINGS

Our legal system is classified as an "adversary" system. The plaintiff and the defendant are viewed as contestants locked in a struggle in which each is in quest of a favorable decision. Each litigant, whether he be embroiled in a trial or an appeal, has the opportunity to present his side of the case and to challenge the position taken by his adversary. The astuteness with which the litigants carry on their offensive and defensive maneuvers plays a significant part in shaping the outcome of the litigation.

The adversary system patently offers a better chance to succeed to the litigant who can most masterfully recruit and make use of the instruments with which a lawsuit must be waged. Legal counsel, expert witnesses, and investigators may be crucial elements in determining how a court will rule. Here the party with the greater financial resources enjoys a distinct advantage. An indigent, simply because of his indigence, may be destined to lose. Due to his lack of resources he may not be able to effectively present his position nor counter his opponent's moves. His own maneuvers may be but a shadow of what they might have been if he had the wherewithal to obtain the essential tools of litigation.

The principle of *in forma pauperis* has long served as a basis for courts extending limited assistance to indigent parties. *In forma pauperis* means "to proceed as a poor person." To be allowed to proceed in such a fashion an indigent must ask the court to be excused from paying particular court fees or from having to comply with court rules which require him to incur expenses. Under this principle a poor person does not have a right to proceed as a poor person. *In forma pauperis* is a privilege to be granted or withheld in the discretion of the court. To decide if permission should or should not be granted the court evaluates the probability of the indigent's success in the proceeding. If the court decides that it is improbable that the poor person will succeed, his request will be denied. This doctrine is not intended to accord the same legal rights to all indigents or to treat the poor and the affluent alike. At best, it serves to ameliorate, to a degree, the harshness of the discrimination the legal process makes between the poor and the rich.

179

In Griffin v. Illinois,[1] decided in 1956, the defendant challenged a state criminal appellate procedure which required an appellant to pay for a transcript of the trial court proceedings. Due to his lack of funds the defendant was unable to appeal his conviction. In striking down the state practice the Supreme Court did not rule that a state is obliged to make appellate review available to whomever is convicted of a crime. However, it declared that if a state does choose to make appellate review available it may not make it available to the rich and deny it to the poor. A standard tied to the ability to pay was condemned as a denial of due process as well as an invidious discrimination in violation of the equal protection of the laws clause of the Fourteenth Amendment.

Since *Griffin* the Court has acknowledged that in practice it is impossible to place the poor and the rich on exactly the same footing. It is assumed that perfect equality is unattainable. But the Constitution does outlaw differences in the "access to the instruments needed to vindicate legal rights" which are based on nothing more than the defendant's "financial situation." Simply because one accused or convicted of a crime is destitute he may not be denied the opportunity to make use of any process which would be open to him under federal or state law if he were affluent.

The Sixth Amendment governs federal criminal proceedings. It provides that an accused shall "have the assistance of counsel for his defense." This right is enjoyed by all defendants, the very wealthy and the very poor. If a defendant cannot afford to pay for an attorney, and a lawyer is not otherwise made available to him, the federal court is obliged to assign him counsel. By rule, the Supreme Court has provided that in all but "petty" criminal cases, "petty" being left undefined, federal magistrates must inform one accused of a crime that counsel will be furnished him or her at the expense of the government if he or she is too poor to hire an attorney. Attorneys assigned by the federal courts to represent indigent defendants are paid by the federal government in accordance with a fee schedule established by Congress.

The due process clause of the Fourteenth Amendment requires that a state give one accused of a crime the opportunity to retain counsel. In 1932 the Supreme Court ruled that under particular circumstances one charged with the commission of a very serious crime had a constitutional right under the due process clause of the Fourteenth Amendment to demand that the state provide him with counsel if he lacked sufficient funds to personally retain an attorney. In the Court's opinion certain circumstances, such as the defendant's age or his inability to read or write, might render a trial a meaningless gesture if the accused did not have counsel to assist him.[2] For the next thirty years the Court followed a circumstances test. It would rule a state conviction unconstitutional if it appeared after "an appraisal of the totality of facts" that a defendant, convicted of a felony, too poor to retain counsel and not assigned counsel by the state, had, in the absence of counsel, been denied "fundamental fairness, shocking to the universal sense of justice." In 1963, in Gideon v. Wainwright,[3] the Court abandoned the circumstances test. It proclaimed that regardless of the circumstances it was a denial of due process for a state to try one charged with a serious crime without extending to him the opportunity to have counsel assigned to assist him in his defense. As yet the Supreme Court has failed to rule whether or not one accused of a "petty" crime is entitled to demand that counsel be assigned to assist him if he lacks adequate funds with which to retain an attorney. State law may provide that counsel assigned to assist an indigent defendant is to be paid out of public funds.

While an indigent defendant in a criminal proceeding has a constitutional right to counsel he does not have a constitutional right to demand that the federal or state court supply him with the services of experts or investigators. Congress has provided that a trial court, if satisfied that such services are "necessary" may, at the expense of the federal government, arrange to furnish them. State law may offer similar assistance at public expense to indigent defendants.

The principles found in *Griffin* and *Gideon* are confined to criminal proceedings. In other kinds of cases an indigent does not have a constitutional right to assigned counsel. Congress has provided that a federal court may, in its discretion, request an attorney to serve as counsel for an indigent in a civil action. A court cannot compel an attorney to comply with such a request. If the attorney agrees to serve he is not entitled to compensation from the federal government. Ordinarily a court will undertake to supply legal services "only if the likelihood of success is more than just doubtful." Only in exceptional cases will a court request an attorney to assist an indigent who wishes to prosecute a case to obtain money damages. State laws empower state courts under stated conditions to assign counsel to assist indigents in civil cases. Government and privately sponsored programs supply legal services for indigents in a variety of ways in various types of civil proceedings.

The Supreme Court has ruled that persons who are on welfare may not be denied the opportunity to obtain a divorce simply because they cannot afford to pay the fees the state usually requires of those who wish to sue for a divorce. To bar poor persons from seeking a divorce, a form of relief which could not be obtained other than by litigation in a state court, was found to be a denial of due process.

A court may invoke the doctrine of *in forma pauperis* to excuse an indigent in a civil proceeding from having to pay filing fees or satisfying court rules which necessitate the expenditure of funds. For example, an indigent may be permitted to appeal without having to

---

3. 83 S.Ct. 792, 372 U.S. 335, 9 L.Ed.
2d 799, 93 A.L.R.2d 733 (1963).

file printed briefs with the appellate court. A less expensive form of reproduction, such as typing, may be authorized.

A society which lauds individual achievement and is dedicated to a work ethic understandably looks with dismay on persons who, although physically and mentally capable of working, fail to do so. State vagrancy statutes reflect approval of individual achievement and a work ethic. Such statutes treat as criminals those persons who fail to comply with the tenets of this ethic. While the precise content of vagrancy statutes varies, in general they strike out at idleness, making it a crime for a person, able to work, to be found simply loitering or strolling about without being able to give a good account for such behavior or having no visible means of support. Vagrancy statutes are inconsistent with present day concern with the plight of the nation's poor. Already a number of states have repealed such legislation. Some courts have struck down vagrancy statutes as unconstitutional on such grounds as: (1) the requirement that one must give a "good account" of his behavior is too vague and therefore violative of due process of law which requires that a state give a person reasonable notice of what the law requires of him, (2) the words "loitering" and "strolling" and the phrase "no visible means of support" are unconstitutionally vague, (3) the statute assumes "that idleness and poverty are invariably associated with criminality" and it seeks to punish persons who may not in fact be guilty of criminal behavior, (5) and it makes "a crime out of status or condition as opposed to behavior," treating "idleness or indigency coupled with being able-bodied" as a crime.

While debtors' prisons fell into disuse a long time ago only recently has the Supreme Court ruled unconstitutional a state practice which kept one convicted of a crime in prison after he had served the maximum period of imprisonment allowed by law because he was too poor to pay the fine also imposed upon him. The Supreme Court has declared unconstitutional a state statute which provided that one found guilty of violating a traffic regulation had the option of paying a fine or going to jail to work off the fine. The Court ruled that it was a denial of due process to imprison a poor person simply because he was unable to pay the fine while one who had funds with which to pay the fine could avoid imprisonment.

GRIFFIN v. ILLINOIS

Supreme Court of the United States, 1956.
76 S.Ct. 585, 351 U.S. 12, 100 L.Ed. 891, 55 A.L.R.2d 1055, rehearing denied
76 S.Ct. 844, 351 U.S. 958, 100 L.Ed. 1480.

The petitioners were tried and convicted of armed robbery. Illinois law provided that all persons convicted of a crime had a right to appeal. If one wished to have the appellate court review the trial court's proceedings in their entirety he had to submit to the appellate court a certified copy of the trial court record and a transcript of the proceedings. The petitioners requested the trial judge to supply them with these two items at state expense on the ground that they were too poor to pay for them. Their request was denied. They claimed that the court's refusal to accede to their demands denied them due process and equal protection of the laws. The petitioner's challenge to the trial court's decision in state post-conviction proceedings was unsuccessful. Certiorari was granted.

MR. JUSTICE BLACK announced the judgment of the Court and an opinion in which THE CHIEF JUSTICE, MR. JUSTICE DOUGLAS, and MR. JUSTICE CLARK, join.

* * *

Providing equal justice for poor and rich, weak and powerful alike is an age-old problem. People have never ceased to hope and strive to move closer to that goal. * * * In this tradition, our own constitutional guaranties of due process and equal protection both call for procedures in criminal trials which allow no invidious discriminations between persons and different groups of persons. Both equal protection and due process emphasize the central aim of our entire judicial system—all people charged with crime must, so far as the law is concerned, "stand on an equality before the bar of justice in every American court." * * * In criminal trials a State can no more discriminate on account of poverty than on account of religion, race, or color. Plainly the ability to pay costs in advance bears no rational relationship to a defendant's guilt or innocence and could not be used as an excuse to deprive a defendant of a fair trial. * * *

There is no meaningful distinction between a rule which would deny the poor the right to defend themselves in a trial court and one which effectively denies the poor an adequate appellate review accorded to all who have money enough to pay the costs in advance. It is true that a State is not required by the Federal Constitution to provide appellate courts or a right to appellate review at all. * * * But that is not to say that a State that does grant appellate review can do so in a way that discriminates against some convicted defendants on account of their poverty. Appellate review has now become an integral part of the Illinois trial system for finally adjudicating the guilt or innocence of a defendant. Consequently at all stages of the proceedings the Due Process and Equal Protection Clauses protect persons like petitioners from invidious discriminations. * * * Statistics show that a substantial proportion of criminal convictions are reversed by state appellate courts. Thus to deny adequate review to the poor means that many of them may lose their life, liberty or property because of unjust convictions which appellate courts would set aside. * * * There can be no equal justice where the kind of trial a man gets depends on the amount of money he has. Destitute defendants must be afforded as adequate appellate review as defendants who have money enough to buy transcripts.

The Illinois Supreme Court denied these petitioners relief under the Post-Conviction Act because of its holding that no constitutional rights were violated. In view of our holding to the contrary the State Supreme Court may decide that petitioners are now entitled to a transcript, * * *. We do not hold, however, that Illinois must purchase a stenographer's transcript in every case where a defendant cannot buy it. The Supreme Court may find other means of affording adequate and effective appellate review to indigent defendants. * * * The Illinois Supreme Court appears to have broad power to promulgate rules of procedure and appellate practice. We are confident that the State will provide corrective rules to meet the problem which this case lays bare.

* * *

Vacated and remanded.

WILLIAMS v. ILLINOIS

Supreme Court of the United States, 1970.
90 S.Ct. 2018, 399 U.S. 235, 26 L.Ed.2d 586.

Convicted of petty theft Williams received the maximum sentence allowed under Illinois law: one year imprisonment and a $500 fine. He was also taxed $5 court costs. State law directed that one who failed to pay a fine or court costs must remain in prison after the completion of his sentence until he "worked off" the fine and court costs at the rate of $5 per day. While in prison Williams filed a petition asking that the order that he remain in prison beyond one year because of the nonpayment of the $505 be vacated. He informed the court he had been and was without funds with which to pay the fine and costs. His petition was dismissed on the ground that it was premature, he having served less than four months of his one year sentence. The state supreme court affirmed, but on the ground that "there is no denial of equal protection of the law when an indigent defendant is imprisoned to satisfy payment of the fine." He appealed.

MR. CHIEF JUSTICE BURGER delivered the opinion of the Court.

* * *

The custom of imprisoning a convicted defendant for nonpayment of fines dates back to medieval England and has long been practiced in this country. At the present time all States and the Federal Government have statutes authorizing incarceration under such circumstances. Most States permit imprisonment beyond the maximum term allowed by law, and in some there is no limit on the length of time one may serve for nonpayment. While neither the antiquity of a practice nor the fact of steadfast legislative and judicial adherence to it through the centuries insulates it from constitutional attack, these factors should be weighed in the balance. Indeed, in prior cases this Court seems to have tacitly approved incarceration to "work off" unpaid fines. * * *

The need to be open to reassessment of ancient practices other than those explicitly mandated by the Constitution is illustrated by the present case since the greatly increased use of fines as a criminal sanction has made nonpayment a major cause of incarceration in this country. Default imprisonment has traditionally been justified on the grounds it is a coercive device to ensure obedience to the judgment of the court. Thus, commitment for failure to pay has not been viewed as a part of the punishment or as an increase in the penalty; rather, it has been viewed as a means of enabling the court to enforce collection of money which a convicted defendant was obligated by the sentence to pay. The additional imprisonment, it has been said, may always be avoided by payment of the fine.

We conclude that when the aggregate imprisonment exceeds the maximum period fixed by the statute and results directly from an involuntary nonpayment of a fine or court costs we are confronted with an impermissible discrimination which rests on ability to pay, and accordingly, we reverse.

* * * In the years since the *Griffin* case the Court has had frequent occasion to reaffirm allegiance to the basic command that justice be applied equally to all persons. Subsequent decisions of this Court have pointedly demonstrated that the passage of time has heightened rather than weakened the attempts to mitigate the disparate treatment of indigents in the criminal process. Applying the teaching of the *Griffin* case here, we conclude that an indigent criminal defendant may not be imprisoned in default of payment of a fine beyond the maximum authorized by the statute regulating the substantive offense.

A State has wide latitude in fixing the punishment for state crimes. Thus, appellant does not assert that Illinois could not have appropriately fixed the penalty, in the first instance, at one year and 101 days. Nor has the claim been advanced that the sentence imposed was excessive in light of the circumstances of the commission of this particular offense. However, once the State has defined the outer limits of incarceration necessary to satisfy its penological interests and policies, it may not then subject a certain class of convicted defendants to a period of imprisonment beyond the statutory maximum solely by reason of their indigency.

* * *

The mere fact that an indigent in a particular case may be imprisoned for a longer time than is a non-indigent convicted of the same offense does not, of course, give rise to a violation of the Equal Protection Clause. Sentencing judges are vested with wide discretion in the exceedingly difficult task of determining the appropriate punishment in the countless variety of situations which appear. The Constitution permits qualitative differences in meeting punishment and there is no requirement that two persons convicted of the same offense receive identical sentences. Thus it was that in Williams v. New York, * * * (1949), we said "The belief no longer prevails that every offense in a like legal category calls for an identical punishment without regard to the past life and habits of a particular offender."

Nothing in today's decision curtails the sentencing prerogative of a judge because, as noted previously, the sovereign's purpose in confining an indigent beyond the statutory maximum is to provide a coercive means of collecting or "working out" a fine. After having taken into consideration the wide range of factors underlying the exercise of his sentencing function, nothing we now hold precludes a judge from imposing on an indigent, as on any defendant, the maximum penalty prescribed by law.

It bears emphasis that our holding does not deal with a judgment of confinement for nonpayment of a fine in the familiar pattern of alternative sentence of "$30 or 30 days." We hold only that a State may not constitutionally imprison beyond the maximum duration fixed by statute a defendant who is financially unable to pay a fine. A statute permitting a sentence of both imprisonment and fine cannot be parlayed into a longer term of imprisonment than is fixed by the statute since to do so would be to accomplish indirectly as to an indigent that which cannot be done directly. We have no occasion to reach the question whether a State is precluded in any other circumstances from holding an indigent accountable for a fine by use of penal sanction. We hold only that the Equal Protection Clause of the Fourteenth Amendment requires that the statutory ceiling placed on imprisonment for any substantive offense be the same for all defendants irrespective of their economic status.

*   *   *

Judgment vacated and case remanded.

PROBLEMS

1. The defendant informed the trial judge that he lacked funds with which to retain counsel. He then rejected each of ten attorneys assigned to him on the ground that none of them were of sufficient stature to fully comprehend the intricacies of his case and that he clearly saw legal issues which none of them could see. He insisted that the court assign him one of the five lawyers he named. Each was a prominent and an experienced attorney. When asked by the court to assist the defendant each declined on the ground that he had several cases pending in which he was representing an indigent defendant. At that point the court assigned another attorney to assist the defendant. The defendant told the judge he did not want that attorney to represent him. The judge told the defendant that the named attorney would be available for aid and would remain in court throughout the trial. The defendant refused to proceed to trial. The judge ordered the prosecution to select a jury and proceed to trial. During the jury selection, as well as during trial, the defendant remained mute. The jury found him guilty and he was sentenced to

a term of 10 to 30 years in prison.   On appeal he argued he had been denied due process of law.   What judgment?

2.   State law did not provide that an indigent accused of a crime was entitled to the service of experts at the expense of the government.   When charged with violating a state income tax statute the defendant asked the court to assign a certified public accountant to assist him to put his records together and to help him establish that he did not owe the state the money the state charged he had failed to pay.   The defendant informed the court he had almost no knowledge of income tax law and was very "poor" with figures.   He told the court he had no funds.   The court denied the request, stating that while one might have a constitutional right to counsel one did not have a constitutional right to the services of a certified public accountant.   The defendant appealed.   What judgment?

3.   The defendant was a member of the armed forces.   When charged with having violated the Uniform Code of Military Justice he asked that he be assigned counsel to assist him.   He was told that he was free to hire and personally pay outside counsel but the only available counsel for assignment to assist him was an officer who had served as defense counsel in "hundreds of cases" but had never formally studied law.   Does the defendant have a constitutional right to have the government supply him with the services of a person formally trained in the law?

4.   The indigent defendant, convicted of grand larceny, was sentenced to four years in jail.   On appeal his attorney presented to the appellate court the results of a recently completed study of sentencing practices which revealed that in the county in which the defendant had been tried persons who earned more than $20,000 per year immediately preceding their conviction for grand larceny were sentenced on the average to six months in prison.   Persons who earned less were, on the average, sentenced to four years in prison.   He asked the appellate court to set the defendant's sentence aside or reduce his sentence to six months.   What judgment?

5.   Under state law an attorney who was assigned to represent an indigent defendant charged with the commission of a felony was entitled to receive a fee of $500.   In "special circumstances" the trial judge might authorize a larger fee.   An indigent defendant challenged the statute, claiming it denied him due process and equal protection of the laws because the specified compensation was inadequate and that no "responsible" lawyer would exert his best efforts for such a small fee.   What judgment?

6.   The petitioner purchased merchandise which she claimed to be defective.   When she sought to commence a proceeding against the seller in Small Claims Court she was informed that it cost $3.01 to begin the action.   She told the clerk that she needed all of her money for food, clothing, and shelter.   When he refused to allow her to com-

mence her suit without paying the $3.01 she petitioned the court for an order directing the clerk to permit her to commence the suit without her paying the usual fee on the ground that the only way she could obtain relief was by court action and she lacked funds with which to commence action. What judgment?

Chapter 21

THE SHELTER DEPRIVED

Since the latter part of the 1930's federal, state, and local governments have enacted legislation to assist those whose housing needs have not been satisfied by the private sector of the economy. To carry out this policy government has made use of public funds to take private property and to finance the building and operation of apartment dwellings. Sometimes government has assumed the role of landlord and sometimes it has chosen to act as the overseer of those facilities it has set aside for use by those it has made the beneficiaries of this form of government largess.

Federal and state governments possess the power of eminent domain. This power permits government to take private property for public use. When this power is exercised the Constitution requires that property owners be justly compensated for their loss. When public support of private housing was in its infancy the constitutionality of governmental seizure of private property to provide housing for the shelter deprived was questioned. In a leading case the state legislature had authorized the condemnation of slum properties and the subsequent construction and operation by private enterprise of middle income housing. The court found that the state legislature might properly find that slums were a public evil, causing social and economic loss to the state. Governmental seizure of private property followed by the destruction of slum properties and the erection of apartment dwellings was found to constitute a public purpose. In the court's opinion the fact that a private builder and landlord might make profit did not matter since replacing slums with new housing would enhance the "public good."

To a limited extent government has traditionally acted as a landlord, owning and operating office buildings and courthouses and at times owning, operating, and leasing for private use such things as stadiums and auditoriums. In regard to these kinds of properties courts determine the rights and duties of government by distinguishing between government acting in its "governmental" capacity and in its "proprietary" capacity. Government acts in its "governmental" capacity when it owns or uses property to perform a function usually entrusted to government, such as maintaining public office buildings or military installations. When it owns and leases property for a purpose ordinarily fulfilled by private enterprise, such as a stadium or an auditorium, government is said to be acting in its "proprietary" capacity. Should a court find that government has acted in its governmental capacity it resolves the litigation by invoking the rules which are exclusively applicable to governmental action. If it finds that government acted in its "proprietary" capacity, the rules applicable to private landlords vis-à-vis tenants and other persons are used to determine the rights and duties of the government vis-à-vis its tenants and other persons.

The restrictions the law places on private landlords differ substantially from those generally imposed on government. For example, few constitutional restraints are applicable to private landlords. Only when their behavior is closely akin to governmental action is the propriety of their behavior tested by constitutional standards. A private landlord who provides a "public" street, "public" road, or "public" parking lot is supplying a facility commonly supplied by government. In such cases constitutional guarantees such as freedom of speech and press proscribe how and when he may control what other persons say or the materials they make available to others on such streets, roads, or parking lots.

Under the "governmental" versus "proprietary" approach government would be free to treat tenants in public housing as if they were residing in privately owned and operated facilities. Initially courts followed this classification procedure. For the most part it has now been abandoned in favor of the principle that when government acts as a supplier of housing it is subject to the same constitutional restraints as when it goes about any of the functions traditionally carried on by government.

Courts envision legislation which involves government in the building or operation of housing for the shelter deprived as an expression of legislative intent to confer a property right on those who qualify for such housing. By classifying the right to public housing as a property right courts require public officials to show the same deference to the right of persons to secure and reside in public housing as the Constitution requires they show to other kinds of property rights.

Unless specifically prohibited by law, a private landlord may accept or reject a prospective tenant with or without reason. He may require a tenant to sign a lease which provides that either the landlord or the tenant can terminate the tenancy by doing nothing more than giving the other party thirty days notice that he desires to do so. The tenancy can be brought to an end with or without reason. If after the tenant has received the notice he refuses to vacate the premises as he has agreed, the landlord can obtain a court order authorizing the tenant's eviction. Public housing officials, on the other hand, must act in accordance with a body of objective and reasonable criteria when taking action against a tenant or prospective tenant. When the demand for public housing exceeds the supply, housing officials may not select persons on the basis of favor or partiality. They may make use of a lot system or a first come first served arrangement. Even if the lease signed by a tenant provides that his tenancy may be terminated with or without reason on thirty days notice it may not be so terminated unless there is in fact a reasonable cause for such action. A tenant who qualifies for public housing may not be evicted simply because his conduct does not meet the moral standards of particular public officials or even society at large. Eviction may not be used as a means of punishing a tenant for his past wrongs. The fact that one has committed a crime does not *per se* make him subject to eviction. One may have a right to remain in public housing even if he is guilty of some forms of criminal behavior. But one entitled to public housing may be required to meet the minimum standard of conduct essential to sustain a civilized community. A tenant can be evicted if he is guilty of behaving in such a way that his continued presence in public housing constitutes a danger to the housing facility or to other tenants.

Government may not condition one's receipt or retention of public housing on his surrender of a constitutionally protected right. For example, individuals enjoy the right to freely associate with other persons. One may not be denied public housing merely because he refuses to sign a certificate of non-membership in organizations designated subversive by the Attorney General of the United States. Due process requires that one have notice of the charges against him and a hearing before government may deprive him of his property. Housing officials may not evict a tenant from public housing unless they first inform him of the reasons for their contemplated action. He must be afforded an evidentiary hearing with the right to have counsel present to assist him to contest the planned eviction. Compliance with these requirements help prevent one entitled to and in need of housing from erroneously being denied his statutory rights.

The Constitution bars governmental officials from discriminating against persons on account of their race. When deciding the rights of persons to public housing courts follow what they see as an overall national policy of putting an end to practices which keep whites living in one place and non-whites in another. When it appears that a particular housing project is administered in a fashion which will perpetuate the existence of racial ghettos, a court may order that for a period of time persons once kept out of the project because of their race thereafter be accepted as tenants because of their race. For example, if a neighborhood is predominantly white, and the tenants already residing in the project are predominantly white, the court may direct that housing officials establish a quota system which for a period of time insures access to the project by a stated number of non-whites. This form of racial discrimination in favor of non-whites has been found not to be invidious and therefore constitutional.

Generally before new publicly supported housing can be built existing housing must be torn down. Many of those displaced are among the nation's shelter deprived. Their quest for housing after eviction is often torturous. Recent legislation requires that governmental officers assist such displaced persons in their search for a suitable place in which to live. Courts recognize that because of past and prevailing housing practices non-whites usually find it more difficult to find new living quarters than white persons. Because of this disparity of opportunity, it has been held that when formulating a plan to assist those who will be displaced by the disruption of existing tenancies to make way for new housing governmental officials must pay attention to the special needs of non-whites. Their failure to do so has been found to deny such persons equal protection of the laws.

It is unconstitutional for public officials to discriminate against shelter deprived non-whites by providing those parts of the community in which they live with "grossly" inferior public services such as sewers, paving, school buildings, recreational facilities, and traffic signals. An "other side of the track" approach which allots more and better services to white than non-white neighborhoods has been found to constitute the sort of invidious discrimination prohibited by the Fourteenth Amendment.

Some zoning laws make it difficult or impossible for poor non-whites to obtain housing in all or part of a community. For example, a zoning ordinance may direct that one family homes can be built on no less than one acre of land or it may severely limit the number of apartment dwellings which may be built. Restrictions on apartment houses may necessitate costly construction. Prescribed room arrangements may render the dwellings unfit for use by poor persons with large families. Courts are now being asked to strike down such forms of legislation on the ground that they are an invidious form of discrimination against poor non-whites and therefore unconstitutional.

NORWALK CORE v. NORWALK REDEVELOPMENT AGENCY

United States Court of Appeals, Second Circuit 1968.
395 F.2d 920.

The Norwalk Chapter of the Congress of Racial Equality, two non-profit tenants' associations made up of low-income black and Puerto Rican persons, and several individual blacks and Puerto Ricans brought an action against the Norwalk Housing Authority, its Administrator and members, the City of Norwalk, its mayor, several building contractors, and the Secretary of the Department of Housing and Urban Development (HUD). In their complaint the plaintiffs alleged: (1) HUD had refused to require the construction of low-income housing when it approved the sale of six acres of land for an urban renewal project; (2) blacks and Puerto Ricans who had been living in houses located on such property would be displaced as a consequence of the renewal project; (3) there was insufficient housing for such low-income displaced persons in Norwalk; and (4) the failure of the defendants to take steps to build low-income housing in Norwalk would require the displaced persons to leave the city. The plaintiffs asserted that (1) HUD had violated § 105(c) the Housing Acts of 1949 and 1954 which require that when federal funds are used for urban renewal provision must be made for the future housing of displaced persons and (2) the failure of the defendants to take special account of the unique and especially difficult task of low-income blacks and Puerto Ricans to find housing in Norwalk denied them equal protection of the laws. The District Court dismissed the complaint. The plaintiffs appealed.

J. Joseph Smith, Circuit Judge:

* * *

The District Court never reached the merits of this claim for it concluded that

Members of the public, whether living inside or outside a project area, ordinarily have no standing to challenge planning of an urban renewal project * * * nor, by alleging civil rights violations, do they gain standing they would otherwise not have [citing cases]. If residents of a project area cannot challenge a project while it is in the planning stages and before construction has begun, certainly they can have no standing to assert the same kind of challenge at a time when planning has been implemented, most of the land has been purchased and conveyed to developers, and construction of new buildings has been almost completed.

We consider first the issue of standing. The courts will not, it is clear, entertain a suit by one who does not have some personal stake in the outcome of the litigation. * * *

Even where a plaintiff has a personal stake in the outcome of a case, he may be denied standing to sue on the ground that the right which he is attempting to assert is not one which the courts will recognize. * * *

The plaintiffs in the case before us are in a very different position. Their stake in the outcome of the case is immediate and personal, and the right which they allege has been violated—the right not to be subjected to racial discrimination in government programs—is one which the courts will protect. Their standing to sue is clear * * *.

What plaintiffs' complaint alleges, in substance, is that in planning and implementing the Project, the local defendants did not assure, or even attempt to assure, relocation for Negro and Puerto Rican displacees in compliance with the Contract to the same extent as they did for whites; indeed, they intended through the combination of the Project and the rampant discrimination in rentals in the Norwalk housing market to drive many Negroes and Puerto Ricans out of the City of Norwalk. The argument is that proof of these allegations would make out a case of violation of the equal protection clause. We agree.

Section 105(c) of the Act provides that contracts for loans or capital grants entered into under the Act shall require the availability or the provision of relocation housing for displacees which meets the standard set out in that section. That standard is designed, as the District Court recognized, to prevent displacees from suffering a change for the worse in their living conditions. It is no secret that in the present state of our society discrimination in the housing market means that a change for the worse is generally more likely for members of minority races than for other displacees. This means that in many cases the relocation standard will be easier to meet for white than for non-white displacees. But the fact that the discrimination is not inherent in the administration of the program, but is, in the words of the District Court, "accidental to the plan," surely does not excuse the planners from making sure that there is available relocation housing for all displacees. "Equal protection of the laws" means more than merely the absence of governmental action designed to discriminate; as Judge J. Skelly Wright has said, "we now firmly recognize that the arbitrary quality of thoughtlessness can be as disastrous and unfair to private rights and the public interest as the perversity of a willful scheme." * * *

Since the plaintiffs are admittedly displaced as a result of the Project, there is no question of the presence of "state action" within the meaning of the Fourteenth Amendment. Where the relocation standard set by Congress is met for those who have access to any housing in the community which they can afford, but not for those who, by reason of their race, are denied free access to housing they can afford and must pay more for what they can get, the state action affirms the discrimination in the housing market. This is not "equal protection of the laws."

What we have said may require classification by race. That is something which the Constitution usually forbids, not because it is inevitably an impermissible classification, but because it is one which usually, to our national shame, has been drawn for the purpose of maintaining racial inequality. Where it is drawn for the purpose of achieving equality it will be allowed, and to the extent it is necessary to avoid unequal treatment by race, it will be required.

We hold that plaintiffs' complaint alleges a denial of the equal protection of the laws, and that the District Court should have proceeded to consider that claim on its merits.

* * * The question we must answer is whether actions taken by HUD and local public agencies under section 105(c) are ever subject to judicial review.

The proposition is now firmly established that "judicial review of a final agency action by an aggrieved person will not be cut off unless there is persuasive reason to believe that such was the purpose of Congress." * * * We have concluded that plaintiffs are aggrieved, and that there is no persuasive reason to believe that Congress intended to cut off judicial review.

The defendants maintain that plaintiffs cannot obtain judicial review of action under section 105(c) unless they can show that Congress, in enacting that section, intended to confer upon them a "legal right" to protection. A "legal right" to protection means, in the abstract, nothing at all. The specific and practical question here is whether or not plaintiffs may seek enforcement of the section, and the cases make it clear that the answer turns on whether Congress' purpose in enacting it was to protect their interests. * * * That was precisely Congress' purpose, as the legislative history of the Act clearly indicates:

* * *

Congress was deeply concerned that slum conditions be eliminated, not merely displaced to grow up elsewhere. * * *

The relocation requirements of section 105 (c) were not enough, of course, to ensure the elimination of slum conditions, and Congress recognized this fact. But they were designed to work toward that end by guaranteeing that, in clearing slum areas, government would not be driving into still worse conditions the people who lived in those areas. * * *

We have found no reason to believe that Congress intended to cut off judicial review under the Act. Nothing in the Act or its legislative history indicates such an intent, and we do not think that it can be inferred from the nature of the subject with which the Act deals. * * *

We hold, then, that judicial review of agency action under section 105 (c) of the Act is available to displacees. * * *

Judgment reversed. Remanded for further proceedings not inconsistent with this opinion.

———

RANJEL v. CITY OF LANSING

United States Court of Appeals, Sixth Circuit 1969.
417 F.2d 321.

The Lansing City Council approved a "spot" zoning ordinance which rezoned a 20 acre site from a one family residential district to a district in which one hundred low rent townhouse units and a low rent five-story apartment building containing one hundred and fifty units for the elderly could be built. The City's Charter provided that in cases in which the Council approved a zoning change, on the filing of a petition signed by at least 15% of the City's electors, the zoning ordinance could not take effect unless it was approved by a referendum. After the requisite number of persons signed a petition requesting that a referendum be held the plaintiffs, poor black persons and Mexican-Americans, brought a suit against the City to enjoin the holding of the referendum on several grounds, one of which was that the referendum was "racially" motivated and therefore unconstitutional. From a judgment in the District Court in favor of the plaintiffs, the City appealed.

Per Curiam.

* * *

It must have been a "shock" to the City for plaintiffs to claim, and for the District Court to hold, "that the conducting of this referendum makes the City of Lansing a partner in discrimination in violation of the Constitution," * * * for it was the City that established the Housing Commission; that originated the project and applied to HUD for the financing of it; that enacted the ordinance providing for the variance in the zoning; that approved the plans and specifications of the developer; that refused to accept the referendum petition; that resisted the mandamus action in the Circuit Court; that appealed the adverse decision of the Circuit Court to the * * * Court of Appeals; that co-operated in every respect with the housing project until the mandamus decision became final, when the City had no choice but to place the issue on the ballot as ordered by the Court or take the consequences of being held in contempt.

 *   *   *

In holding that the referendum was motivated by racial factors, the District Court necessarily had to reach that conclusion by searching the minds of 15% of the electorate who signed the referendum petition, and the remaining 85% who were enjoined from voting, none of whom were called as witnesses to testify in the case.   *   *   *

The Court relied upon opinion evidence to support its findings as to discrimination. City Planner Guernsey, who attended a public meeting, testified that residents in the area were opposed to low income people being moved there, many of whom were black. He did not indicate that the opposition was on racial grounds. He testified that there was opposition to overloading the schools in the district, and to the change of zoning from "A" one-family, to the higher density and multiple family housing.

People also stated that they had purchased their homes when the area was zoned for single family residences and did not think it was proper to change it.   *   *   *

The District Court also relied on testimony of Dr. Goldner, not a resident of Lansing, who undertook to give his opinion that the motivation of the middle class whites would be to exclude black and poor people from the neighborhood. Although he had no experience in Lansing, Dr. Goldner testified:

"Unless the people of Lansing that we are considering are much different than other people that have been studied rather extensively, I would say that their motivation is to keep out black and poor people."

On cross-examination, however, he limited his previous answer:

"Q Now, you did state, however, that the motivation of the people of the City of Lansing was to keep out black and poor people.

"A No, sir. I said that, as I recall my own remarks, I said that I was not commenting upon the intent but upon the effect of their actions."

In our judgment, this type of opinion evidence does not support the findings of discrimination made by the District Court. But if the electors had a legal right to a referendum, their motive in exercising that right would be immaterial.

Initiative and referendum is an important part of the state's legislative process. Being founded on neutral principles, it should be exempt from Federal Court constraints. * * *

Reitman v. Mulkey, 387 U.S. 369, * * * (1967), relied on by the District Court, is inapposite. In that case an effort had been made by a mandamus action to keep the proposal to amend California's Constitution off the ballot, but the Supreme Court of California ruled it would be more appropriate to pass upon the legal questions after the election rather "than to interfere with the power of the people to propose laws and amendments to the Constitution and to adopt or reject the same at the polls." * * * The California Supreme Court considered the proposal after election and held that it did more than merely repeal existing law but authorized discrimination in the housing market and was unconstitutional. The Supreme Court of the United States affirmed.

Reliance on Otey v. Common Council of City of Milwaukee, * * * is misplaced. In that case the District Court did indeed enjoin an election on an initiative proposal which prohibited the City Council of Milwaukee from enacting any ordinance restricting the right of owners of real estate to sell, lease or rent property. The Court held that the proposal, if passed, would be unconstitutional. Another reason of the Court for enjoining the election was to prevent a threatened riot.

We believe the better practice was that followed by the Supreme Court of California in *Reitman*, which allowed the election to proceed and ruled on the validity of the measure after its passage.

Nor do we think that citizens should be deprived of their right of suffrage merely because a riot was threatened. It would be more appropriate to enjoin unlawful acts of rioters than to deprive the electorate of their right of franchise. In the present case no riot was even threatened.

The judgment of the District Court is reversed and the cause is remanded with instructions to dismiss the complaint.

PROBLEMS

1. A municipal zoning ordinance provided that 80% of the apartments in new housing developments must have one bedroom and the remainder two bedrooms. Plaintiffs, a husband and wife with four children, brought an action to have the statute declared unconstitutional on the ground that it arbitrarily discriminated against persons with large families. The city defended the ordinance on aesthetic grounds as well as on the ground that there was a shortage of sanitation and educational facilities within the city's limits. What judgment?

2. A suburban town enacted a zoning ordinance which provided that only one-family homes could be built on the town's remain-

ing undeveloped area of about 5,000 acres. A suit was brought by poor blacks to have the ordinance declared unconstitutional. They claimed that the law precluded them from having an opportunity to live in the town. What judgment?

3. A city amended its zoning regulations to permit the construction of nothing other than luxury apartment dwellings along waterfront property. The proponents of the ordinance claimed it was essential for the city to attract persons with money. Such persons could not be attracted unless adequate luxury housing was available. The plaintiffs, a husband and wife who together earned $17,500 a year, brought a suit, asking that the zoning regulation be declared unconstitutional on the ground that it discriminated against the less affluent members of society who were already among the shelter deprived. What judgment?

4. The City of New York enacted an ordinance which provided that landlords of houses built after a certain date would be entitled to a stated schedule of periodic rent increases. The plaintiff, a landlord of a building constructed before the date specified in the statute was subject to an earlier statute which permitted him to periodically increase his rentals at a lower rate. He challenged the City's rent control scheme as arbitrary and unreasonable and in violation of the equal protection of the laws clause. What judgment?

5. The petitioner, a tenant in a housing project, in part paid for with federal funds and operated by the respondent, a municipal housing authority, was evicted without first having been notified of the reasons for her eviction and without an opportunity to challenge her ouster. A HUD regulation issued after the eviction proceedings were begun required that a tenant in such housing, prior to being evicted, had to be informed of the reasons for the eviction and had to be given an opportunity to contest it. The petitioner claimed that she was entitled to the benefit of such procedures. The respondent insisted that she was not, pointing out that the lease agreement between the petitioner and the respondent provided that the respondent was only required to give the petitioner 15 days notice and in any event the HUD regulation was issued after the eviction proceedings had been started. What judgment?

6. The petitioners asked the court to enjoin the city from evicting them from their homes. The city wished to evict them to raze the buildings in which they lived so that the street could be widened to comply with plans drawn to effect urban renewal. The city's budget director had not as yet received the proposal to widen the street, the city had not as yet approved final plans to proceed with the project, the plans formulated for the project had not been acted upon for 10 years and there was a possibility that one of the participants in the ten year old plan would withdraw. What judgment?

Chapter 22

WELFARE RECIPIENTS

Welfare law is predicated on acceptance of the proposition that it is a proper function of government to take money from some members of society and redistribute it to those in need. Since legislatures have the power to assess and collect taxes and provide for the allocation of public funds they alone can direct who shall pay the cost of welfare and who shall benefit from it. Executive officers and administrators are responsible for carrying out legislative policy. Courts play a limited but vital role in welfare law. They serve as the guardians of the constitutional and statutory rights of those who are taxed and those who receive welfare benefits.

The Poor Law passed by Parliament during the reign of Elizabeth I has greatly influenced this nation's approach to welfare. This 1601 statute entrusted parish officials with the task of assessing and collecting local taxes sufficient to satisfy the barest of needs of the parish's poor. This statute's objective and format, to meet the needs of the poor by local action, has its counterpart in our present day array of welfare programs. Today's general welfare programs are established and administered by the states. County, municipal, and town governments are intimately involved in the administration of such programs. While the federal government has yet to enter generally into the welfare field, its public assistance programs play a significant part in the nation's overall welfare scheme. At present federal funds are made available under four programs: (1) Aid to Families with Dependent Children (AFDC), (2) Aid to the Permanently and Totally Disabled (APTD), (3) Aid to the Blind (AB), and (4) Old Age Assistance (OAA).

While federal public assistance programs call for dispersal of federal funds the federal government is not directly involved in placing money in the hands of the poor. This is the task of state and local governments. State and local governments obtain federal funds to supplement their own when state and local laws and practices satisfy the general demands set forth in Congressional welfare legislation.

The Supreme Court envisions the right to receive welfare payments under state and local programs which are in part funded by federal money under a federal public assistance program as a federal right protected by the Constitution and federal law from unreasonable, arbitrary, or capricious action by federal, state, and local officials. To a formidable extent the right to receive welfare is protected in the same fashion as a property right. What property is to a property owner, receipt of welfare payments is to the indigent. In most cases the unlawful failure to make welfare payments to an indigent portends far graver consequences for the indigent than does the unlawful taking of ordinary personal or real property from its owner. In the case of an indigent, a wrongful refusal to pay a small sum of money can result in grave physical and mental injury, at times even death. In the case of a property owner, unless his need for the property is in fact akin to an indigent's critical need for food, clothing, and shelter the result of an unlawful seizure is much less appalling.

The Supreme Court has struck down as unconstitutional (1) legislation which denied welfare payments to persons who otherwise qualified for assistance but failed to satisfy a minimum one year state residency requirement placed on those requesting welfare benefits and (2) a local practice which permitted the termination of welfare payments without the recipient first receiving notice of the cause of the proposed termination and an opportunity to contest such action.

State and local governments which elect to supplement their own welfare funds by accepting federal funds under a federal public assistance program are not free to follow their own wishes as to how their own welfare program shall operate. They are obliged to comply with the constraints Congress has placed on the operation of state and local program in part funded under federal law. Should a state or local policy conflict with one or more Congressional directives the federal mandate must be followed. On this ground the Supreme Court has struck down a state statute which denied welfare assistance to otherwise qualified children if their mother cohabited with a man other than her husband. The Court found that the state's desire to discourage "illicit sexual behavior and illegitimacy" ran counter to the overriding desire of Congress to require participating states to give financial assistance to needy children. The Court interpreted federal law as prohibiting a state from using its own evaluation of the moral or immoral quality of one's behavior as a criterion of eligibility for welfare assistance. Similarly, state and local governments must (1) satisfy a federal directive which calls upon them to increase the number of persons eligible to receive assistance under their programs and (2) not redefine their standard of need in a fashion which would circumvent a Congressional directive that state and local governments receiving federal funds carry out a "cost-of-living reappraisal" for welfare recipients.

The Supreme Court has acknowledged that state and local governments have limited resources with which to fund their welfare programs and that federal public assistance legislation does allow for "striking differences in the degree of aid provided among the States" so long as prescribed federal requirements are satisfied. The Court has refused to "second-guess" state and local legislators and decide what type of welfare program would be best for each state, county, municipality, and town. It has sustained a state law which placed "an upper limit on the total amount of money any one family might receive." The fact that under such a program children who were members of small family units would receive more funds to satisfy their individual needs than those who were members of large units did not, in the Court's opinion, constitute an invidious discrimination within the meaning of the equal protection of the laws clause of the Fourteenth Amendment.

Welfare recipients, like those who do not receive welfare, enjoy the constitutional rights to freedom of speech, press, public assembly and association, to petition government for the redress of grievances, and freedom from compulsory self-crimination and unreasonable searches and seizures. But, as pointed out in previous chapters, constitutional rights are not absolute. The measure of their protection is determined by the setting in which they are sought to be exercised and the nature of the government's interest in restricting their use. The government's interest in the proper administration of its welfare programs can in particular instances serve as a valid basis for limiting a welfare recipient's right to the unbridled enjoyment of one or more of his constitutional liberties. For example, the Supreme Court has ruled that it is not unconstitutional for a municipality to terminate payments to a welfare recipient who has refused to allow a single municipal caseworker familiar with the recipient to visit her home after a request had been made for permission to do so. In the case before the Court the caseworker was not seeking entry to conduct a criminal investigation. The Court found that the procedure followed by the municipality was marked by sensitivity to the recipient's right to privacy except for a very limited intrusion for a very limited purpose. The reasons for the daytime visit were to learn whether or not welfare funds were being used for their intended purpose, if the recipient was receiving the services to which she was entitled, if dependent children were being neglected, and to assess the recipient's eligibility for future assistance. The public, in the Court's opinion, had a sufficiently compelling interest to demand access to the recipient's home for the stated purposes. The municipality's conduct in relation to the stated objectives did not constitute an unreasonable search and seizure within the meaning of the Fourteenth Amendment.

GOLDBERG v. KELLY

Supreme Court of the United States, 1970.
90 S.Ct. 1011, 397 U.S. 254, 25 L.Ed.2d 287.

Plaintiffs, New York City Welfare recipients, brought an action against the City Commissioner of Social Services. In their complaint they alleged that their welfare payments had been, or were about to be terminated, without their first having been notified of the reasons for the termination. They did not have an opportunity to challenge the termination before it took effect. They claimed that this procedure denied them due process of law. After the suit was begun the City adopted a procedure which barred the stoppage of welfare payments until recipients were notified of the cause of the planned termination. Each recipient had an opportunity to submit a written statement to a designated welfare official setting forth why the payments should be continued. If the official approved of the termination the recipient would be informed of such action and the payments would then be stopped. The plaintiffs also challenged this new procedure. The District Court ruled in favor of the plaintiffs and the Commissioner appealed.

MR. JUSTICE BRENNAN delivered the opinion of the Court.
* * *

The constitutional issue to be decided, therefore, is the narrow one whether the Due Process Clause requires that the recipient be afforded an evidentiary hearing *before* the termination of benefits.
* * *

Appellant does not contend that procedural due process is not applicable to the termination of welfare benefits. Such benefits are a matter of statutory entitlement for persons qualified to receive them. Their termination involves state action that adjudicates important rights. The constitutional challenge cannot be answered by an argument that public assistance benefits are "a 'privilege' and not a 'right.' " * * * Relevant constitutional restraints apply as much to the withdrawal of public assistance benefits as to disqualification for unemployment compensation, * * * or to denial of a tax exemption, * * * or to discharge from public employment, * * *. The extent to which procedural due process must be afforded the recipient is influenced by the extent to which he may be "condemned to suffer grievous loss," * * * and depends upon whether the recipient's interest in avoiding that loss outweighs the governmental interest in summary adjudication. Accordingly, as we said in Cafeteria & Restaurant Workers Union, etc. v. McElroy, 367 U.S. 886, 895, * * * (1961), "consideration of what procedures due process may require under any given set of circumstances must begin with a determination of the precise nature of the government function involved as well as of the private interest that has been affected by governmental action." * * *

It is true, of course, that some governmental benefits may be administratively terminated without affording the recipient a pre-termination evidentiary hearing. But we agree with the District Court that when welfare is discontinued, only a pre-termination evidentiary hearing provides the recipient with procedural due process. * * * For qualified recipients, welfare provides the means to obtain essential food, clothing, housing, and medical care. * * * Thus the crucial factor in this context—a factor not present in the case of the blacklisted government contractor, the discharged government employee, the taxpayer denied a tax exemption, or virtually anyone else whose governmental largesse is ended—is that termination of aid pending resolution of a controversy over eligibility may deprive an *eligible* recipient of the very means by which to live while he waits. Since he lacks independent resources, his situation becomes immediately desperate. His need to concentrate upon finding the means for daily subsistence, in turn, adversely affects his ability to seek redress from the welfare bureaucracy.

* * * Welfare, by meeting the basic demands of subsistence, can help bring within the reach of the poor the same opportunities that are available to others to participate meaningfully in the life of the community. At the same time, welfare guards against the societal malaise that may flow from a widespread sense of unjustified frustration and insecurity. Public assistance, then, is not mere charity, but a means to "promote the general Welfare, and secure the Blessings of Liberty to ourselves and our Posterity." The same governmental interests which counsel the provision of welfare, counsel as well its uninterrupted provision to those eligible to receive it; pre-termination evidentiary hearings are indispensable to that end.

* * *

* * * The requirement of a prior hearing doubtless involves some greater expense, and the benefits paid to ineligible recipients pending decision at the hearing probably cannot be recouped, since these recipients are likely to be judgment-proof. But the State is not without weapons to minimize these increased costs. Much of the drain on fiscal and administrative resources can be reduced by developing procedures for prompt pre-termination hearings and by skillful use of personnel and facilities. * * * As the District Court correctly concluded, "[t]he stakes are simply too high for the welfare recipient, and the possibility for honest error or irritable misjudgment too great, to allow termination of aid without giving the recipient a chance, if he so desires, to be fully informed of the case against him so that he may contest its basis and produce evidence in rebuttal."

* * *

"The fundamental requisite of due process of law is the opportunity to be heard." * * * The hearing must be "at a meaningful time and in a meaningful manner." * * * In the present context these principles require that a recipient have timely and adequate notice detailing the reasons for a proposed termination, and an effective opportunity to defend by confronting any adverse witnesses and by presenting his own arguments and evidence orally. These rights are important in cases such as those before us, where recipients have challenged proposed terminations as resting on incorrect or misleading factual premises or on misapplication of rules or policies to the facts of particular cases.

* * *

The city's procedures presently do not permit recipients to appear personally with or without counsel before the official who finally determines continued eligibility. Thus a recipient is not permitted to present evidence to that official orally, or to confront or cross-examine adverse witnesses. These omissions are fatal to the constitutional adequacy of the procedures.

* * *

In almost every setting where important decisions turn on questions of fact, due process requires an opportunity to confront and cross-examine adverse witnesses. * * * Welfare recipients must therefore be given an opportunity to confront and cross-examine the witnesses relied on by the department.

"The right to be heard would be, in many cases, of little avail if it did not comprehend the right to be heard by counsel." * * * We do not say that counsel must be provided at the pre-termination hearing, but only that the recipient must be allowed to retain an attorney if he so desires. * * *

Finally, the decision maker's conclusion as to a recipient's eligibility must rest solely on the legal rules and evidence adduced at the hearing. * * * To demonstrate compliance with this elementary requirement, the decision maker should state the reasons for his determination and indicate the evidence he relied on, * * * though his statement need not amount to a full opinion or even formal findings of fact and conclusions of law. And, of course, an impartial decision maker is essential. * * * We agree with the District Court that prior involvement in some aspects of a case will not necessarily bar a welfare official from acting as a decision maker. He should not, however, have participated in making the determination under review.

Affirmed.

SHAPIRO v. THOMPSON

Supreme Court of the United States, 1968.
89 S.Ct. 1322, 394 U.S. 618, 22 L.Ed.2d 600.

The District of Columbia and the States of Connecticut and Pennsylvania denied welfare assistance to persons otherwise qualified for such assistance who had not resided within the jurisdiction for at least one year immediately before asking for aid. Applicants for welfare assistance in each jurisdiction who did not satisfy the one year residency requirement brought a suit in a District Court asking the Court to declare the requirement unconstitutional. Each Court ruled in favor of the applicant. The defendants appealed.

MR. JUSTICE BRENNAN delivered the opinion of the Court.
* * *

There is no dispute that the effect of the waiting-period requirement in each case is to create two classes of needy resident families indistinguishable from each other except that one is composed of residents who have resided a year or more, and the second of residents who have resided less than a year, in the jurisdiction. On the basis of this sole difference the first class is granted and the second class is denied welfare aid upon which may depend the ability of the families to obtain the very means to subsist—food, shelter, and other necessities of life.   *   *   *

We do not doubt that the one-year waiting period device is well suited to discourage the influx of poor families in need of assistance. An indigent who desires to migrate, resettle, find a new job, and start a new life will doubtless hesitate if he knows that he must risk making the move without the possibility of falling back on state welfare assistance during his first year of residence, when his need may be most acute. But the purpose of inhibiting migration by needy persons into the State is constitutionally impermissible.

This Court long ago recognized that the nature of our Federal Union and our constitutional concepts of personal liberty unite to require that all citizens be free to travel throughout the length and breadth of our land uninhibited by statutes, rules, or regulations which unreasonably burden or restrict this movement.   *   *   *

Thus, the purpose of deterring the in-migration of indigents cannot serve as justification for the classification created by the one-year waiting period, since that purpose is constitutionally impermissible. If a law has "no other purpose   *   *   *   than to chill the assertion of constitutional rights by penalizing those who choose to exercise them, then it [is] patently unconstitutional."   *   *   *

More fundamentally, a State may no more try to fence out those indigents who seek higher welfare benefits than it may try to fence out indigents generally. Implicit in any such distinction is the notion that indigents who enter a State with the hope of securing higher welfare benefits are somehow less deserving than indigents who do not take this consideration into account. But we do not perceive why a mother who is seeking to make a new life for herself and her children should be regarded as less deserving because she considers, among others factors, the level of a State's public assistance. Surely such a mother is no less deserving than a mother who moves into a particular State in order to take advantage of its better educational facilities.

Appellants argue further that the challenged classification may be sustained as an attempt to distinguish between new and old residents on the basis of the contribution they have made to the community through the payment of taxes. We have difficulty seeing how long-term residents who qualify for welfare are making a greater present contribution to the State in taxes than indigent residents who have recently arrived.   *   *   *   Appellants' reasoning would logically permit the State to bar new residents from schools, parks, and libraries or deprive them of police and fire protection. Indeed it would permit the State to apportion all benefits and services according to the past tax contributions of its citizens. The Equal Protection Clause prohibits such an apportionment of state services.

We recognize that a State has a valid interest in preserving the fiscal integrity of its programs. It may legitimately attempt to limit its expenditures, whether for public assistance, public education, or any other program. But a State may not accomplish such a purpose by individuos distinctions between classes of its citizens. It could not, for example, reduce expenditures for education by barring indigent children from its schools. Similarly, in the cases before us, appellants must do more than show that denying welfare benefits to new residents saves money. The saving of welfare costs cannot justify an otherwise invidious classification.

    * * * Since the classification here touches on the fundamental right of interstate movement, its constitutionality must be judged by the stricter standard of whether it promotes a *compelling* state interest. Under this standard, the waiting-period requirement clearly violates the Equal Protection Clause.
    * * *

    The waiting-period requirement in the District of Columbia Code * * * is also unconstitutional even though it was adopted by Congress as an exercise of federal power. In terms of federal power, the discrimination created by the one-year requirement violates the Due Process Clause of the Fifth Amendment. "[W]hile the Fifth Amendment contains no equal protection clause, it does forbid discrimination that is 'so unjustifiable as to be violative of due process.'" * * * For the reasons we have stated in invalidating the Pennsylvania and Connecticut provisions, the District of Columbia provision is also invalid—the Due Process Clause of the Fifth Amendment prohibits Congress from denying public assistance to poor persons otherwise eligible solely on the ground that they have not been residents of the District of Columbia for one year at the time their applications are filed.
    * * *

Affirmed.

PROBLEMS

    1. State law provided that the state could be reimbursed for money it paid to a welfare recipient by taking from him his real estate, his interest in life insurance policies, and any money he received as a result of personal injuries he suffered due to an accident. The statute did not permit the state to recover any money out of a recipient's wages, salary, or to seize any property he acquired with such earnings. A welfare recipient injured in an automobile accident challenged the statute as unconstitutional. What judgment?

    2. A state vagrancy statute made it unlawful for an able-bodied person to be unemployed and without visible means of support. The defendant, convicted of violating the statute appealed, claiming that it violated the due process clause. The state defended the validity of the statute on the ground that it had a legitimate interest in discouraging abled bodied men who were capable of working from becoming

loafers and public charges and the state might use the criminal law as a means to attain this objective. Is the state correct?

3. May the right to receive welfare assistance be conditioned on the willingness of a recipient to accept employment if offered to him by the agency dispensing welfare funds?

4. State law made it a crime, by wilfull act, to interfere with the proper administration of the welfare law. It provided that no assistance should be given to persons who refused to accept a position for which they were fitted and which they were physically able to accept. The defendant, married and the father of two children, requested and received welfare for himself, his wife, and his children. He was offered a position for which he was fitted and physically acceptable. He refused it on the ground that the wages he would receive would be too low. His welfare payments were stopped but the payments to his wife and children were continued. He was tried and convicted for having wilfully interfered with the proper administration of the welfare law. What judgment?

5. The state legislature allocated funds to pay private camps the cost of one month summer camp for children whose parents were on welfare. The plaintiffs, welfare recipients, brought an action asking the court to direct the state welfare commissioner to provide each of their children with a sum of money sufficient to purchase nessary summer clothing which they could wear while at camp. What judgment?

6. State law provided that if a stepfather resided on the premises with his stepchildren and the children's mother, then the children might not receive welfare payments although they otherwise qualified for such assistance. Is such a statute valid?

ENVOI

Courts are now being challenged to rule in new ways on a variety of social issues which not too long ago were thought of as either not warranting judicial involvement or as already properly governed by prevailing legal doctrines. The following are some of the questions judges are now being asked to consider. To what extent may a prisoner, simply because he is a prisoner, be dealt with by prison authorities without any attention being paid to the usual requisites of due process of law? Are prison authorities free to do as they wish with a prisoner in regard to discipline, his right to associate with other inmates, and the extent to which he may communicate and visit with his family and friends? May state or local law prohibit persons from living in communes? May landlords discriminate against persons who perfer communal living to the traditional family unit? Should those business enterprises which solicit business by advertising their wares be obliged to substantiate every one of the claims they boldly proclaim about the qualities and attributes of their products? Should it be commonplace for consumers to be heard in cases tried before administrative agencies in which the relationship between business and consumers is in issue? Should a debtor have a right to bar a creditor from contacting his employer? Should governmental officials have to obtain a search warrant before they undertake an extended surveillance of one suspected of a crime? May government force integration in housing by directing particular white or non-white persons to move into areas in which there are few if any of their race then residing? Should persons other than a child's natural parents have a right to the custody of the child if an exceptionally intimate relationship has developed between such persons and the child, with the child having had little if any contact with his natural parents? Should a childless husband and wife who wish to adopt a child be denied the opportunity to do so simply because they are more than fifty years of age? Can parents be required to send their children to a state operated school if the state decides that the religious school the children are attending fails to satisfy state established criteria of acceptability? Do parents have a right to insist that their children be excused from required sex education classes offered as part of an elementary school curriculum? Should bar examinations be discontinued since they may work a hardship on educationally and culturally disadvantaged persons who wish to practice law? Should job tests be outlawed on the ground that they perpetuate poverty and work an undue hardship on illiterate persons? Should poor persons have a constitutional right to have counsel assigned by the federal or state governments to assist them in any form of proceeding in which if they had funds they would be permitted to have the assistance of retained counsel?

208

Within the next decade as yet unpredictable social issues will be pressed upon the courts for adjudication. The 1970's promise to be an exciting period. It will also be a painful one. Persons will be forced to accommodate to the rejection of old and trusted shibboleths and learn to abide by new legal standards of right and wrong.

*

INDEX

References are to Pages

INDEX
References are to Pages

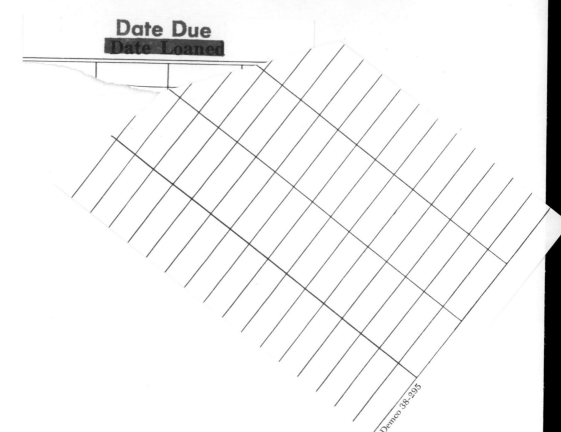

Date Due

Date Loaned

Demco 38-295